The Football Tourist

by
Stuart Fuller

www.ockleybooks.co.uk

Published by Ockley Books Ltd

First published 2013
All text & images copyright of the author

The moral right of Stuart Fuller to be identified as the author of
this work has been asserted

ISBN 978-0-9571410-25
Front Cover designed by Proworx

Printed & bound by:

Scandinavian Book
Hamilton House
Mabledon Place
Bloomsbury
WC1H 9BB

To the real CMF, twenty-years of great memories....some even featuring both of us.

Contents

Introduction

Tourist: [too-r-ist] noun - A person who travels to and stays in places outside their usual environment for leisure, business and other purposes.

Modern football is crap. How many times have I heard that throwaway comment in recent years? There have even been a couple of books that eulogise about times gone by and how much better the beautiful game was when we only had three TV channels, sand for pitches and steak 'n' chips with light ale on the side for a pre-match meal.

But it's not really crap is it?

That's actually a load of rubbish.

In fact it's bloody wonderful.

Technology means that the global game is now in the palm of your hand. At this very moment I'm writing these words for my publisher on an iPad as my train passes under the English Channel. I have the fixtures for every league in the world at my fingertips for plotting my next little trip, whilst Twitter is keeping me up to date on the Ebbsfleet United v Macclesfield Town pitch inspection. On Sunday I will be able to sit in my armchair at 10am and watch live football from Italy, Germany, Scotland, England, France and then South America without moving a muscle.

Modern football is crap?

Rubbish.

A trip to the football no longer means getting on a Football Special. Those stadiums we used to see on Sportsnight, built up to be such places of mystery and wonder, are now within a £20 flight (with tax, luggage charge and environmental levy on top of course) from an airport near you. The internet has given us a wonderful opportunity to broaden our horizons and experience the true meaning of the phrase 'The Beautiful Game'.

Those who know me well will understand my values in life. We have been given a fantastic opportunity through technology and the ways of the world today to experience things that our parents only dreamed of. At the last count I had seen football in a mere thirty-seven countries. I say "mere" because I know people who have seen double and even treble that. That's progress in anyone's book. I value that glorious freedom more than almost anything else in life, as we all should.

This book is the story of 20 months of that very existence. Nearly two years of balancing a stressful job, a wonderful family and a passion for watching football in some of Europe's furthest corners. Whereas once I could only dream of watching the Rome derby on Channel 4's Football Italia, I was now very much a part of an epic twice-a-year stage-play featuring a cast of 60,000 and full of heroes and villains.

Again, modern football is crap, right?

Again, rubbish.

In searching for a title for this book, David Hartrick and I threw a number of titles around before deciding on 'The Football Tourist'. I never think of myself as a tourist, just like trying to fit in as many new grounds into a weekend trip never makes me a 'ground-hopper'. I've always been happier with a map rather than a novel, wandering off the beaten track and trying that dish that looks like dog food (on a trip to Turkey once it actually turned out to be dog food – long story).

If I had to describe myself, I suppose without ego I sometimes I feel like a pioneer, breaking virgin ground for those to follow. That is one of the reasons why I have always documented my travels, hoping that others get as much pleasure from following in my footsteps and avoiding the occasional pitfalls that have occurred. Back in 2006 I wrote my first blog post after a trip to Moscow. It was a natural progression from researching and writing factual information about details of European Football Grounds. I'd travelled across the continent drawing maps and making notes in my little black book without ever putting in the emotions, the joy and the beauty of watching the world's favourite sport in various different languages. So from that moment onwards I vowed to try and share my experiences. Whether I liked it or not, I'd become a Football Tourist.

Along the way I had met many like-minded people who have become firm friends. You may well know some of them already. Others you will meet for the first time on these pages. No names have been changed to protect the guilty or the innocent, the events have been recorded more or less as they happened.

People who know me through my football travels often find it hard to believe I have time in my life for anything else apart from being the Football Tourist. But I do. And despite what you may believe, it's bloody hard work and often stressful. Getting to airports at 5am is not fun when you have a day full of meetings in some far-flung place and you can only look longingly at those enjoying their pre-holiday pint in Weatherspoons. But occasionally (yes, only occasionally) the two worlds collide and I have been able to sample some real hospitality that has crossed cultural barriers and made even the biggest Euro-sceptic forget their stereotypes for ninety-minutes.

And then there's my family. Yep, despite my frequent forays

into foreign lands I have a family back at Fuller HQ. They are my support team, not in any illegal performance enhancing cycling way, but keeping me sane and organised. My wife has come to expect the weekly request for permission to go to some far-flung corner of Europe, even now dropping the slow shake of her head when I ask. My daughters see me as some kind of school project, telling teachers and classmates about "where in the world is my Daddy today?" One couldn't ask for a better set of friends, let alone close family.

As for those that share my passion and enthusiasm for "one more game" at 11am on a Sunday in Prague? Well, it would be unfair to single out Danny Last for leading me astray in this way, but life is unfair and I would doubtless travel less if it weren't for his suggestive text messages. The best part of all this though is that we've proved we are not alone in our wanderings and general wanderlust, and you will meet a cast of many throughout this book. The term 'football tourists' has never been more apt for those who share the addiction I have with Europe in the palm of our hands and an ever-expanding year-long fixture list.

So what do I want you, dear reader, to take away from this book? I hope to inspire you to not spend every Sunday afternoon with Martin Tyler and Gary Neville for company but to embrace something new every now and then. Remember when you tried Yorkshire puddings with your roast chicken dinner for the first time instead of beef? Well that's what I want you to feel, excited, giddy, a little bit scared of the unknown, but overall knowing that the combination of a couple of things you already know and love could just be something very special.

Ladies and Gentlemen, I am The Football Tourist and this, for better and for worse, is my story.

Foreword

By Kenny Pavey

Man must become comfortable in flowing from one role to another, one set of values to another, one life to another. Men must be free from boundaries, patterns and consistencies in order to be free to think, feel and create in new ways.

Luke Rhinehart - The Dice Man

I still get a kick about saying the words "I am a professional footballer" even after all these years. The sheer thrill of having 30,000 fans shouting your name, sharing your emotions and knowing that you can make their day, week or year by simply doing something right or wrong. I'm fortunate that the slice of luck you need along the way came early in my career, and the bold decision I made has rewarded me with league titles, cups, European campaigns and the odd award over time. Not many English players can lay claim to that in the modern era. Oh, who am I? Sorry, let me introduce myself. I'm Kenny Pavey - the ultimate accidental football tourist.

I can still see you scratching your head, trying to place my name among the Premier League clubs, but you won't find me there. For the past fifteen years I have been playing my game in Sweden, under the radar of the English press. Whilst Michael Owen has graced the Bernabau for Real Madrid and Beckham can lay claim to AC Milan, Madrid, LA Galaxy and now PSG as employers, I have been playing games in places few people outside of Scandinavia have ever heard of, let alone visited. Ljungskile, Sundsvall, Landskrona, Växjö. Names that roll off the tongue to me these days. Why Sweden? Well, that's why I am a football tourist.

Back in 1998 I was on the verge of a move to the big time. I had been spotted by a Premier League scout whilst playing for Sittingbourne, then in the Southern League. My dream of a move to Aston Villa fell down after the two clubs could not agree a fee for me. I'd always been taught to fight for what you really want, so whilst this door slammed shut with crushing disappointment, another one opened in the town of Ljungskile in the Västra Götland region of north-west Sweden. A town with a population so small that they could all squeeze into Sittingbourne's Central Park stadium. I was on the path to becoming a football tourist.

Ljungskile SK were plying their trade in the Superettan, the second league in Swedish football. I had swapped trips to Rothwell Town for Motala FC, St Leonards Stamcroft for Landskrona and King's Lynn for Kristianstads. Where were they on the map? I had no idea. But soon I would find out. The club had ambition, having risen from the fifth tier of Swedish football, and would rise again to the Allsvenskan, the top table in Svenska. Some of the days were cold, colder than you can ever imagine, but I was living my dream. Ljungskile SK was a good friend to me in particular in those first few months where my Swedish consisted of

'Bra', 'Slutspurt' and 'tack sa mycket'. I learned quickly, I was only a few hundred miles away from home but I could have been on the moon. I had now officially become a football tourist.

I thought that life couldn't get any better then in 2006 I moved to 11 times Swedish champions, and the biggest club in the country, AIK. I was heading to the bright lights and expensive beers of Stockholm. After a season outside of the top flight, the Gnaget were building for the future and I was part of those plans. I approached every training session and every game with the same positive mental attitude and a will to win. The notorious fans of the Black Army were soon singing my name as we won an unprecedented league and cup double. I had found my home. My family were all around me and football made my life complete. I was no longer a football tourist, I was a local.

I met Stuart for the first time after a Svenskan Cupen game in the wilds of Ängelholm in 2010. We'd struggled to break down a dogged second division side in what was a real potential banana skin for AIK. We were officially the best team in Sweden and everyone wanted a shot at us. But here on a Monday night, miles from where tourists would normally venture, was Stuart, camera in hand. We greeted each other with a smile, a handshake and finally a manly hug. After all, any Englishman who had made the long trip into the Swedish countryside on a school night deserved my ultimate respect. Here, I realised, was the real football tourist.

Last autumn my contract with AIK expired. I could have taken the easy option and come back home to south-east London. But that's not what I am anymore. Being a football tourist has changed my life. Breakfast to me is a kanelbulle rather than a bacon sandwich, the occasional beer (when I'm not training of course) is low alcohol and winters mean proper snow. So I decided to stay, moving to newly promoted Östers IF in the central town of Växjö for one last shot in what is the best job in the world. Once again, I was a football tourist.

So why do we do it? Why do we travel thousands of miles just to watch 22 men kick a bit of leather around a bit of grass? Because it is the beautiful game. And thanks to the internet, budget airlines and a new generation of football fans who want to experience something new, we are willing to fly here, there and everywhere just to say "I've been there". I may be on the other side of the white line but I get the same kick from playing somewhere new as I did 20 years ago when my career started.

Yeah, sure, I could have taken the so-called 'traditional' English approach when that Sweden-shaped door opened up for me in 1998 and put on a video of Only Fools and Horses, opened my copy of The Sun and tucked into my roast beef Sunday lunch. But I didn't. Little did I realise it at the time but I had become a football tourist.

Since our meeting back in 2010, Stuart and I have chatted frequently about the game, the Swedes and the West Ham / Millwall rivalry. I've read with interest some of his travels, taking the whole concept of football tourism to a new level. In some ways I'm jealous, reading about places I've always wanted to visit. But I still have a job to do here. So for now I begrudgingly hand over the title of the Football Tourist to Stuart, but one day I want that title back. Read on, take notes, dare to be brave and follow in our footsteps. You will be rewarded for your efforts.

Be lucky.

Kenny Pavey
Växjö
April 2013

The Cast

"To say that these men paid their shillings to watch twenty-two hirelings kick a ball is merely to say that a violin is wood and catgut, that Hamlet is so much paper and ink..."

J.B. Priestley

Like any Hollywood blockbuster, there would be no huge explosions, no steamy sex scenes or horrific blood baths without a crew of experts behind the scenes. The Football Tourist is exactly the same....apart from the blood, C4 and the sex. Yes, let's not forget the lack of sex. But what there has been over the past couple of years is a group of top people who have been Pacino to my De Niro, Hattie Jacques to my Barbara Windsor and Katie Price to, well, nobody really. So in no particular order, this Ockley Books production has been brought to you by:

The Current Mrs Fuller (CMF) - Patient, understanding wife of nearly 15 years. We met in a bar, arguing about whether Pearce or Dicks was the best left back in England. Twenty years later we still don't agree. Loves it when I come home from a weekend away and immediately start planning another one with just a bunch of petrol station flowers as a bargaining chip. Thinks that the Lewes FC toilets are worst in world and will not come to a game at The Dripping Pan until new ones are installed.

Lolly Fuller - Not her real name but one of those embarrassing (for her) nicknames that was devised when she was a baby. Although based on her constant teenage demands to "borrow" money from me, the name is very apt. Loves going to football, but as long as she can put her make up on first. Bought Tom Daley's book just to look at the pictures.

Littlest Fuller - Not really that little now having just turned ten. Hates football with a passion because of the illogical nature of the offside rule, but can be bought with a free ice cream or if the game was between Hello Kitty City and Moshi Monsters United (whatever they are).

Danny Last - "Lasty" to his mates, "Danny" to me and "oh God where are you going now?" to Current Mrs Fuller. Creator of EuropeanFootballWeekends.co.uk, a man's best friend who loves Brighton & Hove Albion, taking jolly good pictures, a beer or two (but never before breakfast), speaks pretty good Spanish but rubbish Serbian. Once scored a goal at Bognor Regis Town FC, but doesn't like to talk about it.

Big Deaksy - A gentle giant of a man who turns into an internet troll after a few beers on a Saturday night. Loves nothing more than an away day, especially if it involves a few beers in a new pub somewhere and slagging off part-time fans.

Cynical Dave - People may think he is a being of mythology but Dave exists, ruler in his own world of obscure football trivia, huge complex football bets and pointing out the failings of non-league referees. Doesn't do European trips unless it involves going to Belgium in Fuller's Taxis to stock up on tobacco.

Huddo Hudson - Newcastle misses an angel when Andy Hudson goes on tour, which is basically every weekend. Recently made the high-profile move from Hebburn Town to Jarrow Roofing FC (as marketing manager) but still retains his passion for a trip or two. Always up for a laugh, with a story or five. Has an eye for the ladies, especially when he's 'splashed it all over'.

Kenny Legg - Weymouth's loss was Düsseldorf's gain when he upped-sticks for work to head for Germany. King of searching out the most ridiculous tin-pot games, finding dogs wearing scarves and can multiply any two digits together within seconds. Kenny is single, ladies.

Stoffers - Michael Stoffl is a German giant of a man. Lives in Berlin, fan of Munich 1860 although spends more than 50% of the year in various corners of the world watching football, spreading happiness and joy. Can order a drink in 76 different languages, carries maps for every town in the world as well as an emergency bottle of beer in his 'secret' pocket.

Shep - Phil Sheppard is our West Country correspondent, happy with life and modern day football. Haha – fooled you! Shep hates modern football, laments the good old days of watching Forest Green Rovers without the vegan menu, loves his Stone Island jacket and the tear ups between Swindon Town and Swindon Supermarine.

Adam Lloyd - Lives in a villa (paid for by work) in a small town overlooking Rome. Drives to work in a brand new Alfa Romeo (paid for by work), eats at the finest restaurants in Rome (paid for by work) and is a regular in the Stadio Olimpico supporting AS Roma. Jealous? Too bloody right! Has a fine eye for a good picture. Reading's loss was Rome's gain.

Dagenham Dan - A man who thinks nothing of dropping everything and heading off to Europe for the weekend when Dagenham & Redbridge are away. Getting married shortly, so I expect his volume of trips will increase. Owns more football shirts than Stevie G (probably).

Chapter One

Welcome to Spakenburg
The maddest local derby in Europe

6th November 2010
SV Spakenburg 2 IJsselmeervogels 3
Sportpark de Westmaat

7th November 2010
FC Utrecht 1 PSV Eindhoven 2
Stadion Galgenwaard

*"...whichever way you looked you had thousands of flashing
Viking hats in your eye line..."*

I woke up and tentatively opened one eye. Something didn't feel quite right. Firstly, I had to think about where I was. The bright light, the cold hard floor and a towel as a pillow suggested that I was in a bathroom. A hotel bathroom. A Dutch hotel bathroom. I carried out a quick assessment to ensure everything else was in some sort of order.

Trousers on?

Check.

Phone in hand (but dead)?

Check.

Money spilt over the floor?

Check.

Temporary IJsselmeervogels tattoo on my arm?

Check.

It must have been a good night...

The sound of the Match of the Day theme tune started to fill my ears. I slowly got up, held onto the towel rail and peered round the corner into the room. Still asleep on the bed was Danny Last, fully clothed (including shoes) and clutching a bottle of Malibu.

Saturday night was all a bit of a blur. I do remember a man with a goat at some point and a taxi-driver called Willem who claimed he was once an extra in Coronation Street, buying a bag of bon-bons from Mavis Riley no less. I remember a school disco, a bloke dressed as the Pope, Stoffers walking around with 25 beer glasses on his head and finally, 'Smullers Spicy Crockets'. It dawned on me I was in Utrecht, Holland's fourth largest city and home to the 'Museum of Automatically Playing Musical Instruments'. Welcome to the world of European Football Weekends.

Danny woke up looking worried that John Motson was talking to him from the TV at the end of his bed. He scanned his attire, confused that his shoes were still in place yet he had no socks on. He looked even more concerned about the bottle of Malibu in his hand, especially as it was completely empty, he didn't drink spirits and it smelt faintly of wee.

We tried to piece together the answers to those questions in some sort of order. Motty was on the TV because BBC One can be received in Holland. He had no socks on because on the way back to the hotel he stood in a puddle that turned into a small swimming pool (although I have no idea why he then put his shoes back on). I had found the bottle of Malibu in a bathroom sink in a bar in the village of Bunschoten and gave it to him as a present.

Ah, yes, mystery solved. We're in Bunschoten which is, of course, the home of SV Spakenburg.

As a seasoned football watcher I have seen some of the biggest games in the world in my time. I've seen AC Milan annihilate Inter 6-0 in the San Siro. I've seen Brøndby fans set fire to Parken, home of FC Copenhagen whilst losing the "New Firm" derby. Back home in England I've seen more police than fans at a West Ham versus Millwall game. Even taking all that into account and many more experiences I won't bore you with (yet), when Danny suggested we come to watch the Spakenburg derby I have to say I looked at him as blankly as I do when the Current Mrs. Fuller utters the words "a cracking craft fair".

But then he showed me some pictures he'd been sent from a local journalist in the lowlands of Holland. Of course pigs painted in the team colours. Of course a twenty-foot inflatable Viking. Of course an airplane drop of hundreds of toilet brushes over the away fans.

Welcome to the SV Spakenburg versus IJsselmeervogels, or to give it a more appropiate name - the spell-check derby.

Few people have ever heard of the game outside of the Netherlands, let alone the actual place. This meant we went as pioneers for European football tourists everywhere, brave warriors looking to return with a bag full of memories that would tempt others to follow in our trail-blazing footsteps. It wasn't hard forming an advance party to journey into the unknown and legendary world football sightseer Michael 'Stoffers' Stoffl was the first name on the list. So famous is Stoffers now in his home city of Berlin that there are plans to create his very own action doll for Christmas complete with interchangeable silk scarves of various obscure football teams to put around its wrist.

Next on the list was Shep, without a shadow of a doubt the single most pessimistic football fan in the world. Shep lives in a small village not far from Nailsworth in Gloucestershire, which of course is famous for being the home of an incredibly steep hill at the top of which can be found the New Lawn, home of Forest Green Rovers. Shep is disillusioned with Rovers thanks to a new owner who has banned meat from the match day menu. To him that is tantamount to banning beer from pubs. "It's just not right Stuart, men need meat at football, it's in our DNA, it's part of who we are" he told me on the flight over. Several times. However this weekend he is accompanied by his brother who is, of course, also called 'Shep', is much happier with his lot in life and keeps the mood up throughout.

There would be other characters that would drift in and out of our weekend's entertainment but it was the five of us (me, Danny, Stoffers, Shep and Shep) who met at an ungodly hour on the concourse of Amsterdam's Schiphol airport. Our destination was the tiny little town of Breukelen, about 30 minutes south of Amsterdam. There we were to be picked up by Pat, another man who spent far too much time travelling around the world to watch football than was healthy. Pat would then drive us to Bunschoten, home of the two teams, and it would be time for the fun to start.

Spakenburg and Bunschoten developed as two separate villages but urban sprawl has meant they are now one and the same place. Nice pretty Dutch houses, a small harbour and a population of just less than 20,000 people. This is a commuter town for the cities of Amsterdam and Utrecht for those with a sleepy outlook on life, the kind of place where an abandoned bike would make the front page of the local paper. Everyone knows everybody here and washing the car on Sunday is frowned upon.

For 50 weeks of the year everybody goes about their lives in an orderly and civil fashion; for the other two the whole place goes a bit mental. Just like Manchester, Milan and Munich, the place is divided by whether you are a blue or a red - the blue of SV Spakenburg or the red of IJsselmeervogels. On Bunschoten Derby Day (capitalised as it should be on the calendar of any self-respecting football fan) there is no in-between.

Within a small community, these two team's histories have been intertwined for the best part of eighty years. The blue half of the village was first formed back in 1931. They joined the Eerste Klasse in the 1970–71 season under coach Joop van Basten, father of the legendary Dutch striker Marco van Basten, and clinched their first amateur league title in 1974. They became champions again in 1985 when they also won the overall Dutch Amateur league title, and again in 1987, 2000 and 2008. Over in the red corner IJsselmeersvogels were formed in 1932 as Na Arbeid Sport ('Sport after Work') and have followed a similar pattern to SV Spakenburg. They came into the newly-formed Topklasse division as one of the favourites, but as we're all well versed in footballing clichés by now we know that in these games the form book usually goes out of the window.

In 2005 NOS Studio Sport broadcast a documentary about the recent renewal of hostilities between the two clubs called 'Rood of Blauw, een week uit het leven van een gespleten dorp', or for those not quite fluent in Dutch like, ahem, I am - 'Red or Blue: A week in the life of a village split in two'. Since they first played each other in the Eerste Klasse in 1972 the clubs had met thirty-one times with the blue half slightly edging things with eleven wins to IJsselmeersvogel's ten. Despite the relative anonymity, this as big a game as you can get in Dutch third-tier football. Woof!

We were early, or possibly Pat was late - either way with time to kill we headed for some food. For those of you who have never sampled Dutch railway station fare, until you have you can never call yourself truly adventurous. Holland is the home to 'Febo', a fast-food brand that can lay claim to be one of the oldest in the world. Outdating McDonalds by some 7 years, Febo first opened its doors in Amsterdam in 1941. Today it is simply known as the place with the spicy potato 'Krokets'. Each branch is a wall of little doors with hot food in each one. You put your money in the slot, open the door and taste the goodness inside. Not too dissimilar to the Banana Bar in Amsterdam really in a way, except you can touch the goods on offer in Febo.

Sated with tasty savoury Dutch treats and a cheeky bottle of Amstel, Danny updated us on the plan for the day. Apparently we were heading to someone's back garden for a party, then onto the football, followed by a school disco or two. Bunschoten doesn't do things by half it appears. He explained that the local mayor had decreed that an alcohol ban would be in place until after the game finished to try and stop some of the tomfoolery that had taken place over previous years (such as said toilet brush drop from a great height earlier). You could see his point as tensions had run so high in the past that the Dutch Football Association kept the two sides in separate divisions for extended periods.

Just like the old battles between the ICF and Headhunters across London, time and gravity catches up with everyone and so the troublemakers of yesterday are now the peacemakers of to-day, happy to have a cup of coffee and a nice little sit down rather than tearing it down the high street high on Heineken. The game is played in an almost carnival atmosphere, albeit one where rip-ping the piss out of your opposition in the most creative way is positively endorsed and encouraged, and this was what piqued Danny's initial interest. A game in a small town surrounded by parties and piss-taking? Tick, tick, tick and tickety-tick.

This was the first time the game had been played in the newly remixed Topklasse division, the third tier of Dutch football. The Dutch FA had seen the development of the two clubs and had 'encouraged' them to join the league although the move wasn't popular with everyone. The IJsselmeersvogel chairman Arian van de Vuurst (who I really hope is nicknamed 'Expecting the Vuurst' in the manner of QPR legend 'One Size Fitz Hall') was one of the most dissenting voices in the run up to the game, quoted as saying that "professional football does not fit in with our culture."

Pat arrived, his tardiness excused as he explained he'd come straight off his night-shift at Brussels Zaventem airport and then driven straight across the border to meet us, so much was his excitement for the biggest village game in European football. He gave us a rundown of what the local media were saying about the match and it appeared that the SV Spakenburg manager Andre Pope had been arrested for alleged drink-driving in the last week – a fact that the IJsselmeersvogel fans would surely seize upon come game time.

We arrived outside a nice looking house in the backstreets of Bunschoten. Pat checked the address once, twice and then three times like a lady. This certainly appeared to be a strange location for a pre-match party but then the door opened and out came our host Wim Muijs, a SV Spakenburg fan and the most connected man in Bunschoten football apparently. On Danny's request he had not only got us four tickets rarer than Villy van der Vonka's golden ones to a boring old chocolate factory, but we also had an invite to the legendary Muijs house party.

We were directed towards the garage, converted into a club shop for the day, and like a scene from Mr. Benn we entered as English football tourists and as if by magic, exited into the garden bedecked in blue and white with an authentic Viking helmet complete with flashing horns. Just your average Saturday in rural Holland I guess. We donated a sum of €20 to Wim's favourite charity (and quite fine she looked too in her SV Spakenburg bikini) which entitled us to 'help your bloody self to anything you want' in his own words - beer, shots, food from the BBQ, some nice pictures from the front room and, of course, a ticket for the spell-check derby.

All this frivolity meant even Shep the elder broke out in to a rare smile and uttered "bloody lush this lads, best day of my life I reckon." I am sure Mrs. Shep may disagree but for now who were we to sit in judgment on the goings on back in Gloucestershire? We got chatting to a group of Ajax fans who had chartered a coach to come to this game. Eighty fans of Holland's biggest and most storied football club had decided that this game was a must-see event. We were definitely in the right place.

It seemed Wim's party wasn't the only one in the neighbour-hood, a consequence of the alcohol ban only applying to shops and bars selling it, not private parties. All that added up to the fact that the real winners on the day were the local supermarkets who had apparently shipped in a month's worth of supplies just for the event. We walked en masse towards the centre of the village, seemingly at every junction joined by another house party group. Fans of both teams mingled without an issue and few police in sight – hardly the scene you can expect in Bristol when Rovers and City next play each other.

The walk took us through the very picturesque centre of the village and all around Saturday afternoon shoppers without a ticket for the game viewed us with envious eyes. We rounded the corner and then walked into a view that very nearly reduced Stoffers to tears.

Not one football ground, but two.

Two full-blown grounds a mere stone's throw apart.

Another dream scenario achieved.

Not only was this the biggest village game in Europe, but the two grounds were located closer than any other two clubs in the world. Not my opinion but those of Stoffers himself, a man who is known to his friends as 'Judith Chalmers' in honour of his wan-derlust, bettered only by the original bronzed holiday reporter. To give you a sense of perspective, so close were the grounds that an over hit penalty on the IJsselmeersvogel pitch could end up in SV Spakenburg's far net. Just glorious.

It seemed a full-scale weeing-up-the-wall contest was in place from both clubs and their impressive facilities. Despite the game being played at SV Spakenburg's Sportpark de Westmaat, the doors were wide open to the Rood Westmaat next door. Fans wandered in and out, even taking part in a kick about on the pitch. There was a serious case of keeping up with the Van Der Jones's here – one club builds a sports hall, the other builds a sports hall with a sauna. One club builds a stand with 500 seats, the other will build one with 501. One club installs a 3G plastic pitch, the next minute a 4G appears across the way. You wee, we wee higher and so on and so forth.

With a good hour to go to kick-off the ground was almost full to the rafters. The huge twenty-foot inflatable Viking stood guard over the tunnel area whilst the teams warmed up on the pitch. We manoeuvred ourselves as close to the IJsselmeersvogel fans as we could, although whichever way you looked you had thousands of flashing Viking hats in your eye line. The official capacity of the ground is 8,500 but with people sitting in trees overlooking the ground, on roofs of double-decker buses in the car park and in every other nook and cranny, there was certainly more than that there on derby day. One man walked up and down the away terrace 'blessing' the fans. This man was dressed in the ceremonial gowns of the Vatican City and every so often he would run at full pelt and weave in and out. After a few minutes it registered through the beer what he was doing, of course – a reference to Mr. A Pope and his driving misdemeanours. Nobody bothered to remove him from the pitch and throughout the game he kept popping up on the touchline behind the goal, dishing out what I'm sure was welcome advice to the home side.

Whilst no beer could be taken out of the clubhouse (a.k.a. the school gym, more on that later) you could drink to your heart's content inside – although in theory not until half time. Note the words 'in theory'. What this of course translates to in these circumstances is 'Slip us €5 and you can fill your pockets with those strange little cups that you only get in Holland'. Stoffers came back from an expedition almost double the size, an achievement for such a tall man, and then proceeded to feed us beer like our Lord Jesus Christ and those loaves and fishes, hidden in specially sewn pockets in his coat.

T-minus one minute until kick off. Suddenly blue smoke started to fill the air and the noise was turned up past 11. Judging by the reaction of the crowd around us, something was happening. It's all right if you have inside knowledge but we poor English football tourists had no idea what was occurring beyond the blue fog. When the smoke finally subsided it turned out the game was underway. Apparently, according to a local next to me, the teams had run out, there had been a streaker run across the pitch with a rude message on his bum aimed at the away fans, who in turn had sent the Pope on to mediate. At least I think that's what he said, it could have been "I have no bloody idea you Cockney Muppet." Whatever it was the roar of the crowd as the home side won a corner distracted our intentions and we actually watched some football for a bit.

I'm sure you are not particularly interested in what happened over 90 minutes in third-tier Dutch football so I won't dwell too much on the detail. Despite the home side being top of the league and in good form, IJsselmeersvogel sneaked a 3-2 win in a very entertaining game. The reds took the lead in the 23rd minute when Raymond Bronkhorst bundled the ball home but could only hold on for 4 minutes before Hans van de Haar equalised.

The second half saw the only non-Dutch player in the starting twenty two score the third goal of the game as Suriname's Cerezo Fung a Wing put IJsselmeersvogel back in the lead. This in turn led to a mini-pitch invasion that was soon brought to order by the Pope himself. Their lead was extended in the 73rd minute by Nick Kuipers before Spakenburg reduced the arrears to 3-2 when Ivo Rottiné scored with ten minutes to play. Despite six yellow cards and a frantic period of extended injury time IJsselmeers-vogel held on for a famous 'away' win. Whilst the red half of the village celebrated, the blue raised their Viking horns in defiance and headed to the bar.

We had watched the second period with two English ex-pats who had made the trip especially to say hello to Danny and myself. This has become standard form on such trips - there are always these little cameo appearances from individuals that various social media networks have thrown up. We've built up quite a network of ex-pats and locals who love obscure football matches as much as we do. Thomas Archer and Dan Richardson had got in touch via Twitter and were sold on the history of the game like us.

Tom had come to Holland on a rugby tour a few years ago, got lost in the Red Light District in Amsterdam and decided it was easier to stay. Mr. Richardson was another West Country chap, albeit one who now lived in Slovakia, working on a rig in the North Sea whilst also being an ADO Den Haag and a Slovan Bratislava season ticket holder. Clear as mud really. Somehow Dan had managed to convince his girlfriend that he could come to this game, despite the fact she was well over 8 months pregnant. It was only an eighteen-hour drive back to Bratislava after all and I reassured him that first-born babies tend to be born after twenty or so hours of labour so he would be fine if the emergency call came through. I made that bit up but it seemed to offer reas-surance, if any were needed that is.

With the game now over it was time for the fun part. Whilst the atmosphere at the derby had delivered on the hype, it was the post-match parties (yes that should be a plural) that had really got our interest piqued. Whilst there was a party on the Thursday before the match when the women's teams played against each other (SV Spakenburg won that game 7-0), it is the Saturday night shenanigans that had really seen us all sign up for the trip. Our host Wim had tried to describe what would be in store for us. When he started his description with "you know those DVD's where all the women take their clothes off" I blacked out. All I really remember was Danny clicking his fingers in front of my eyes to bring me round.

It seemed that both clubs hosted almost identical post-match parties; however the winning side's one tended to be the better one for obvious reasons. We had some loyalty to our hosts and so we kicked off with the blues bash. The DJ was trying to get things going, but with their team's defeat the fans weren't really in the mood. It was still brilliant in there, but we had to move on. Two hours later and without anyone looking, we sneaked out, walked across the pitch of the Rood Westmaart stadium and into their party. In Danny's very own words "chaps, we've done it, we've found Nirvana."

He wasn't just talking about the DJ playing 'Smells like Teen Spirit' either. The IJsselmeersvogels team were on the main stage of course, fans were standing on tables and chairs singing all around us, and there in the middle were the ladies, just like Wim had said. It was as if IJseelmeersvogels had won the World Cup. Whilst the blue half of the village would have to lick their wounds tonight, they would have the last laugh on their neigh-bours later in the week when they took over 1,500 to Eindhoven for the Dutch Cup match with 21-time Dutch Champions PSV.

Holland loves its Munts. Wherever we go in the Netherlands it seems that our cash is simply not good enough for football clubs. They don't want our Euros, they want Munts. Small round plastic discs that you have to buy and then exchange for beer. Lovely, Dutch beer. We did our bit for the crumbling Eurozone that night, creating a beer tower that soon rose higher than Stof-fers and he is of course taller than a giraffe standing on a step ladder doing a Peter Crouch impression. The night ended with the inevitable swinging of a shoe on the dance-floor. We danced to a traditional mix of Euro techno pop, football party tapes and, ahem, Coldplay. The Pope was there of course. We danced with him too although we resisted the urge to kiss his ring, which was I think what he wanted us to do. It sounds silly now, but the most popular dance of the night was some sort of Hokey-Cokey num-ber. I say silly, but when you've had a skin full of beer and you're on your holidays, it is tremendous fun whether you have a clue what's going on or not.

If you've ever wondered what happened to all the dry-ice machines that were made redundant after Top of the Pops ended, don't. Turns out they've all been bought up by the folk of Spakenburg. Dry-ice filled both sports halls all night. This was, and still is, the party of the year in Bunschoten and everyone was out and dressed to impress. It's rumoured that the birth rate peaks nine months after these games and having been, I can understand why.

At some point in the evening we made our way back to the centre of the village. We had been joined by a couple of locals, who for some reason thought that Shep was a member of the CIA and wanted to arrest their neighbour for growing fake weed. Then the truth struck us. We were stuck in the middle of a village in the heart of the Netherlands, there was no public transport to where we needed to go and most pressingly, where did we need to go? Danny had mentioned Utrecht but now all he could say was "there's a wild wind blowing down the corner of his street". It appeared he was suffering from Coldplayitis, from which there is no cure no matter how hard we try to *ahem* fix you. Shep used his black ops contacts to rustle up a cab for us. We searched Danny and found a confirmation email in his pocket, handed it to our driver and we were off.

Fast forward ten hours and here we were, Match of the Day on the TV and wondering where the bottle of Malibu that smelled of wee fitted into our previous night's fun. We headed down to breakfast and lo and behold there were Sheps One and Two plus Stoffers. Of course, the events of Spakenburg started to come flooding back and giggles were the order of the day along with our full English.

As most seasoned European football weekenders will tell you, there is no point in having an opportunity of a weekend away and only getting one game in. Granted this trip was arranged to take in the surreal atmosphere in Spakenburg, but those lovely chaps at the Dutch FA had kindly scheduling had meant that just down the road FC Utrecht were taking on PSV Eindhoven on this very afternoon. Would we be there? Too bloody right.

Tickets to see games in Holland aren't easy to get – that is unless you have friends like Football Fans Frans (say that quickly with a hangover – we couldn't) who had sorted out our seats for us with a nod and a wink. Frans runs one of the best European Football websites the world has ever seen (FootballFans.eu) and had only been too happy to help out the "crazy English fans" when we had shared our plans for the weekend. Before you could say Sportvereniging Roda Juliana Combinatie Kerkrade he had secured tickets for us all.

Any good football fan will know that FC Utrecht was formed on the 1st July 1970. I was supposed to have been a Sixties child myself but I stubbornly refused to make an appearance until the 6th day of 1970. Looking back now I think there would have been much more kudos to say I was born in the 1960s but nature decided it was not to be. Like FC Utrecht I missed out on all the orgies, drugs and loud flowery shirts, but like FC Utrecht I've made up for it since. Except for the orgies and drugs bit. Love a flowery shirt, me.

The owners of three local teams, DOS FC (Denial of Service? That was an in-joke for us technical geeks, trust me if you worked in I.T. right now you'd be laughing your head off), USV Elinkwijk and FC Velox had a bit of a chat over a pancake whilst watching the 1969 Moon Landing (probably) and decided that one club would be better than three so they agreed to merge. Hmm, now where to play and what to call themselves? Well as they were all in the city of Utrecht one bright spark came up with the perfect name, FC Utrecht. And a ground for this new club to play in? Well what about that unused football pitch to the south of the ring road, you know, that Stadion Galgenwaard place? Sorted. One professional team sir, fit and ready to start the next season.

The seventies wasn't the best time to be a new professional club in Holland. Ajax dominated the game in Holland and across the continent winning 5 Eredivisie titles and 3 European Cups, whilst the other 5 titles were shared by PSV Eindhoven and Feyenoord – sound familiar? In the 2009/10 season Utrecht had exceeded expectations and a Europa League spot was grabbed, catapulting them into a tough group with ex-European Cup winners Steaua Bucharest, Liverpool and former Italian giants Napoli. Four games in at the time of our visit and three draws had seen the club still in with a chance of progressing, assuming they beat Napoli in December.

The club were enjoying the most impressive home form in Holland having dropped just two points in the season to date but they were up against PSV Eindhoven, a team who had scored ten just two weeks previously in a remarkable game against Feyenoord.

Disappointingly, PSV had only sold a thousand tickets for a game that was about an hour away (everywhere in Holland is 'about an hour' away) but there would still be a police presence that would put the total armed forces in a number of small countries to shame.

After our hearty breakfast we took to the streets of Utrecht, wandering along the canals that criss-crossed the centre as befits the Dutch stereotype. Our plan was to meet Frans at the ground early where he would open a magic door to a member's bar for us. Not just any old bar either, but one that had managed to find 6 different TV stations that were all showing speed skating, different races as well I should add. Impressive stuff.

We were joined by some of the very finest Anglo-Dutch bloggers (if a category like that did indeed ever exist anywhere). As well as Frans the PSV diehard, we were also joined by Abby, a masters student from down the road who is also Seattle Sounders fan and knows more about European football than your average TV pundit (a classic quote was "Mario Balotelli has only once scored twice and been sent off in his career before today and that was against Brescia in the Italian Cup in 2006").

Pre-match drinks out of the way we piled into the stadium. The signs outside made it very clear in no uncertain terms that all bombs should be disposed of before we entered, and that tickling anyone below the knee was strictly forbidden. Common sense we all thought. We changed our cash for Munts of course, and filled our pockets with small Dutch beers. As I stood waiting to be served I noticed movement to my right. From a distance it appeared that the players were miraculously descending down a magic staircase onto the concourse to join the queue for refreshments. Of course they weren't really, but this was the Utrecht's crazy take on tunnel architecture. The players descend a glass staircase that runs across the concourse, so that the fans can press themselves up against the windows and leer at the teams. Apparently last season in the game versus Ajax one buxom young lady whipped her top off and exposed her breasts with the words (in Dutch of course) 'Ajax suck on these'. The kick off was delayed whilst the squad formed an orderly queue (I better add an 'allegedly').

The Galgenwaard is similar in design to the shy and retiring Dave Whelan's DW Stadium in Wigan with one exception; this place had an atmosphere. The PSV fans made some noise as the teams came out, knowing full well that a win here coupled with

Ajax's shock defeat at home to ADO Den Haag would put some light between them and the chasing pack.

The first twenty minutes weren't particularly exciting. Utrecht tried to play long diagonal balls but the PSV defence was well marshalled enough to cope. It was no surprise that they eventually took the lead on 24 minutes when then-PSV-but-soon-to-be-Barca-midfielder Ibrahim Afellay delivered a cross from the right and Ola Toivonen forced then-Utrecht-but-soon-to-be-Swansea-goalkeeper Michel Vorm into a diving save with a glancing header. The rebound fell to Balazs Dzsudzsák who produced a low left-footed dipping shot that squirmed under the body of the keeper and into the bottom right-hand corner of the net.

Ten minutes later and it was the turn of the home fans to celebrate as PSV's Jonathan Reis received a straight red for an elbow on Utrecht's Alje Schut. Harsh perhaps but as Alan Hansen would say in this situation "If you lead with your elbow you are asking for a red card son, now where the hell am I, what the hell's a 'Munt' and why is no one speaking English here?"

The second half saw Utrecht throw the proverbial kitchen sink at the PSV defence. They had gone to a 4-5-1 and looked dangerous on the break. Of course it is always harder to play against ten men, because that makes logical sense to everyone apart from the manager whose team cannot beat a team with ten men. This is football cliché law after all.

In this instance PSV soaked up the pressure, broke with speed, Toivonen wriggled his way into the box and fell over the leg of Jacob Lensky. The referee immediately pointed to the spot and showed Lensky a straight red card, failing to consult with the linesman who was up with play and had a much better view. Dzsudzsák stepped up to convert the resulting spot kick and enraged the home fans by taking over two joyful minutes to walk back to the centre spot.

The crowd noise swelled again although this was in part due to Utrecht drowning out any natural hustle and bustle by playing recorded sound over the loudspeakers, apparently to stop the abuse being heard by the referee as they are sensitive chaps here in Holland and may start to cry. A few minutes later Franck Demouge scored for the home side with an overhead kick, which then started two key debates:

1) What is the difference between a traditional bicycle kick and a plain old overhead kick?

2) What is the best example of either you have seen?

Nobody has answered question one conclusively yet but the overwhelming Twitter poll (the only medium that matters in this modern footballing world) winner of number two is Trevor Sinclair for QPR v Barnsley in the FA Cup in 1997. I can only imagine his delight at the news and if you're reading this Trevor, there is a small trophy in the post.

Please note if you are Trevor Sinclair there is no small trophy in the post. Loved your work at West Ham and at the 2002 World Cup, but no trophy for you as the correct answer is now Zlatan's v England in 2012 - huge apologies

Time was up for Utrecht. PSV had been the big winners of the weekend and their fans celebrated in the only way they knew how by trying to tear down the fences in the stadium and setting fire to the seats. Great to see such glorious traditions preserved for the younger generation.

With that, our weekend was almost over. There was still time for a couple more drinks and some of the obligatory spicy potato crockets as we discussed where our quest to conquer the great obscure games in Europe would take us next. Above us, a TV showed the Liverpool versus Chelsea game but do you know what? Nobody really cared about John Terry's latest fall from grace, Ashley Cole's bitter and twisted outburst or the fact that Fernando Torres still hadn't scored a goal. All of those fans at Anfield were getting worked up into a rage about teams and players who couldn't care a jot about them and gave very little back, yet just an hour away on an airplane was a hidden world of fun where for two afternoons a year, a small harmonious village turns into the party capital of Europe. Where would we go next? Well one thing was for sure; it wouldn't be Liverpool.

Chapter Two

Stockholm Syndrome
Flares, fire-crackers and Kenny Pavey

4th April 2011
Djurgården IF 0 AIK 0
The Råsunda

"...minutes after the teams came out they were ushered back
down the tunnel as smoke engulfed the stadium..."

Look to the stars
Let hope grow in your eyes
And we'll love and we'll hate and we'll die
All to no avail, all to no avail

Lyrics from 'Stockholm Syndrome' by Muse

What's the biggest game in world football at club level played on a regular basis?

Many will immediately say Real Madrid v Barcelona, others the Derby d'Italia between Juventus and Internazionale, some might even say Manchester United and Liverpool on size of global fan bases alone. While it's difficult to track something as ambiguous as 'the biggest', there are patterns you can follow to help you make a decision.

For instance, what is clear is that in most domestic leagues the bigger games tend to be the local derbies. Take for instance the Superclásico in Argentina, Boca Juniors versus River Plate, a big enough event to genuinely stop the traffic in Buenos Aires. Anyone who has experienced the Eternal Derbies of either Rome or Belgrade will feel the passion coursing through the streets of those cities on those days more than any other. Whilst the story is a bit different in Spain and, to an extent, France, nothing has quite the passion of a big city rivalry. Childhood friends become enemies for the day, families split in two with a clear line down the middle and romances are often conducted like modern day Montagues and Capulets thanks to the teams people choose to support in their youth.

During the past few years I have been lucky enough to experience some of the biggest derbies in the world. Internazionale 0, Milan 6 will always rank up there in my most treasured footballing memories, as will the rampant destruction of Parken (home to FC Copenhagen) by Brøndby IF fans in 2010 in one of the fastest growing inter-city rivalries. One game I had yet to tick off but had always wanted to see was the Stockholm derby, a simmering affair flying under the radar of some, between Djurgården IF and AIK.

Stockholm is a three-team city but since the relegation of IF Hammarby in 2009, the rivalry between the two left in the top tier has grown to proportions that are normally only seen in South America. The two teams, ironically, share so much. Both were founded in 1891 separated by just a single month, and both are originally from the northern part of Stockholm. As the city has spread its tentacles into the suburbs, the clubs have moved too. Today they are almost in different towns with AIK based in Solna to the north of the city centre, and Djurgården in the eastern district of Östermalm.

They are historically the two biggest and most successful clubs in Sweden, with 11 League titles each. The Djurgården versus AIK rivalry on the pitch is considered by far the biggest in Sweden and maybe even the whole of Scandinavia because of its rich history. Today however, there is huge animosity between the two clubs and both sets of fans with the Järnkaminerna or Blue Saints of Djurgården on one side, and the notorious Black Army of AIK on the other.

Swedish football is a hard one to explain. Being one of the few countries that play a March to November season, by the time the Allsvenskan winners kick off their Champions League campaign in mid-July, they are often without their star Championship-winning players and struggling to find the form that won them the league the previous year. The previous seven seasons have seen seven different sides win the league, further underlining the unpredictable nature of football in the country. It's not only the traditional big clubs who find themselves in pole position either. IF Elfsborg and Kalmar FF can lay claim to winning the Allsvenskan in the past five years, two clubs that few outside of Sweden will have ever heard of.

Every season the team that seems to do well is the one that has the most home-grown players. With Sweden playing March to October they essentially only have the August transfer window to make their changes, by which time the league is often all but over. As a result clubs develop their squads, do well and win the league and then sell off all of their best talent to eager clubs across Europe. Of course for the title-winners this means that by the time the Champions League campaign starts the following July the heart of their squad has often gone and more often than not, their campaign is over quicker than they dared hope for. This season (2011) was no different. Last year the champions had been undoubtedly Sweden's biggest club, AIK, but come the first derby of the year they were second bottom with just two points and one goal to show for their first five games.

I am lucky enough to travel quite frequently for work purposes. With some freedom on my itinerary I am able to wind down at the end of a busy day with some football. As luck would have it on the very date I planned to be in Stockholm, the first derby game of the 2011 season was due to kick off at 7pm.

Strange that.

Almost as if I planned it.

Stockholm is often missed off the European footballing week-end radar because of the cost of...well...basically everything apart from the football. Whilst you can often pick up a bargain flight to the city you'll then end up on a two-hour bus trip from some remote Ryanair-served airport, or the £40 train ride on the super-fast Arlanda Express.

From there you can of course save money by not eating or drinking anything in the city centre. Fancy a McDonald's? Then be prepared to pay one of the highest prices in the world for your Big Mac. The quarterly Economist BMI (Big Mac Index) puts Sweden in third place globally for your beef, bun, lettuce, on-ions, special sauce, cheese and gherkin that nobody likes all wrapped up in a sesame seed bun. Tempted by the Bishops Arms just a stone's throw from the station? Then be prepared not to see much change from your 100 Kroner note (usually about £11) for a drink.

But on the other hand - football tickets? Well, they are yours for the price of a shandy and an Apple Pie. Due to the previous instances of trouble in the derby it wasn't just as easy as log-ging onto Ticnet.se and printing your tickets at home this time. Thanks to some trademark Fuller charm I had established a good working relationship with the Djurgården press office, which of course meant that obtaining a pass for the most antici-pated game of the season was straight forward once they realised it was for *ahem* 'England's best looking and wittiest Swedish football reporter'.

Stockholm is a wonderful city. Over thirty percent is parks and green spaces, and another thirty percent is waterway. It is perfect for simply finding a spot to rest and watching the Swedes go about their daily business. Thanks to the novels of Stieg Larsson, and subsequent Millennium Trilogy of films, we are now very familiar with the city. From the historic buildings in Gamla Stan to the attraction-filled island of Djurgården, it just begs to be explored.

After various trips to Stockholm in the past I was looking for-ward to visiting the historic Olympic Stadion, home of Djurgården for this game. The Olympic Stadion, or simply Stadion for those in the know, hosted most of the events in the 1912 Summer Olympic Games including the Tug of War competition. Well, not really much of a competition to be honest as only two nations competed (Sweden represented by the Stockholm City Police and Great Britain represented by the City of London Police) and the event was held in less than 30 minutes on just the one day.

If that fact wasn't enough for you then did you know that it also hosted part of the Olympic Games in 1956? Yep, whilst the running, shooting, pushing, pulling and throwing was going on in Melbourne some 9,609 miles away in Australia, the equestrian competition was held in the Olympic Stadion due to quarantine issues. The answer to a pub quiz question you've yet to be asked.

Knowledge my friends, knowledge.

All this was jolly exciting and I had of course made a simple assumption that the game would be played at Djurgården's 13,000 capacity arena. And I would have happily headed off in that direction if it wasn't for one of the chaps in our Stockholm office pointing out that Solna is only a 5-minute journey from my hotel.

Solna?

No, I'm heading out to Östermalm.

Aren't I?

Well you'll be Jonathan No-Mates the Second out there, came the all-too-knowing answer. It seems that all big games like this are played at the Råsunda, home of AIK.

AIK are the team that everyone wants to knock down. Every country has one, whether it be for financial reasons, fan base or simply a perceived arrogance. They are the best-supported team in the country, although some would point to the fact they are allowed to play at the national stadium (the Råsunda) as a clear sign of favouritism from the Swedish FA.

However, things are due to change. Having survived for decades in old stadiums with poor facilities, all three Stockholm sides will have new homes within three years. Two brand new stadiums are due to pop up in different parts of the city that will see AIK become the major tenants at the 50,000 all-seater Friends Arena in Solna at the start of the 2013 season, whilst Djurgården and IF Hammarby will share the new Tele2 Arena in Johanneshov from August 2013 in the south of the city centre.

But for now it was the historical Råsunda that would see the first Battle of Stockholm in 2011. The Råsunda is one of two stadiums in the world to have hosted World Cup finals for both men and women. It hosted the men's final in the 1958 World Cup and the women's final in the 1995 Women's World Cup (the other stadium with this honor is the Rose Bowl in Pasadena, California, USA which hosted the 1994 World Cup and the 1999 Women's World Cup – knowledge again, see).

This wasn't my first trip to the stadium. Back in early 2010 I had come to see the man that had won the hearts of the AIK faithful, a man who was every bit a South Londoner as I was, yet was a virtual unknown in England. A hard-tackling and committed player who the fans loved and still speak of in only the most revered terms. A footballer who showed a level of integrity, humility and above all respect for his profession that put the majority of other players to shame worldwide. In a time when we were crying out for a decent right full back in our national team, here was one who had just won the double with AIK. Step forward Kenny Pavey.

An infectious smile comes across the face of every AIK fan when you mention one name: Kenny Pavey – crowd favourite, idol of the North Stand, legend. If you wanted a definition of a whole-hearted, passionate and fan-driven player then I would give you Kenny Pavey. But this isn't just an English clogger, this guy has skill to go with the occasional reducer.

I had been lucky enough to meet Kenny on my previous visit in 2010. The first question was obviously how he came to be plying his trade in a land best known for IKEA, Volvo and long summer nights. Pavey made his debut at his local club Affenley FC in South East London before moving to his boyhood favourites Millwall as a schoolboy. Unfortunately the dream of playing for the Lions didn't come through and so he moved down the A2 to Ryman League Sittingbourne where he made his debut in one of the most progressive non-league clubs around, so progressive in fact that he almost found himself on his way to Aston Villa where he seemed to have impressed when on trial in 1998. The clubs couldn't agree on a fee and just a few seasons later he was catapulted into the world of Swedish second division football.

His success here is down to the way he has integrated himself into the Swedish way of life, learning the language and throwing himself into his passion – football. He has won plaudits in and around the game for his attitude, commitment and the drive which last season saw him win the ultimate honour of a League and Cup winner's medal.

When we met Kenny prior to this game I asked him what I could expect from my first derby;

"It is one of the best football experiences of my life, my first derby match was a crowd of just under 35,000. Fans make it an amazing experience with Tifos, fireworks and flags. We won 3-1 that night which made the experience even more special. Family and friends that have been over say they have never seen anything like it, it always makes me very proud of the fans we have here."

Kenny isn't the only ex-Millwall player to have played in the Stockholm Derby of course. Back in 1985 Djurgården IF's star striker was none other than Edward "Teddy" Sheringham. Teddy was nineteen at the time and pushing to break into the Millwall first team. With Sweden playing summer football it was seen as an ideal opportunity for him to gain some experience. Thirteen goals in twenty-one appearances saw Teddy become a cult hero here and return to South London to a first team place for the Lions. Teddy would go on to play over 750 games in his career, but his only experience playing abroad was in Sweden.

Back to the game and both teams had suffered poor seasons in 2010. The home side's 10th place finish was at least an improvement on 14th in 2009 but still a long way from their domestic double in 2005 and subsequent jaunt into the Champions League. AIK also went through a season of hell in 2010 after winning the treble in 2009, finishing in 11th place. The Allsvenskan is a hot potato that no team wants to hold for more than a season it seems. Seven different winners in the last seven seasons did not bode well for both of these sides, especially as Swedish blogging expert Huddo Hudson had confidently tipped an eighth, Örebro, for the title in 2011.

With a full day's work under my belt I headed north up to Solna ready and prepared for what was about to hit me. The journey to the stadium should have been straightforward - five stops from T-Central straight to the stadium - but those little rascals the AIK fans decided to trash a metro train so we weren't going anywhere fast. What was obvious was that the railway workers had recently been on a customer experience course hosted by South-Eastern railways as the confusing messages being relayed to the thousands of football fans on the platform were a great help in getting us all nowhere.

Still, thanks to a helpful policeman I did a little shufti one way, a shimmy the next and before you could say Martin Kayongo-Mutumba I was at the Råsunda stadium. I was welcomed with a warm smile, a press-pass and personally escorted to my seat. Despite being there forty-five minutes before kick-off, one end was rocking. I will give you a clue which one. They play in black and yellow. AIK had almost filled the 'away' end, which was actually the same end they have when they play at home at the Råsunda. At the other end the 'home' fans had a decent turn out (many were still stuck due to the train incident) but it did all beg the question; why not play this at genuinely at home in the first place?

The bad news when the team sheets arrived was that 'our Kenny' was only on the bench. He consoled himself by giving fellow sub Ibrahim Bangura a piggy-back race around the pitch as the teams warmed up. The good news was the atmosphere was cracking, up there with the best I have ever experienced in my life, and one that would have any Premier League fan cowering underneath their seat. A little bit too cracking for the referee and the police in fact because minutes after the teams came out and lined up they were ushered back down the tunnel as the smoke engulfed the stadium. Few fans actually knew that they had disappeared until the smoke had dispersed. I've seen some fireworks before but this put London on New Year's Eve to shame. Add in AIK's fans singing a version of KC & The Sunshine Band's Give It Up and the Djurgården X-Factor style ticker tape raining down and I'm still only giving you a fraction of the picture.

The yellow and black smoke to my left soon turned to a red glow of a thousand flares being held up high, whilst to my right the blue and red smoke billowed upwards. Five minutes later the referee reappeared. He chatted to a few people and disappeared again just as more loud bangs reverberated around the stadium. Was the game in doubt? Of course not, according to my fellow journalists. This was now all part of the match planning. Set it for 7pm and it would really kick off at 7.15pm.

If this was a 'tame' derby in terms of games around the world I cannot imagine what a 'lively' one would be like. The noise rose to deafening as we had to sit and wait. Eventually some fourteen minutes later the home side got the game underway to comparative silence as both sets of fans regrouped and planned their next shows of strength.

It took some time to remember I was here to actually watch a game and not the two sets of fans. Two minutes in and the home side nearly got the dream start when Sebastian Rajalakso's drive from the edge of the box narrowly went past the post with Turina in the AIK goal well beaten. That brought the Djurgården fans into song. Ah if Teddy was here tonight he would have been in tears as the Djurgården fans broke into a chorus of "No one likes us, we don't care" but in Swedish (well that is what it sounded like to me).

With eighteen minutes on the clock, AIK had a massive shout for a penalty turned down. After Daniel Gustavsson outpaced the home defence and lifted the ball over Pa Dembo Touray in the Djurgården goal, the shot was cleared by a defender straight onto his own hand and out for a corner. Nothing given and outrage all round. To try and rouse the home fans the Djurgården mascot made an appearance, a big cat with an upside down saucepan on his head of course. Now as bizarre as that sounds I had already seen most things in this game so it wasn't too much of a surprise.

Chances were few in the first half with both keepers only really tested from distance. Half time saw a few exchanges between the fans and the police as missiles were thrown down from the Djurgården fans behind the goal onto a small group of AIK fans in the stand along the side of the pitch. For the first time in the evening I started noticing how chilly it had become. Just because it was April doesn't mean winter has disappeared here in Stockholm. Snow was still on the ground in outlying areas and some of the rivers were still frozen over. What we needed to warm us up was 45 minutes of decent football.

"One Kenny Pavey" sang the AIK fans as he was brought on at the start of the second half to inject some pace down the right hand side for the 'visitors'. With both teams attacking it was going to be 45 minutes for the brave of heart. The noise built beyond what I thought possible and it was now difficult to keep an eye on what was going on during the game for fear of missing something from either set of fans.

By now there was an almost constant stream of flare smoke, synchronized bouncing, fire crackers and songs with English tunes. Do the Premier League officials not look at games like this and wonder where the passion and spectacle comes from? This cannot be bottled and sold as part of your monthly subscription. These are fans who haven't been priced out of the sport and are looked after by a Football Association who respects them and treats them as a bigger part of the game than the clubs. Nearly 29,000 of them were here in the stadium right now, less than half you would get at The Emirates but I bet twenty times as loud and passionate.

And with added flares.

Inevitably the game ended in a draw on and off the pitch. A nil-nil did little for either team's league position but both went straight to the top of the charts for their fan displays. If nothing else the bragging rights had been shared and therefore work was bearable for both sets of fans the following morning.

Contrary to the cliché, football was not the winner, but passionate support definitely was. Would I want to see supporters like this every week?

Hell yes.

I headed down to the tunnel post match to have a chat with Kenny. I waited for him to complete his Swedish interviews, conducted in perfect local dialect of course, before he greeted me with a smile and a big hug. Sod the fact that the rest of his team-mates were waiting on the coach outside, he wanted my opinion on the game and more specifically my first derby. He also wanted to know whether Millwall could get to the play-off final and whether it was true that Lilly Allen had been lined up to replace Cheryl Cole on X-Factor. Good, exceptional, no, and unfortunately yes (that one never did pan out) were my answers.

Twenty-four hours later and I still had the sound of the game ringing in my ears and the smell of the acrid smoke in my nostrils. I wanted to be back in the Råsunda, standing shoulder to shoulder with the Black Army holding a flare aloft. I shared my feelings with my work colleagues, who didn't seem in the least bit surprised.

"It gets to us all, the Stockholm Syndrome in full effect."

And they were right, the definition of the condition is irrational feelings or emotions towards a captor or an aggressor who may intermittently harass, beat, threaten, abuse, or intimidate the other. That sums up perfectly how I felt.

Surely no game could top that one for atmosphere? Well, there was only one way to find out. Next stop Copenhagen - the Capital of Cool and Carlsberg, and also home to a derby that had hit the headlines for all the wrong reasons in the past.

Chapter Three

A New Way of Life
Why Denmark is brilliant (apart from the bacon)

8th May 2011
BK Avarta 3 Frederikssund IK 0
Espelundens Idrætsanlæg

IF Brøndby 1 FC Copenhagen 1
Brøndby Stadion

"...ever spent any time in Copenhagen, Stu? Okay, let me
rephrase it, ever fancied living in Copenhagen, Stu?"

In June 2009, my life changed dramatically after my regular weekly meeting with my boss. It was at the end of the financial year, one in which we had exceeded all expectations in terms of performance, but I was in a difficult place. Essentially I had outgrown my job and was looking for a new challenge. He knew that and wanted to talk about "the future".

"Ever spent any time in Copenhagen?" he opened with. It was a rhetorical question, as he very well knew. I had been a regular visitor since we acquired a company out there in 2007, using my work trips to catch a game or three.

"Ok, let me rephrase it. Ever fancied living in Copenhagen?"

I was, as they say, gob smacked. I was being offered a very senior role, essentially running one of our subsidiaries with offices across Scandinavia. Part of the deal was a riverfront flat in the posh part of town, free food and as many football matches as I could take in. Well, the last part wasn't exactly written into my contract but it was a given. After a discussion with the Current Mrs. Fuller, it was agreed that I would move to Denmark whilst she stayed back in England with the Little Fullers. I would travel out on a Monday morning and come back to Fuller Family Headquarters on a Thursday.

Well, sometimes a Friday, mainly in weeks when, coincidently, there was a Europa League match on.

I was going to be having my Copenhagen cake and eating it. Being posted to a foreign country is a traumatic experience; ask any Brazilian footballer who has tried to settle in Manchester and they will tell you how quickly they get homesick with nobody around to help them integrate into a new environment, learn a new language or try new food (one wonders who first showed Robinho black pudding and told him it was okay, it's just blood and fat really). My trauma lasted all of seven minutes on arriving in the office.

Firstly, they had laid on a welcome banquet for me. I was not only inheriting a fantastic office and a great team of people, but also two chefs who cooked lunch for everyone every day and boxed up the leftovers for me to take home. A fine spread of Danish treats including herring done every way imaginable, raw mince with an egg on top and Danish Blue cheese had me reaching for the suitcase full of Pickled Onion Monster Munch, although the first of many Tuborgs went down very well, even if it was 10am.

I wasn't actually going to be on my own. Work colleague and

general top chap Ben had already beaten a path for me in Copenhagen. He was posted here back in 2008 on a short-term project, then ended up staying after putting the financial controller in an awkward position (and I don't mean with his expense claims). Today, along with their beautiful daughter Isabella, they are a happy family, although I am not sure Christina was looking forward to my arrival as much as Ben was, to share his love of beer and football Danish style.

In my first year in the capital of cool I saw 29 games in Scandinavia. Every week I scanned the fixtures in Denmark, Sweden and Norway, planning games around my travel (or was it vice versa?). No level was ruled out, as long as it was after work. You don't have to go far down the leagues to get to roped off pitches and cars doubling as dressing rooms in Denmark, in fact teams in the fourth tier often play in front of one man and his Danish dog. With so few teams in their league pyramid the Danish Cup often throws up real David v Goliath games, especially as a tiny club only needs to win two games before they could find themselves running out at the mighty Parken to play FC Copenhagen.

I soon developed an intimate knowledge of the Danish railway network, the South Western Swedish bus network and the ferries that crisscrossed the harbour in Oslo. I started to learn Danish through reading the sports pages in the newspaper. My lunchtime conversations with my work colleagues became more meaningful and thought provoking as I was able to offer up opinions on OB's false nine, Stale Solbakken's flawed Champions League tactics away in Cyprus and whether this was going to be the year when Brøndby finally won the league again.

Slowly I became known as a bit of a Danish football expert. With the national side qualifying for the 2010 FIFA World Cup in South Africa, the English media were falling over themselves to have "experts" for each country. I was now the go-to guy for all things Danish, dispelling such myths as the fact Carlsberg was still being brewed in Copenhagen, that Danish bacon was the best or indeed anywhere near the best in the world, and that Nicklas Bendtner was actually any good.

The 2010/11 season brought more new games, with my own take on the Road to Wembley, following one side from the first round all the way to the final at Parken without actually having to travel outside of Copenhagen. Highlights of the season included watching a penalty shoot-out interrupted by a dog attacking the ball in the first round of the Danish Cup, the final game prior to the winter break in temperatures dipping as low as minus twenty in a snow-filled paradise called Randers in the North of the country, and England's visit to Copenhagen in February 2011 where I ended up acting as the local guide for the gathered press pack.

One game that I tried to always get to was the El Vidunderlig Classico or 'New Firm' derby between FC Copenhagen and IF Brøndby. There is certainly no love lost between these two sides, which had moved in opposite directions in the last few seasons. Amazingly, the rivalry only started in 1992 when the face of Danish football was changed forever. At the time Brøndby were the dominant force in the domestic game, but struggled when they dug out their passports and went travelling in European competition. So, a plan was hatched to create a "super team" who could compete not only in the SuperLigaen but also in European Competitions. The plan was to merge KB and B1903, two of the most successful clubs in the city, and play under the name FC Copenhagen. To help things along, the new side was installed in the National Stadium, Parken. A legend was born.

This season, FC Copenhagen's dominance was such that by the winter break they were sixteen points clear of second place, and with a goal difference of +30 to match. They had also come within a few minutes of beating Barcelona in the Champions League group stages and all but wrapped up a place in the knock-out stage for the first time. Brøndby on the other hand were floundering in mid-table, although second place and a Champions League qualifying spot was still a distant possibility.

The derby game had provided more incident off the pitch than on in recent years. Back in 2007 I had witnessed my first encounter, with FCK winning not only the three points but the SuperLigaen title at Brøndby. That night the atmosphere had been one of the best I had experienced, with the Faxe Tribune literally shaking with the bouncing of the home fans. After the game a photographer approached Ben and I, hearing our English accents and asked to take our picture. Some six months later we appeared in the Daily Express in an article about English football fans who looked abroad for their 'kicks', complete with a picture of us with our hoods up and scarves wrapped around our faces. My Mum was so proud although questioned why we were wrapped up so warm for a game in mid-May. Three years later after Parken had gone through a multi-million Kroner refurbishment, the Brøndby fans welcomed the modernization by setting fire to the seats in the away end.

To try and stop any trouble at the first derby game of the 2010/11 season at Parken, the police decided that they would fingerprint every away fan who wanted to purchase a ticket. In a country where civil liberties are cherished as much as the Little Mermaid, there was a huge outrage and the Brøndby fans subsequently boycotted the game.

With my time in Copenhagen coming to an end, Ben suggested a trip to the final derby of the season at Brøndby Stadion. FC Copenhagen had already been crowned Danish Champions so the focus would be on whether the home side could hold onto a Europa League spot, after the dream of a runners-up spot had headed over the horizon in the shape of OB from Odense. A quick phone call to FCK's Press Officer, who was also an English expat, and media passes were arranged for the 'Cockney Boys' as we had become known in the office.

But before any main event you need a warm up act. Brøndby had pulled out all of the stops for this game and had arranged for Outlandish to play live on the pitch before the game. What do you mean you've never heard of Outlandish? The Danish hip-hop group is an institution in these parts, famed for foot tapping songs like 'Man binder os på mund og hand'. One look at the dodgy outfits on the promotional literature had me reaching for the good old crystal football to see if there were any other pre-match options. Once the mist cleared, there, right in front of our eyes was the perfect answer. Just over a mile away BK Avarta versus Frederikssund IK would be kicking off some three hours before the main event in the Danish 2nd Division (East).

What do you mean you have never heard of the Danish 2nd Division (East)?

The third tier in Danish football is basically comparable to your Ryman or Evostik Leagues. The average attendance is around 270, with the bigger sides getting nearer 600. Their moment in the sun often comes in the early rounds of the cup when they can find themselves facing one of the big boys. However, few grounds at this level have the luxury of floodlights – with a four-month winter break they are simply not required. If a team progresses in the cup then they often have to play games midweek during the afternoon. A few years ago an amateur team from the north of Zealand (the island where Copenhagen's located) called Elite 3000 made it through to the third round of the cup and drew FC Copenhagen. They declined any offers to switch the game to Parken, home of FCK, and instead took on the league champions at 2pm on a Wednesday afternoon.

I had seen most clubs play in and around Copenhagen, but BK Avarta were a new one on me. They are located in the western suburb of Glostrup, around 20 minutes away on the train. It is sort of a Danish equivalent of an English commuter town, sitting on the edge of a 'Concentric-Zone Model', for those who spent far too much time awake in urban planning lectures. It isn't really known for much although it is the home of Madeleine Dupont. What do you mean you've never heard of Madeleine Dupont?

Well Mads is the former Danish Women's National Curling Team Captain no less, who skippered the side to the second place in the 2007 World Championships. Pretty amazing stuff I'm sure you will agree and something you feel better for knowing. Of course you won't be interested in the fact that she also appeared topless in a calendar produced to promote the sport are you? Madeleine had no issue whipping her top off, saying that "if the pictures of me can get more people watching the sport on TV then it's a good thing".

Like any good famous boy reporter, I did some extensive research into BK Avarta (meaning I read their Wikipedia page). The club had only spent two years in their 58-year history playing at a higher level. Their Espelundens Idrætsanlæg ground had a capacity of 6,000 although the average was just over 400. The players are all part time, although they do have a disproportionate number of Morten's in their squad (15% of them) and a centre-forward named Mohammed Ali.

My Super Sunday, or Super Søndag as Sky would say in these parts, started in the most English way. Bacon sandwiches and a big cup of tea. Ben's girlfriend Christina is a big football fan herself being a former season-ticket holder of IF Brøndby, but two's company and three's a crowd in the Bang-Anderson house these days with little Isabella not quite getting the finer points of the offside rule. So whilst the Cockney Boys would be watching the football, the Danish girls would be going to the zoo. She had laid on breakfast, which of course featured Marmite. The English breakfast staple was currently unavailable to buy in any shops in Denmark due to its high vitamin content. This is the country that invented hardcore pornography, where bestiality is legal as long as you don't harm the animal (and that also means mental harm by not phoning when you say you would or at least buying them dinner first) and where they have a place called 'Pusher Street'. Anyway, not only were we sticking two fingers up in the face of authority with our choice of savoury spread, but Christina had acquired some proper Danish bacon.

If you are ever offered bacon in Denmark think twice before accepting. The wealth of the nation has been built on exporting the Western world's favourite food product, so much so that they only keep a small amount for themselves. What they do keep are the bits that no-one else wants, meaning the only way they can eat it is burnt to a crisp. When my Danish colleagues come to England they salivate at the prospect of some proper bacon, ironically normally Danish, from the café across the road. So Christina had pulled a blinder by somehow acquiring some of the proper stuff in a way that only reminded me of the League of Gentlemen and their 'special stuff'.

After our perfect English breakfast it was time to negotiate the complexities of the Danish Klippenkart public transport ticketing system, and head into the western suburbs of Glostrup for a double dose of delightful Danish. The sun was shining and the world seemed a very happy place. If you think the UK currently has strange weather then Denmark trumps it with four aces. In my two years living here I have experienced one of the coldest ever days on record (when I travelled north to Randers to see FCK play the thermometer went as low as minus 20), one of the hottest days where the mercury hit 35 degrees, and the wettest 24 hours on record.

But today was a perfect early summer's day. As we walked up from Brøndbyosyter station we came upon a huge crowd queuing where the football ground entrance was. Surely this wasn't for the football? Surely others hadn't had the same idea of a Super Søndag as us? After waiting for a few minutes in the crowd we scanned the people around us. They all seemed to be dressed in a…how you would say this if you were being tactful? They were all dressed in a 'down-beat' way, meaning they all looked liked they had been shopping in charity shops for some time now. Hardly your typical cool-suburban Danish football fan. So we jumped to the front of the queue despite the protestations and found out this was the queue for Copenhagen's largest flea market, held every Sunday here at 1pm. Ah, the football was next door, where that big sign said 'Football Here'.

Going to watch Avarta was like coming home to one of my regular haunts. If Lewes FC had a Danish cousin then it would be here in Espelundens Idrætsanlæg (pronounced Idrætsanlæg – got it? Good). Of course the sunshine made the magic happen, but still for a small club they had got so much right. The joy of watching football in the sun was the winner but there were many other reasons to be happy.

The Danish Kroner to the pound has strengthened by around 30% since I have been travelling out this way but even so, 60DKR (£7) for admission was a bargain. We walked through the gates and heaven opened up in front of us. Espelundens is a simple ground like so many of the very best, one smart newish stand running down one side of the pitch and a decent size clubhouse behind one goal. What set it apart were the huge grass banks that rise up from the pitch on three sides. You can see now how such a modest club can accommodate 6,000 fans, although I wouldn't fancy standing on there in the pouring rain.

On a sunny day like today everyone was laying back with a beer in their hand, enjoying the sunshine and the promise of a decent game. Did I mention the beer? Well how about this for a bonus, it was the cheapest beer in Copenhagen. Carlsberg Pilsner or Dark for just 25DKR – about £2.75. Northerners may bang on about this still being "bloody expensive" but bear in mind a normal local bar in Copenhagen will see you pay double that, whilst a tourist trap on Nyhavn will see it top the 80DKR mark. It was worth the admission money alone.

We were feeling rather pleased with ourselves, sitting here in the sunshine, drinking our cheap beer and looking at some of the stunning Danish women on display (in a non-sexist and very PC fashion of course, we are the epitome of modern men and we like the chicks to know it). It was good to have Ben's local knowledge and translation skills on hand. He may know only a smattering of Danish words but the words "Pølser er klar" ("Sausages are ready") were translated at double quick time and we were at the front of the queue. Two of your big ones please sir with a dollop of your special sauce of course.

For me the best part of the ground was the tunnel. Nothing unusual about that you may say – after all most players emerged from a tunnel, but this was a real tunnel. A proper tunnel. A huge concrete pipe, one that would normally be carrying sewage under the street that had been bored through the grass terrace. I have never seen a finer football entrance in all my watching days and what's more, I probably never will.

The game started at quite a pace. Boldklubben Avarta, in a fine

Lewes-esque green kit, had Luka Modric in midfield. If the Croatian ever needs a body double to fool the fans in London then the Avarta number 6 is your man - same hair, same hair-band, same boots and the same bowlegged passing style. He pulled the strings in the game, setting up the opening goal in the tenth minute from a corner that was headed in by the big centre-back (actually both centre backs were huge so it was the bigger of the two) Morten Foge. Of course his name was Morten.

There was a definite end-of-season feel about proceedings. Neither side were in with a shout of promotion to the BetSafe Liga, the second tier of Danish football which is also known as the 'Elephant's Graveyard' or 'Elefanter Kirkegård' where some of the former biggest reputations in the domestic game now lived. With the creation of FCK and the emergence of relatively young but well funded clubs such as FC Midtjylland and FC Nordsjælland, teams such as 10 times League winners AB from Copenhagen, Esbjerg and AGF Arhus have found it difficult to establish themselves in the new order, one minute hosting FC Copenhagen or Odense, the next playing away on a cold winter's night at Avarta. The technical areas were set up with picnic chairs for the coaches to sit in and the presence of some scantily clad female fans certainly caught the eye of the substitutes warming up, as they carried out a series of overly-enthusiastic groin stretches and lunges.

The second half saw Avarta continue to dominate and score two further goals towards the end of the game – both scored by Mortens (Asmussen and Seifert). Of course their names were Morten. It really was a pleasant way to spend an early afternoon. Our view from high up on the grass bank was suddenly spoiled. We were strategically positioned above what can only be described as a WAG's bikini picnic, although before we get labelled 'dirty old men' we had sat there first (and anyway 42 is not old these days now we're living longer is it. Is it?).

They had arrived early in the game, laid out their towels and stripped off, ignoring the football completely. One slip and we would have been squashing their Ambre Solaire. However, a rather strange chap arrived on the scene towards the end of the game, positioning himself in the space between us and the girls. He wore socks and sandals, which is never a good look, but combine that with Benny Hill-esque shorts pulled up so far that they reached his nipples – oh, and before you wonder how I knew that, he was topless, and it was only a matter of time before he offered to rub some lotion into their backs. The final whistle came and whilst it was tempting to see whether the chap would get a slap, arrested or both, we had another game to go to, thirty minutes walk down the road.

Finding our way wasn't difficult as just behind the Brøndby stadium is the biggest flagpole in Scandinavia (apparently this is true but I have one question, who measured all the others?) that stands 47.74 metres tall. Of course rather than go by this we could have also just followed the thousands of fans decked out in yellow and blue as we made our way down Brøndbyvester Boulevard to one of my favourite stadiums in Europe.

Back in 2000, when we were all young, I came to Copenhagen for the first time. I was lured by the images of the Little Mermaid, the home of Carlsberg and of course, the Erotic Museum that marketed itself as having the biggest collection of '70s hardcore pornography on public display in Europe. The Current Mrs. Fuller was more than happy to come, although I didn't really share that last tourist attraction detail with her. I didn't even want to go to the museum in truth but I thought I better just look in to make sure it was as disgusting and shameful as I hoped. I mean feared.

Back then the short hop due east was only serviced by British Airways and SAS meaning flights were ridiculously expensive. Thanks to some free flight vouchers with Virgin Express (remember them kids?) we were able to make the trip, via Brussels. An easy 80-minute journey took us four hours. This was back in the day when smoking was just being banned on flights in Europe and an Italian chap, unaware of the new rules lit up a big fat cigar causing panic in the cabin. He was told that he couldn't smoke so he simply went to the toilet, which back then weren't fitted with the 'highly sensitive' smoke alarms the stickers warn of.

The reason I chose Copenhagen for the little break wasn't really all about legendary aquatic creatures, beer and pornography. There was also football. IF Brøndby had finished in second place in the previous year's Superligaen (the winners, BK Herfølge winning their one and only title) and thus went into the qualifying stages of the Champions League. Their first game would be at home to KR Reykjavik, coincidentally on the night we arrived in Copenhagen – what were the odds of that unless you plan it meticulously, source a ticket, work out how near your hotel is to the ground and only tell the wife once you're safely on

Danish soil, eh? Pretty slim let me tell you. Even better, let the Current Mrs Fuller tell you, she knows.

At the time the Brøndby Stadium was coming to the end of a 46 million Kroner redevelopment programme that made it the most modern stadium in Denmark. Just a few years before it had been a very different affair, scaffold-constructed stands that stood over the original athletics track had been replaced by modern seating, executive boxes and most importantly, a roof. Whilst the Current Mrs Fuller sat back in our plush room at Nyhavn 71, watching the boats come and go with a very little Lolly (that was the reason why she hadn't been keen on visiting the biggest porn collection in Denmark – the fact we had our 3-month old daughter with us, I was so disappointed to go on my own let me tell you), I saw the Danes beat the Icelandic champions 3-1.

This period in the club's history was supposed to be full of promise. A newly redeveloped stadium, regular Champions League appearances and an unenviable youth development programme should have lead to the Brøndby dynasty ruling Danish football. Alas, as often is the case, off-the-field distractions caused the on-the-field bubble to burst. In 2002 Michael Laudrup arrived as manager, with 'couldn't hit a barn door from 3-yards in an Arsenal shirt' John Jensen as his assistant. Four years later they could boast a domestic double plus three runners-up spots, as well as a decent run in the UEFA Cup that had seen them run Barcelona very close. But Laudrup and Jensen left an already sinking ship in 2006, to date the last time the blues finished in the top two.

Six years after they won their last title there were signs that life could be coming back into Brøndby. Last season they had finished in third place, and this season they seemed to be making more of a fight of second place with OB, the upstarts from Odense. FC Copenhagen on the other hand had just cruised to their eighth title in ten seasons with the minimum of fuss. Despite losing to Chelsea in the Champions League knock-out phase in February, they continued their dominance domestically, coming into this game on the back of five consecutive wins.

So back to today and the mouthwatering prospect of another derby game. As we arrived at the stadium so too did the police, but this was not quite your normal riot squad. They were in big trucks and wearing more body armour than was necessary for a group of football fans having a bit of a ruck.

"That looks like the bomb squad," said Ben.

And sure enough it was.

A threat had been received and consequently the game would be delayed. Bar? Why not, after all the Erotic Museum was miles away and probably shut.

Considering the animosity between the two clubs, you would struggle to imagine the scene on the other side of the ground. It was almost like a village fete with a beat the keeper game, human table football and various other games for the kids, as well as grills selling an array of sausages that would make a German weep, beer by the tanker-load and all manner of Danes stripped down to enjoy the blazing sunshine.

The tifosi, however, were starting to get restless, wanting to get into the ground and prepare their pre-match displays. With the delay approaching the hour mark, there was some mutterings that we may even miss the pre-match Outlandish show if we were lucky, I mean unlucky (I don't). The fans in these parts have become used to disappointment, but missing the Danish hip-hop legends would take it to a new level.

Finally the all clear was sounded and we could pile into the stadium. Whilst the hoi-polloi jostled to get in through the turnstiles, Ben and I walked the red carpet and up into the media lounge. Despite the sun still shining, in the shade and high in the main stand it was freezing. Fortunately blankets had been dispensed to us and we huddled up ready for the start of the action on and off the pitch.

Despite the wait we were not disappointed when it came to some fan action. FCK had filled the top tier of their allocated stand, with the vast majority of the fans having received the email this morning about dressing in all black. They had been bussed direct to the ground to avoid any problems, although the bomb scare had meant they had gone on a bit of a magical mystery tour around the Copenhagen suburbs before they could be let in. Not to be outdone, the home fans in the Faxe Tribune opposite had launched into a riot of yellow and blue flag waving as Van Halen pumped out of the speakers.

Unlike the regulations in Sweden the game started with flares and smoke filling the stadium. Both sets of fans created a huge noise despite the fact less than 20,000 were in the ground. It appeared that this game was not the draw it was a few years ago. Whilst not at the intensity level of the Stockholm derby it certainly put any game in England to shame due to its noise, colour and passion of the fans. What more could you ask for on a

Sunday afternoon? Well what about some free beer?

Sometimes rules are just plain silly, and the rules on who could and couldn't get a beer were strange at Brøndby to say the least. Prior to kick off we went back down to the lounge to get a Carlsberg as you do at such occassions.

"Two beers please"

"Do you have a press card?" the young lady asked us both. I directed her eyes to the pass around our necks we were given upon arriving at the ground.

"No, you need a press accreditation card to get your free beer" she told us with that stern look Danish girls can give you.

Hang on, free beer?

"You mean one of these?" I said as I whipped out my Accredited International Press Society card and handed it over.

"Yes, like that."

She waited for one from Ben but alas, he didn't have one of the special cards, although producing his Blockbuster membership was a stroke of genius that nearly fooled her.

"No – you cannot use that and you cannot have a beer!" she said defiantly nodding at the yellow and blue card that said '10% off all rentals' in Ben's hand. Suddenly and most welcomely, inspiration arrived.

"Do I have to show this every time I want a beer?" I asked, pointing at my press card.

"Yes, EVERYTIME!" she emphasized as she poured me a beer.

I took the drink and had a small sip, beautifully crisp with that lovely tang you only get when it's free. Having checked to make sure it was good I handed it to Ben, smiled back at the girl with my card in hand.

"Can I have a beer please?"

She smiled and poured another immediately. I was playing by her rules, she was perfectly happy with that. We had bonded.

Not only did we get a beer but also an ingenious lid that sat on top of your cup filled with peanuts. Bang and Olufsen, Lego, Pandora, the biggest collection of '70s hardcore pornography on public display, and now nuts-topped beer. Is there nothing these Danes can't do?

And so to the game itself.

Amazingly FC Copenhagen could only name six substitutes after a last minute injury to Johan Absalonsen. If they'd have asked I would have been on that bench like a shot, after all, I was very nearly the same age as Jesper Grønkjær (although admittedly one or two pounds heavier as I was still carrying some *ahem* holiday weight). Any talk of player crises was banished after five minutes when the league's leading scorer Dame N'Doye, no relation to Dame Maggie Smith before you ask, chipped the advancing Brøndby keeper. Home spirits were soon lifted when Remco van der Schaaf, no relation to the US Toy manufacturer who made the Star Trek utility belt before you ask, rose unmarked to head the equalizer. N'Doye should have had a second just before half time when he headed against the bar, and César Santin, no relation to the dog food manufacturer before you were bound to ask, missed the rebound with the goal gaping wide-open in front of him.

The long hike up to the press box was a step too far in the second half so we used our passes to sit in the posh seats, which had notably better blankets. The game itself was destined to be a draw with neither side creating a clear chance. Off the field, however, the fans were at least trying to win the game of one-upmanship with their passionate and noisy support. As a single fan held up two flares in the Brøndby end you could make out his mask, lit by the flames. Here was Guy Fawkes holding up two sticks of dynamite, ready to complete the gunpowder plot some 406 years too late and in the wrong country.

At full time we headed down to the fabled 'Mixed-Zone' where players, staff and VIPs mingle with the press. We hoped to see one of the Laudrups who had been part of the TV punditry for the day, as well as have a quick word and photo if possible with Danish football anchorwoman Ulla Essendrop. As it turned out with our combined Danish stretching to 'thank you for food' (verbatim), 'sausages are ready', and 'where are my trousers?' our questioning abilities were severely limited. In the end we just stood and listened as others asked questions that weren't about eating or slacks.

The basic gist seemed to be that a point was a fair result, Brøndby would have liked all three in their hunt for a Champions League spot but they would take one game at a time (dull football clichés translate into many languages the same) and nobody felt too poorly done to. Unfortunately, it seemed as if Ms. Essendrop was otherwise engaged so we made our way home. The point kept FCK a mere twenty-six points clear of second place OB, and effectively ended any hope of a Champions League return for Brøndby.

The one lesson I learnt living here is the Danes will always have "one for the road". Meeting a work colleague on the bus on the way back to Glostrup station he suggested a quick beer in the city centre. Eight hours later we were still going strong, or as strong as you can be after eight hours drinking.

"Ladies and Gentlemen, please welcome the one, the only, Mr. Stuart Fuller!"

I bounded onto the small stage in a bar on Østergade to grab the microphone from Mr. Anderson to sing my solo in 'Don't Let The Sun Go Down On Me', which ironically now at 4am was actually coming up rather than down.

I had to be at work bright and breezy in 3 hours.

Ben was still carrying a bottle of formula milk for his daughter and a block of Lurpak butter (don't ask) that his patient girlfriend Christina was probably still waiting for back at home. It had been another great day, two games, two great grounds for different reasons and twenty-four hours that will always remind me of what is brilliant about life in Denmark.

Next up? The Isle of Wight of course, a wonderful trip to the dear old Isle of Wight.

Chapter Four

A Trip to Pleasure Island

Almost too good to be true

26th June 2011
Gotland 2 Isle of Man 4
Westwood Park

Rhodes 2 Greenland 1
Vicarage Lane

Åland Islands 3 Saaremaa 3
Beatrice Avenue

Isle of Wight 4 Ynys Môn 0
St Georges Park

"...I was on my way to see the finest festival of football the Isle of Wight (the British Ibiza) had ever seen... "

Let's not beat around the bush here. Let's 'keep it real' as the kids would say.

Major football tournaments are invariably a letdown.

Whether it be the FIFA World Cup, European Championships or London Evening Standard Fives, the expectation and anticipation often outweigh the promise of the players and teams on offer. They are hyped for weeks, even months in some cases, yet when they arrive they soon go flat with a drab opening game here or a series of cagey draws there.

Those of us who have been lucky enough to have travel halfway around the world to watch one of the big ones know what it is like to be treated with suspicion wherever you go. Then there's the being told what you can and cannot eat by the sponsors, being told what you can and cannot drink by the sponsors, constantly as fans be made to play second fiddle to the sponsors, and having to fight for every ticket because they have been allocated (on complimentary terms of course) to, you've guessed it, the sponsors.

But what if you knew nothing about a tournament before it started? What if you had no clue who the major players would be, who the favourites were or even what colours the teams played in? What if the organisers did everything in their power to organise that tournament around the spectators and then virtually give the tickets away for free? And what if all that was on your doorstep?

Sound too good to be true?

Well it isn't.

I pondered the answers to these questions with a smile as I stood on the deck of a ferry, watching the coast of Southern England disappear into the distance. I felt like the luckiest man alive. Whilst others would be having a lay in, reading the Sunday papers and thinking about whether to wash the car or cut the grass, I was going to one of the biggest football tournaments being played that season. Yes, the 2011 CONCACAF Cup may have the glitz and showbiz that only the US could provide, yes the 2011 Under17 s World Cup in Mexico may be a spicy affair, and yes the 2011 Women's World Cup was due to start in a few hours and it would feature a German team who felt that as a pre-tournament warm up they would get their kit off and pose for Playboy, but I was on my way overseas to see the finest festival of football the Isle of Wight (the British Ibiza as no one calls it) had ever seen – the 14th International Island Games.

This was effectively the Olympic Games for those places on earth that craved independence from their masters. Those island nations that seemed to be good enough when contributing valuable cash to the economy but suspiciously overlooked when it came to major sporting events. Where else could you see Bermuda take on Minorca, the Shetland Islands play the Caymans, or Frøya clash swords with deadly rivals Hitra?

Some of these islands have populations of less than the number of people through the door of Faces nightclub in Essex on a Saturday night. Sark (pop. 600) was now the smallest island to have taken part in the competition that started back in 1985 and now has over 1,000 competitors in 14 sports over a full week of events. The premier event in the bi-annual tournament is the football competition. No guesses where we were heading on this promise-filled Sunday morning.

The last time the tournament had been held on these shores was back in 2005 when the Shetlands had hosted and run out winners of the football tournament themselves, beating a talented Guernsey in the final. Since then Rhodes and Åland had hosted the games, whilst lined up for 2013 was a small matter of a trip to Bermuda.

The Isle of Wight was a great choice for the 2011 games. Britain's most populous parliamentary constituency is a county in its own right these days. Whilst it is probably best known for its '70s music festivals, prisons and for being home to one David Icke, the arrival of the 14th International Games were sure to boost the local economy for the week. Fifteen Islands were to take part in the men's football tournament, now due to start at 2pm when Gotland took on the Isle of Man in Cowes. Danny, the never more aptly named Cynical Dave and I were heading over the water to see eight of these teams do battle in the ultimate day of international football. With admission set at £3 per game and the venues all within 10 miles of each other (everything in the Isle of Wight is 10 miles apart as we found out during the day) it was going to be the ultimate football day out.

In the week leading up to the games there was talk the tournament may be reduced to 14 teams. The poor old Falkland Islands, the country with the longest journey, were grounded due to a volcano in Chile. They had to postpone their warm-up game at Blue Square Bet South Eastleigh due to delays in their travel plans, and would potentially arrive on the day of their opening game in far from ideal circumstances.

Three times winners Jersey were sure to be the favourites, although hosts Isle of Wight would be a tough game for anyone, as too would be Gibraltar who had beaten the Faroe Islands in a warm-up match. My colours were being nailed firmly to the Saaremaan mast having once met a Saaremaan in an Estonian sauna, who then insisted we drank vodka together with just a towel to cover our modesties to celebrate the fact we were both West Ham fans. I was also aware that the Gotland ladies team were well fancied, although I am not sure that was in football terms or simply based on their Nordic good looks (as it turned out it was the latter).

Our day had started at 7am with a full English breakfast in Portsmouth. The sunshine I had left at Fuller Towers in South London at 5.30am had been replaced by thick fog on the South Coast. Surely the weather wouldn't scupper our meticulously planned day. After all, four games in one day is a dream we all have and here we were on the verge of experiencing it for the first time in our lives. Our time on the island would be less than twelve hours. Twelve hours in a footballing utopia.

As our boat docked at Fishbourne, the God of football (Sepp Blatter maybe? Probably not, he's maybe more to do with things downstairs from heaven...) ensured that the fog cleared and brilliant sunshine illuminated our path to Ryde where we were due to pick up our Media passes for the tournament. With none of the major media outlets covering the tournament, we were treated like royalty when we arrived. Perhaps we had bigged up our roles a little bit by saying that we had major newspapers interested in our match reports. Unfortunately we hadn't applied for a pass for Dave but then we spied one in the name of the photographer David Bauckham. We know David well and he wasn't going to be attending until a few days later, so it was only a little white lie by saying our Dave was in fact David. Sorry Mr Bauckham.

We had a few hours to kill so we headed to Cowes for some lunch, a.k.a. beer. Our route took us up the eastern side of island and then down to the waterfront where we crossed the harbour on the Chain Ferry. The floating bridge as it's known is pretty rare in engineering terms in the world today. Discussions have taken place for decades about potentially building a bridge or a tunnel across the water but still the Number 5 ferry makes the 3 minute crossing across the River Medina over 150 times a day, pulled across by a submerged steel chain. Without the ferry you would need to take a ten-mile (of course ten-mile) detour via

Newport to get to West Cowes.

West Cowes is the posh totty of the Isle of Wight. We parked up and wandered along the High Street that would have any aspiring football casual salivating with outlets for Henri Lloyd, Stone Island and Lacoste within a few hundred yards of each other. We looked out of place but couldn't quite put our finger on why. Then Cynical Dave realized something. We didn't have jumpers slung around our shoulders and we weren't wearing canvas deck shoes.

We tried to look the part by buying tea-towels to double for jumpers and purchasing the worst shoes imaginable, but despite our efforts we simply couldn't blend in. With a couple of hours before the tournament kicked off we decided to do what we did best - find a pub, order some beer and laugh at anyone and everything. The most amusing scene was the frequent buses arriving in the High Street that then needed to make a very sharp turn through an impossibly narrow gap to the ferry terminal. As each bus came down the road we said in unison "he's gone too wide" or "he's never going to make it", but of course he always did. We could have sat there all day, but deep down we knew we'd never see them mistime a turn (apparently a bus clips the post once a week on average according to a local source). It was nearly game time so we headed up the "steepest hill in the Isle of Wight" (©Cynical Dave) to Westwood Park, home of Wessex League One side Cowes Sports FC.

Let's get one thing straight from the outset, I am not a ground-hopper. The idea of four games in a day was appealing, sure, the idea of fitting an agenda around this was good as well. But to make it clear, I have no interest in ranking facilities, finding a team sheet, touching the match ball or drinking local ales (Ale of Wight was a lovely pint though). With thirty minutes to go to kick off there were plenty of said folk in the ground already, with their ground-hopping carrier bags and their ground-hopping hats, pouring over ground-hopping maps of the island as to how they were going to get from Cowes to Shanklin in time for the Isle of Man v Gibraltar Ladies game.

However, the best laid plans of mice and men are always at the mercy of the weather. Whilst the mercury was heading towards the 30-degree mark, the early morning fog had delayed the arrival of the Isle of Man kit. It was being brought down at the last minute in the back of a Ford Transit after a sponsorship deal with online betting company SBOBET had been agreed and their name had to be put across the front of their shirts. An impressive lineup of teams under the SBOBET belt now to be fair - West Ham United, Cardiff City and Isle of Man. The Manx fans had also travelled in numbers and were full of confidence. Dave hardly needs an excuse for a bet or two, but he wasn't so sure. "Poor backline, no discipline" was his expert assessment although where that information had been gleaned I literally have no idea.

The game finally kicked off at a quarter past two. At 2.15pm and 7.9 seconds the Isle of Man were 1-0 down. Peter Öhman took the ball, one-step, two-step and then to use a technical term, wellied it in. Now I am not sure if this technically counts as international football, as these were islands rather than countries, but if it did it would have broken the 8.3 seconds of Davide Gaultieri for San Marino versus England, or the 11 seconds of Hakan Sukur from the 2002 World Cup Finals against South Korea. Coincidentally, and this is a massive coincidence that will have conspiracy theorists pondering this long into the night for sure, Cowes Sports had previously been involved in one of the fastest ever goals. In April 2004 one of their reserve players, Marc Burrows, scored after 2 SECONDS in a game against Eastleigh.

Gotland had dominated the opening 8 seconds and so the goal wasn't a surprise although a few of the Isle of Man supporters had missed it climbing the four steps in to the main stand. However, the Isle of Man bounced back and within a minute they had equalised as a ball over the top found Ciaran McNulty and he slotted the ball over the advancing Gotland keeper. Sixty-nine seconds into the tournament and already it had beaten all expectations.

Despite the heat the pace of the game was relentless with the Gotland keeper earning his Dime (Dime's are by far and away the biggest chocolate in Sweden along with Plopp) time and time again, getting every lucky break and deflection along the way. His goal was leading a charmed life. Unfortunately at the other end it was a different story. On a rare foray into the Isle of Man half, Gotland's blonde central midfielder (they were all blonde so it could have been any one of four) lined up a shot that took a wicked deflection past the already committed Manx keeper. Football sometimes isn't just, and the Isle of Man went in at half time somehow 2-1 behind.

The half time speech in the Isle of Man dressing room must

have been delivered by the Lord of Mann (or the Queen as she is known on the island) as the team came out fired up and scored three goals in the first twenty minutes of the half to stun the Scandinavians. Conor Doyle and Nick Hurt did the damage to the Swedes. It was what they deserved. Short neat football, stronger on and off the ball and the approach paid off and set them up nicely for the game on Monday with Falkland Islands. A win there would take them into the semi-finals.

With the game all but over and the ground-hoppers already starting to grade the sugar in their little ground-hopping book, we got in the car and drove ten miles across the island to Brading Town FC. After parking up and walking down a little country lane, we climbed over a fence and came across another contender for the title of 'best little ground in the world'.

Let me set the scene for you. A lush green meadow sloping down towards the coast with a view of hills on each side. Add in a small clubhouse, cars parked around the edge of the field like a village cricket green, and the occasional old London underground train passing at the far end of the ground on the Island's only railway line. Perfect. Whilst the crowd at the opening game was around a hundred people, we had at least double that here with Greenland's whole Games squad in attendance, cheering their countrymen on.

The biggest island in the world that is not a continent and the second furthest away in this competition had brought along their own tifosi, making themselves heard around the pitch and as far away as Ryde. The coldest island in the tournament were taking on the warmest here with Rhodes as the opposition. However someone had obviously given the Greeks some bum information about what to expect in terms of the weather as the coaches and substitutes were dressed in layers of shell suits, jumpers and one even had gloves on.

The Greeks had taken a thirtieth-minute lead when Panagiotis Mathios scored but they were being made to sweat by a determined Greenland team in the second half. With only 56,000 people, the odds on me coming out of retirement to play international football would be slashed to less than 3/1 if I renounce my British passport and became a Greenlander. They needed some inspiration but instead they were distracted by the sound and then the sight of an old London Underground train trundling past at the bottom of the ground. The ex-Metropolitan line train, made up of a four first-class carriages no less, certainly had an impact on the game as the Greenlanders, many of whom will have never seen such a sight, simply switched off. Panagiotis Pompou took advantage to score a second for the Greeks.

Greenland threw everything they had at them and finally got a goal back as the game entered injury time when Pavia Mølgaard turned the ball in from close range. But there was no room for goodwill or Games spirit as Rhodes tried every tactic in the book to waste time. With five minutes of injury time played Lukas Necas was sent off for a playful push on a Greenland defender – one of those you used to do in the playground with someone kneeling behind the victim. Necas stormed off and tried to get into the dressing room, which was locked so he was forced to petulantly kick a plastic cup around for the remaining minute.

He wasn't alone for long as keeper Eleytherios Skylas got a second yellow for handling outside his area. Of course he protested, trying to explain to the officials that the wind/draft of the passing train/a bee had caused him to step outside of his box. He trudged off slowly but as he then tried to get into the dressing room the players noticed they didn't have a spare goalkeeper's shirt. With no subs left the captain agreed to go in goal but first he had to wrestle the shirt off Skylas, which wasted another five minutes. Interestingly, Rhodes would make competition history a few days later when they were kicked out of the tournament for their poor disciplinary record with four sendings off in their opening two games.

Fortunately our comprehensive itinerary for the rest of the day had the word 'pub' next up so no action would be missed. Indeed with half of "Best Day Ever" as we had taken to calling it now complete, we were thirsty. For some ludicrous reason no beer was being allowed outside of the clubhouses so the past couple of hours during the tournament had been dry. It was hardly as if the rival fans fuelled by alcohol would kick off against each other and even if they did, so far the aggregate attendance had been just over 300 so exactly how much trouble could be caused?

We headed off to possibly the finest pub on the Isle, the Horse & Hounds. You know the one, 10 miles from Brading, 10 miles from Newport on that junction. Thatched roof, ivy, you know the score. Three cold Greene King IPA's went down very well as opposed to the pocket-full of stuffing from the help yourself carvery that Dave assumed meant just that rather than actually paying for a meal. We quickly ate all the evidence although it had seen better days, possibly back in 2009 judging by the taste and dryness of everything on offer.

Our third stop of the day saw us heading back up to East Cowes, around ten miles away for the 'Battle of the Baltic' between Åland Islands and Saaremaa, for the chance to be the pride of the Baltic Straits.

Fifteen minutes (and ten miles) after we polished off the final piece of dry stuffing we pulled into the official car park at East Cowes FC, which was essentially the car park for the 5-a-side pitches. Next to us was parked the official Ground-hopper mobile. Out they climbed, complete with comedy hats and out came the note-books in a flash to grade the car park surface.

"Not as black as Torbay from memory – 6 out of 10."

"About 3 inches shorter than West Wight Community College, 4 out of 10."

"Same longitude as Burphem Meadow though – 9 out of 10."

They quibbled at being asked to pay ANOTHER £3 to get in AND a whole 20p for a team sheet. "This is the first Island Games where we have had to pay to get in," said the lead hopper, getting out the red pen to write something bad in his book and looking enviously at our official accreditation knowing we had access to free team sheets, literally dozens of them, we could start a small fire with them or paper the walls. To them we were Kings and we both knew it.

The game hadn't really fired up the interest of the locals. In fact there were more people watching the five-a-side on the far side of the ground than standing around the edge of the pitch. How can they not have realized that this was international football at its best with Finnish Åland taking on Estonian Saaremaa. Each of the Finnish substitutes gave their counterparts a nice badge to remember them by and so to return the favour Åland's back-four gifted Saaremaa with a goal after 20 seconds as Marti Puuk scored from distance. With only three teams competing in Group D, a win here would almost guarantee a place in the semi-final.

The Estonian's doubled their lead four minutes later when Elari Valmas turned, held off a defender and smashed it home. It looked game over for the twentieth richest region in the EU (random Ålander stat for you there) although they got themselves back into the game just before half-time when Peter Lundberg scored from close range, then in injury time Alexander Weckstrøm equalised for Åland.

Alas we were going to commit the cardinal sin in the ground-hoppers bible and thus ruin any chance we had of ever joining their crew – leaving at half time. We could almost hear the tuts and the furious scribbling in their notepads as we exited stage left with a bundle of team-sheets under each arm. We ignored the cat-calls and prepared ourselves for the main event of the day, some ten miles south in Newport as the home nation and tournament favourites were playing their opening game.

I don't think Newport had ever seen anything like it. There was even a queue at the turnstiles as we arrived a few minutes before kickoff. Over 800 had crammed into St Georges Park in the centre of town with a fair few from Ynys Môn, also known as the Isle of Anglesey in North Wales. Most seemed to be queuing for food served by a man with more metalwork in his body than Steve Austin (kids, ask your Dad about the Six-Million Dollar Man AND not the fake WWF wrestler with who looked like a muscly Johnny Metgod with a goatee. While you're there ask them who Johnny Metgod was). This truly was the biggest night out on the island since local band Level 42 played the Guith Morris Dancing Festival back in 1989.

Both teams emerged into the evening sunshine to rapturous applause. There was certainly an air of expectation from the home fans and they weren't backward in their vocal support, perhaps to the extent of influencing the referee in awarding the hosts a penalty in the 14th minute for what seemed like an innocuous challenge. Ian Seabrook didn't let that worry him as he calmly slotted the ball home.

Half-time approached with no further goals scored. It was interesting wandering around the ground to see various other teams there watching the game. Earlier in the day Gibraltar and Alderney had met in the first game in this group, with the former running out 6-1 winners. Based on the first-half performance from the hosts, this group was going to be decided by the meeting of Isle of Wight and Gibraltar on Tuesday.

The game was effectively wrapped up just after half-time as Charlie Smeeton scored, finishing off a great move that Barcelona would have been proud of, and then substitute Levrier scored a few minutes later. With just a few minutes to go Scott Jones scored a fourth to give the final score line a very one-sided look. With that, alas, our day in footballing heaven was over and all we had left was the 10-mile drive back to Fishbourne and a ferry back to the 21st century.

As the sun set over the Solent we sat on the deck of the ferry and reminisced about one of the best days of football you could ever have had. Nineteen goals in four games were a good return but it had been the organisation, the enthusiasm of the locals and organisers, and the surprising beauty of the surroundings that had made the day a winner. Football trips rarely get better than this. Who needs the sunshine of Seville, the culture of Copenhagen, the rustic beauty of Bologna or the beers of Bavaria when the Isle of Wight is on our doorstep. Nothing could better this surely?

Well, perhaps Bermuda in 2013...

Chapter Five

The Seven Deadly Sins

Remember the name 'Jonathan Pereira Rodríguez'

4th August 2011
Neath 0 Real Betis 8
The Gnoll

5th August 2011
Port Talbot Town 2 Cardiff City 2
The GenQuip Stadium

> "...two years ago I even spent my wedding anniversary at
> Cardiff City versus Valencia..."

Every year I embark on a pilgrimage to cleanse my soul, reconnect with my family and generally set me up for the season ahead. The gap between the end of the football season and the start of a new one is often a matter of days. Employing the logic of FIFA (logic and FIFA are two unusual bedfellows in the world of football I know) the season ends each year on the 30th June.

This is the date of the end of most professional footballer's contracts and in theory when all major domestic competitions should be completed. Unfortunately in recent years with tournaments getting bigger there has been an overlap, none more so than the start of the European club cup competitions, with some now starting in June.

My annual trip is to the Gower peninsula and the delights of Swansea. Thanks to the generosity of a man we know only as 'Active Matt', we are able to use his house in South Wales. As a result, for one week in the summer the Swiss-Family-Fuller goes on a summer vacation. Clean beaches, fantastic food, excellent beer and the opportunity to spot the Zeta-Jones playing adventure golf on the Mumbles all contribute to a work-free relaxathon. Did I mention the football? Of course there's football on the agenda - by the time we arrive pre-season is in full swing and you could go to a game a day if your wife didn't threaten you with divorce. As if!

In the past few years I had managed to juggle being a loving husband, doting father, and a bank for all parties with some games at the likes of Newport County, Carmarthen Town, Llanelli and Pontadawe. Two years ago I even spent my wedding anniversary at Cardiff City versus Valencia, not with the Current Mrs. Fuller mind, despite this being one of the first games at the new City Stadium she decided to go to Barry Island with the Littlest Fuller. I'll never understand women and the strange choices they make.

This year I was spoilt for choice but I only permitting myself two football outings during the week. One was a no brainer - Swansea City were making preparations for their first Premier League season with a warm up game against Celtic. The other was a potential stop off on our way home as Cardiff City visited Port Talbot Town, but that still needed to be discussed. Not a bad couple of games I thought. Our wedding anniversary this year fell on a Monday and we spent it on the almost deserted beach at Worms Head, possibly one of my favourite spots in the world. A steep ten-minute walk down to the beach and no facilities once you got on the sand meant your casual sunbather gave it a miss. Consequently you had acres of space all to yourselves. No mobile signal meant work was put out of sight and definitely out of mind as I settled down to the relaxing music of Linkin Park and a cold can of Brains Beer.

A few hours later we hiked up the hill for lunch at the fabulous Worms Head Hotel. I noticed I had a text from local football journalist Mark Pitman. There is nothing Mark doesn't know about football in these parts so I read his news with an excited and open mind.

'You won't believe this but Real Betis are playing at Neath on Wednesday night…a warm up before the Swansea City game'

He was right, I didn't believe it.

Why would a La Liga side be playing against a Welsh Premier League outfit? I had to verify the story so I asked Twitter. Sure enough I was pointed in the direction of Neath's official website by social media's great and good, where I saw the advert with my very own eyes. Real Betis had been due to play Portsmouth last week but technical issues had delayed the return of Pompey from their pre-season tour on the Isle of Wight or somewhere and a lucrative money-making friendly on the South Coast was postponed. Havant & Waterlooville of the Blue Square Bet South had stepped in at the last minute and hosted the Andalucians.

The Spanish team loved the feel of non-league football apparently. The food, the fact you could have a beer whilst sitting on the bench, the non-league dogs wearing scarves and they may actually win the game at a canter. After coming down to Wales on Tuesday to stay at Pontins in Barry Island, they discovered it wasn't as their travel agent had described the 'Costa del Sol of Wales'. Boredom soon set in - after all there are only so many games of bingo you can play around the pool, so they wanted to get a few games in and see some new places. Sort of like a player's ground-hop.

They arranged a friendly with Newport County on Wednesday (3-0 to the Spanish), but wanted to give the whole squad a run out prior to the game against Swansea City. Taking to Google they searched for 'easy teams to beat near Barry Island'; the name that came up was Neath and they arranged to play them just 24 hours later. A romantic wedding anniversary dinner in Rhossili would have to wait for now Mrs. Fuller; the Spanish were in town.

So after a day walking up hills, down valleys and under water-falls in the jaw-droppingly beautiful Vale of Neath, I dropped the

ladies back at Temporary Fuller Towers and made the short trip
down the M4 and up the A483. I was worried that parking may
be a problem with such a high profile game but on arrival it
appeared I needn't have worried. In fact it appeared I was the
only one here.

Perhaps it had been a cruel wind up by Mr. Pitman, taking
revenge for me editing one of his articles I had published on my
website and somehow getting Neath FC in on the gag. But then
I saw it in all its majesty. Real Betis had brought a coach. Not
just a coach borrowed from 'Dave's Coaches, Barry Island', oh
no. They had their own big, green travelling machine, complete
with logos, pictures and a Spanish number plate. Some poor sod
had driven those 1,632 miles from hot and sunny Andalusia to
wet South Wales. That in itself was worth a round of applause.

They love their sport in these parts. The region's sporting heritage has been centered on The Gnoll for decades. Not
only is it the home to the Neath Rugby Union team, one of the
noblest and proudest club sides in Wales producing such players
as Scott Gibbs, Shane Williams and Allan Bateman, but it also
plays host to the South Wales Scorpions who play in the second
level of Rugby League's National Division. With Swansea City
almost on the doorstep and Cardiff City just down the road, the
club has always struggled to get the crowds. Despite attempts to
alter kick off times, reduce ticket prices and attract some well-
known ex-League players, football in the town (and others in surrounding areas such as Llanelli and Port Talbot) always seemed
destined to struggle.

But all of that could be about to change. Swansea's rise to the
Premier League would see them play in front of £35-a-seat (and
the rest) sell-out crowds most weeks in the coming season. Fans
forced out economically and by sheer demand may have to get
their kicks elsewhere and so Neath had invested in this as their
new strategy. The club had spent big bringing in such players as
Lee Trundle and Chris Jones, both ex-Swansea City players who
could arguably still be playing at a higher level. Last season the
club had finished third in the Welsh Premier League, qualifying for the Europa League for the first time after a play-off with
Prestatyn Town – something their Spanish visitors couldn't
boast (a Europa League spot, NOT a trip to Prestatyn). Alas their
European adventure ended after just 180 minutes with a defeat
to the Norwegians, Ålesunds.

Kick-off time and alas, it seemed that the locals hadn't been seduced by the promise of some tiki-taka football or Betis agreeing to put out a first team. I met up with Mr. Pitman who like me, was still pinching himself that the game was taking place. We were joined by Abi Davies who had for the past 12 months reported on every Swansea City game for my website, as well as some of her wilder antics that only a teenage Welsh girl would deem 'normal nights out'. The lass is destined for big things in the world of journalism as long as she sticks to the straight and narrow and I was encouraged by her telling me that she had started to drink coffee for the first time this week. She found the taste unbearable but with a shot of Baileys in it was more palatable. With two it was very nice. She just couldn't understand why Starbucks don't sell it this way.

One look at the team sheet and some familiar names jumped out at us. Canas and Matilla were well known to viewers of La Liga on Sky Sports but it seemed the Spanish weren't exactly packing a punch up front. The line was being led by a player called Jonathan Pereira Rodríguez who must have been one of the smallest players I have seen in years. But as I am often reminded by my five-feet tall wife, great things often come in small packages. Depressingly, I don't think that's a reference to her height, thinking about it.

He may only be five foot five inches tall but by the end of the game Pereira Rodríguez was walking like a giant. Few strikers can boast a four-goal haul in a competitive match, let alone a five-goal salvo ('salvo' being the official term – brace, hat-trick, haul, salvo in that order). Beyond that a double hat-trick is as rare as a funny Michael McIntyre joke, scoring seven in a game is just ridiculous. At 9pm when he left the pitch to a standing ovation, Jonathan Pereira Rodríguez joined an elite club. For not only was his seven goals or fest (see what we did there? Create a new word for scoring seven) the sole difference between the teams on the pitch, but he became the only player currently playing in Europe to score a fest in a competitive match...twice!

He almost opened the scoring after just thirty seconds in when he scuffed a golden chance after Neath had ignored the referee's whistle to start the game. Whilst Betis had Jonathan Pereira Rodríguez, Neath had Lee Trundle who was living on his reputation these days. Slimmer than the Bristol City version from a few years ago, and now playing deeper to try and pull the strings which essentially translates to being too old/unfit to run back to defend from so far up the pitch, he struggled through the game.

In truth he got nowhere near the Spaniards and was lucky not to be red-carded for a cynical knee in the throat of a Betis player as they both fell to the floor midway through the first half.

After fifteen minutes of toying with the Welsh the Spaniards hit first gear. A neat ball was played through to Pereira Rodríguez and his mishit shot dribbled over the line, fooling the keeper who was expecting something with a bit more "Spanish" or at least with pace and accuracy. "GOOOAAAAAAAAAL" came the loud cry from a reporter behind us who was covering the game for the massed throngs in Sevilla who couldn't get a ticket for the game/didn't even know it was on.

One became four within thirty-minutes and the Betis centre-forward was having a field day. He could have put a blindfold on and arse-kicked the ball and it would have somehow gone in. He was in that sort of form that after the game he would have been a fool not to have bought a Euromillions ticket. The crowd by this stage had warmed to him despite playing for the opposition, and every time he got the ball they willed him to try to score a fifth.

Neath's best chance came in injury time at the end of the first half when a Trundle free-kick was charged down by, you've guessed it, Pereira Rodríguez. He proceeded to run the full length of the pitch to get on the end of a cross and make it Neath nil, Pereira Rodríguez five. Even by this stage our Spanish commentator had got bored with events and acknowledged the fifth goal with a muted "y otro" ('and another' for those lacking an O-Level in Spanish).

After some much needed refreshment (Brains Dark Ale – possible the third best beer ever created behind JW Lees Chocoholic and Harvey's Blue Label since you ask) it was time for the second half. Neath took off Trundle (apparently he had to go home and put his daughter to bed – genuinely!), whilst Betis were enjoying themselves too much and kept the same starting XI. This meant more chances for Pereira Rodríguez and he certainly didn't disappoint, adding a sixth and then a seventh in the first fifteen minutes of the half.

He looked genuinely embarrassed by the reaction from the crowd after each goal and when he eventually left the pitch five minutes later as Betis made 10 substitutions (much to the dismay of the fourth official and the announcer) he got a standing ovation from the crowd normally reserved for the likes of Katherine Jenkins and Charlotte Church in these parts.

After that it had the feel of a pre-season friendly with both teams happy to play the ball around without expending too much energy. Betis scored an eighth when aptly named Salva Sevilla scored a beauty from distance. The rest of the non-playing Betis squad by this stage had discovered chips with curry sauce, a change from Gazpacho soup I would image, and weren't paying too much attention to what was going on pitch-wise.

So a useful run out for them prior to playing the game against Swansea in just forty-eight hours. It still had a surreal feel to it, a Welsh Premier League side (probably the equivalent of a step 2 or 3 non-league Club) playing a team from La Liga. When would that happen normally?

Well apart from the previous week when they had started their tour against Havant & Waterlooville of course.

Or when England played Aylesbury prior to Italia 90.

Forget it, you've got the point.

With no formal press facilities I tried to nab a word with the man of the moment, 7-goal hero Pereira Rodríguez, as he headed across the road to board their coach. With his lack of English and my Spanish limited to the question "Cuál es su nombre de hermanos?", the only phrase I could remember from O-Level Spanish, he looked at me rather strangely. This was in part because the whole thing felt bizarre and partly as I had just asked him the name of his brothers. As the coach drove off back towards Barry Island I didn't know what an opportunity I'd missed for a world exclusive. Two days later his goal-scoring feat was plastered all over Marca and was the talk of Spain.

So it had been an unexpected game in my own pre-season training but a very welcome one, and a match I could tell my grandchildren about one day because I'm sure they'll want to know about the night a little Spanish footballer made history.

Won't they?

Just twenty-four hours later it was time to pack up the Fuller tour bus and ready ourselves for the trip back to En-Ga-Luuundddd. Our week of sun, sand and looking at crap tattoos in South Wales was coming to an end.

But wait, what is that I can hear calling me?

Is it a bird?

Is it a plane?

No silly, it's another football match.

And this one was literally on the way home (well a mile diversion off the M4).

Now how could I sell this to CMF and the Little Fullers? Of course! It was Port Talbot Town, home of Richard Burton, Paul Potts and Sir Anthony Hopkins. Hmm, still not enough as I was pretty sure my daughters had not heard of any of them. Well what about the fact that they wouldn't have to actually leave the car itself?

Bingo - we have a winner.

Port Talbot Town's GenQuip Stadium has one unique feature that wins the day for any fair weather fan. You can drive your car into the ground and park it by the side of the pitch (steps back awaiting amazed response). Yep, it is genuinely too good to be true. Certainly something I've never seen since they banned those little blue cars from parking behind the goal at Stamford Bridge for health and safety reasons back in the late 1980s.

So with twenty minutes gone in the game and the steward on the gate departed after having had enough of collecting cash, we drove into the ground for free and parked up on the bank with the best seats in the house. The girls were happy as they had their music, magazines, make up, etc, I was happy as I had some football to watch.

I'd been to the GenQuip Stadium the previous season for a Friday night derby clash against Llanelli. Mr. Pitman had invited me down to sample the fire and brimstone of Port Talbot steelworks by gas light, casually mentioning that the club's new Vice-President would be at the game and I may get to meet him. Nothing too special about that - I've met all sorts of footballing glitterati before so why would this be the compelling event for me to drive 250 miles westwards? Well when the man in question was none other Hollywood A-lister, Brian Clough/Sir David Frost/Tony Blair impersonator Michael Sheen, then it was yet another no brainer.

I told CMF of my plans to meet the great man. She got very, very excited and asked if his brother Charlie would be there. I explained the difference between the two Sheen families and not everyone in the world is related immediately. Her logic that Martin Sheen may well be in town to see his old mate Michael Douglas, currently residing in the Mumbles on the other side of Swansea Bay, and brought one of his sons along was at least plausible I guess.

Sheen (Michael, not Martin or Charlie) was born in the town and had never lost his Welsh roots. With successful films such as The Damned United and Frost/Nixon under his belt you'd have thought that a night out at the Ivy was more his style rather than a quick 99 (like a 69 but with chocolate sauce as added lubricant in these parts) on Afan Lido before catching a game at the GenQuip. The game itself was a 0-0 draw and whilst I never got the chance to actually shake his hand that night, we exchanged nods as we passed in the corridor by the gents in the second half. It was a nod that said 'I respect you and your talent'. I have to say I was pleased with that - I didn't even know he'd read my stuff.

So back to the present. This was Cardiff City's last friendly before the start of the new nPower Championship where they would be kicking off against West Ham United at Upton Park. Consequently only a few of the first XI were being given a run out. Well actually only one - Stephen McPhail. I'm not sure what he had done to offend the manager that resulted in him spending his Friday night in Afan Lido whilst his team mates were in Faces but it seemed a clear sign of discontent in the ranks.

Even with a Cardiff City team of youngsters the omens weren't good for Port Talbot from the kick off as they weathered an early bombardment from the visitors. It only took them three minutes to take the lead when a shot from McPhail took a huge deflection that had the Town keeper beaten all ends up.

I had ventured out of the car, if only for the fact I wanted to watch the small crew of Cardiff City fans trying to antagonise the home fans. The group in question must have had an average age of about twelve and an IQ something lower (combined) as they shared a solitary can of Strongbow . Unfortunately for them, none of the home fans were taking them seriously so they tried to make their own entertainment.

First up they decided to start sending pictures taken on their mobile phones of various undeveloped body parts to random girls. "You're sick man," said one as he realised that his mate had sent a picture of the contents of his pants to his Mum. "Nothing she ain't seen before is it?" he responded much to the amusement of the rest of the group who all nodded knowingly.

A conga around the perimeter failed to see them attract any new fans so they took to trying to roll down the grass banks along the side of the pitch to gain some more attention. It impressed the eight-year-old Littlest Fuller but that was about it. In the meantime Port Talbot scored twice, first when Dylan Blain headed in a Cortez Belle cross-cum-shot and then Lee John scored from distance with one of those shots that hovered just inches above the ground.

After the usual substitutions at half time, the game restarted with Cardiff in the ascendancy. Adam Smith is a name to watch out for in the future and not just for his thoughts on global economics. The wide man was the difference between the two sides in the second half, scoring an equaliser and then hitting the post shortly after, trying to earn a spot on the front seat of the coach for the trip to East London.

Honours even in the end, a two-all draw, and the time for our mammoth journey back to Fuller Towers had come. The home side were quietly confident of an improvement on last season's sixth place finish and would welcome Welsh Premier League Champions TNS (aka The New Saints since the Total Network Solutions money ran out) in a week's time. For the home fans this season would also see them renew their intense rivalry with Afan Lido, based literally around the corner.

My own pre-season training successfully completed for another year, it was now time to throw ourselves head-first into the new campaign with a three day trip to France and Belgium with Danny Last and Andy 'Huddo' Hudson, attempting the ultimate Belgian Beer challenge along the way. Nothing like easing into the season gradually then...

Chapter Six

French Resistance
Non-alcoholic beer and mountains of chips

12th August 2011
Amiens SC 0 Le Havre 1
Stade de la Licorne

13th August 2011
Lens 2 Troyes 1
Stade Félix Bollaert

> "... your dress sense is worse than the Amiens SC
> goalkeeper..."

I still have no real idea how these trips to foreign lands find their way into our collective heads. Normally one of us sees a video on YouTube, a photo on our 'European Football Weekends' Facebook page or an article in a newspaper somewhere. Ideas turn into "what-if" and normally after one email, one, two or even three of us utter the immortal line "I'm in." From that moment until we arrive on distant shores, our heads are full of romantic scenes of huge floodlights, dogs wearing scarves and exotic beers.

These trips rarely feature one game – after all we can see that back at home. What makes a trip that Chalmers, Palin and Pilkington would be truly jealous of is squeezing in three or four games, a night out in some strange bar and even, dare I say it, some culture. Yep, you read that last one correct. Sometimes we even find time for activities that do not involve beer or football. Ok, very, very occasionally then but we at least we think about it, whilst having a beer and watching football.

We football fans do not suffer from 'Winters of Discontent', we suffer 'Summers of Emptiness'. As soon as the season ends, our thoughts immediately turn to when the new season fixtures will come out. Pages of debate are taken up on our Facebook page as to where will be the first country to publish their schedules, but time and time again the French win hands down. Barely has the final whistle blown in the last Ligue 1 games of the season before the French Football Association are firing up the fixture computer, putting in the names and pressing the big red button marked 'Allez'. Twenty-minutes later out pops the next nine month's fun and games (literally).

It seemed rude not to pencil in our first European Football Weekend of the new season as a trip across the la Manche, especially as France staggers their League one and two fixtures across the whole weekend. Friday night, Saturday afternoon and even a potential Sunday game would make a perfect weekend. Throw in a few small bottles of French beer, a plate of steaming coq au vin and we would be as happy as an Essex Girl in a tanning salon with a Bacardi Breezer in her hand.

The initial plan called for a trip to the passion and colour of Racing Club Lens on Friday night, followed by a night out in the wonderful historic city of Gent across the border in Belgium. Who wouldn't want a slice of that footballing pie? Well, Danny Last and Andy 'Huddo' Hudson certainly did, and double portions at that. Both 'reluctantly' agreed to accompany me on my border patrols, with Andy making the additional trip down from the

Northern Metropolis known as Hebburn.

Alas, French TV is as invasive as our cousins down at Sky Sports and ten days before we were due to hop on the ferry, RC Lens's game with Troyes was moved to Saturday lunchtime. Danny kicked into action, finding us an alternative within a few minutes. Just (just!) a hundred miles down the road from Calais is the historic city of Amiens, home of Jules Verne, Peter the Hermit and the Imperial usurper Magnentius. So that was sorted. Two games had become three, and soon became five when the draw for the first round of the Belgian Cup threw up a couple of Sunday afternoon options. Could weekends get any better in terms of raw potential?

The good news was that we would be chauffeured around the countryside of France and Belgium in luxury, taken from stadium to hotel via the bars of Northern Europe. The bad news was that I was the chauffer. Alas, to pack in as much as possible in a limited time frame and to enjoy these trips to the max, I often end up running Stuart Fuller's Taxis (no fare too small, no run too big).

Fortunately, I didn't have a six-hour trip on the Megabus from Newcastle overnight, complete with groups of hens and stags already pissed up from a night out on the Toon and ready for a weekend of debauchery in London.

But Andy did.

As he alighted in the breaking dawn at Victoria Coach Station muttering the words "never again", he truly meant it. Of course a sensible man would have headed to the nearest coffee shop for some refreshment before continuing his journey southwards, but Andy is made of sterner stuff. Who puts a Weatherspoons next to a Starbucks anyway?

Two hours later and we were scratching our heads, pouring over some instructions on how to fit headlight converters in the queue for the Dover to Calais ferry. We suddenly came over all Little England - why do we need to stick these ridiculous things on our cars? They never bother converting theirs when they come over to the UK, bloody political correctness that's what it is. And not only did we have to go through this whole charade, but we also had to buy a fire extinguisher, fluorescent jacket, warning triangle and a first aid kit to be road legal.

Our level of Englishness was now directly proportional to the amount of time it was taking to sort these bloody headlamps out. Seriously what do you need to have in your car to drive in the UK? A Phil Collins CD, a five-year out of date AA Road Atlas and a packet of travel sweets at best. David Cameron can stop bleating about the EU Budget and sort out this sort of complete and utter…wait…they're on, bloody love Europe me. "Drive on the right, drive on the right" I kept telling myself as we rolled off the ferry ramp. Danny and Andy had already got into the holiday mood with a few Stellas on the ferry, whilst I had a Shandy Bass. My fun would come later in the day when the car had been deposited in Amiens. Time was on our side as we headed south. French countryside appeared and disappeared as we covered the miles to Amiens, stopping only to admire the Picardy countryside and to have a pee.

The elitist motorway network in France means that if you have the cash, then your journey is painless. Long empty stretches of toll road meant that we ate up the miles to our first destination. It wasn't hard to find the Stade de la Licorne – after all apart from the 13th Century Gothic Cathedral it is the focal point of the Amiens skyline, rising up above the rooftops like a giant clamshell. Such was the excitement of seeing the stadium on entering the city that we missed our exit on a roundabout, not once but three times. Nothing like being inconspicuous in front of the French Gendarmes sitting on their motorbikes.

The stadium was built in 1999, with that clam-like roof that is certainly unique in terms of football architecture. It was in truth the only reason why we had decided to come to the city. Amiens Sporting Club haven't ever actually set the world of French football alight. One-time division three champions and Cup runners-up in 2001, today they were firmly at home in the lower reaches of the second tier of French football.

Having found the stadium it was now time to find the hotel. As our travel arrangements had been modified at short notice to accommodate French TV, hotels in the centre were at a premium, both in terms of space for three young chaps and in Euros. Our best option was slightly out of town according to the website. Think of Croydon when talking about Covent Garden and you won't too far away from the description of location on the hotel's website. Still, a room is a room, even if it was a single room with three beds shoe-horned in, with one (mine) actually half in the bathroom. Convenient, but at times a bit smelly.

Our original plan of getting public transport to the game was soon abandoned. The one bus took an hour to get back into the city-centre and stopped at 5pm. With torrential rain now the order of the day, I agreed to extend the hours of Stuart Fuller

Taxis (no fare too small, no run too big) for the evening.

After so long in a foreign country without a beer, Andy and Danny were starting to develop a lisp. Fortunately the hotel had a bar. Unfortunately it was closed, after all it was only 6pm on a Friday night – who would want a drink at that ridiculous time? It turned out that the hotel only employed one person and he was currently explaining to a group of Japanese tourists that they weren't in Paris and he couldn't tell them how to get to the Eiffel Tower. Finally we got him to open briefly and sell us our first beer on foreign soil for the weekend. It may have been luke-warm, sickly and tasted vaguely of washing up liquid, but it was still a small treat for the hours of driving so far.

Kronenbourg necked we retraced the journey back to the stadium, passing a coach of Le Havre fans who were being given a police escort to the ground by the police. Whilst this was as close to a local derby in these parts as you could get, the 110 mile journey on a Friday night had put off all but the hardcore travelling Le Club Doyen fans. Of course, it probably doesn't help that the two clubs had played each other here in Amiens in the League Cup just seventy-two hours previously, with the home side running out two-one winners.

With an hour or so still to kick off, we parked up, bought our €10 ticket and wandered around trying to find the bar. All club stadiums have a bar right? Apparently not. The Stade de la Licorne may win awards for architectural brilliance, but it gets nil points for facilities. We did find a Fritteria though. Chips are the national dish of France so we got involved big time. They were literally served in a carrier bag with a pint of mayonnaise poured all over them. French cuisine may have its detractors but this was top notch, best in the world.

Weighed down with a mountain of chips, we headed up the stairs and took our position standing at the back of the stand just as the teams came out. The small section of Le Havre fans waved their flags politely; the Amiens fans in the VIP tent to our right afforded a polite ripple of support. The 12-year-old at the front of our stand led the home fans in the middle section into generous singing.

Eventually we became bored by the carrier bag full of chips and mayonnaise. After fifteen minutes of non-stop eating we were still no closer to finishing them. French cuisine? Way over-rated, worst in the world. What would have been nice would have been a cold beer. With two hours before I had to drive again, even the very strict drink-driving laws in France could afford me one small beer. Danny, like a blood-hound searching out a fallen grouse, spotted a bar. We headed there immediately and joined a queue. Andy nabbed the first one poured, took a swig and immediately turned his nose up. It wasn't sickly sweet like the one at the hotel, but it was watery. Was it non-alcoholic beer? We conferred, debated and thrashed it out before deciding that it must be. We have rules about this sort of thing, so we downed them quickly and headed to a seat at the front of the stand to watch the match.

Neither team attacked with purpose. Perhaps they were also thinking about a night out in the old town after the game as we were. It was no surprise that a cagey first half finished goalless with neither keeper being tested. The high point of the half was the stick the home keeper was getting from the young fans for his choice of attire. An all pink outfit with a nice flowery design, matching boots and gloves did wonders for his street-cred. The atmosphere was muted, the downside of the stadium design being that any noise that is created isn't retained inside the stands, it floats upwards and away into the night sky.

"I reckon we could get a beer in that main stand," said Danny just as the referee signalled for the end of the half. With the main stand having the posh seats and being a few Euros more expensive, we made our way to the concourse that ran around the top of the stadium bowl, blagged our way past security by waving our travel cards and headed straight to the back of the main stand. The VIP tent seemed to be where all the drinking action was. A couple of home fans were coming out of the tent as we arrived. "Your beer, does it have alcohol in?" asked Danny, slightly affecting a French accent. "Oui" shot back the reply. "We'll double up on this round then Andy. Four large beers, one small s'il vous plaît".

As we had made it this far we decided to stay in the posh seats. After all the stadium was only two-thirds full at best and the 'seats' were only bits of plastic bolted onto concrete steps. Andy again was the first to take a gulp of the beer. "This bloody VIP beer is still non-alcoholic, just a bit fizzier". We, of course, vowed never to mention the incident again although we still blamed Danny for not speaking French to the two fans we had met, as if that made any difference at all. With no alcohol to mess with our memory, we took to the football again. Despite the first-half stick he got, the Amiens keeper was still sporting his outfit. As a result of this fashion disaster, it was no surprise that the visitors took the lead after 62 minutes. Football has a simple rule according to Andy Hudson - wear a disgusting top and you will get beat.

Le Havre broke away down the left and a cross that initially appeared to be hit far too high and deep, caught on the jet stream and fell perfectly for Ryan Mendes Da Graça to volley home in style. Nobody wants to really hear about the final thirty-minutes after that do they? In a one sentence summary, Amiens were short of ideas, Le Havre happy with the one goal and the crowd couldn't wait to start their Friday night proper.

We made a sharp exit, wanting to get back to the hotel as quick as we could. Whilst the main reason was to drop the car off, deep-down Andy wasn't just championing my cause to have a beer but he needed that all-important splash of Brut. Andy is a proper Geordie and worships everything Kevin Keegan has ever done, ever said and everpromoted. The 'Classic masculine scent' made by Fabergé was famous in the 1970s, with Keegan telling us famously to "Splash it all over". Rumour has it that Andy was actually baptised with it, making him one of the blessed few 'propa reit Jordeees'.

One twenty-minute taxi ride later and we were in the heart of the city. We had been told that there was a street of bars. The street turned out to be rather small. The street was actually a corner with two bars opposite each other. We headed to the quieter of the two, scanned the menu and waited for some in-different service. "The beer's almost 7 Euros a pint here!" exclaimed Danny. We weren't standing for that and so just as our waiter came over, we perfected the famous French aloofness and left. Desperation set in immediately.

"Is that a pub over there?"

"Na, it's a hairdressers".

And so it went as we wandered around a deserted High Street. Amiens certainly has a nice looking butchers, an underwear shop with a "fit looking lass" in the window according to Andy (aka a mannequin in suspenders) and a cracking Body Shop. Very few pubs though.

Eventually, the decision was very easy. One bar seemed to have monopolised all the beautiful people of Amiens. Of course it was the one that we had left around earlier. Fortunately there was a spare table outside so we took up residence, bit the bullet and ordered the most expensive beers this side of Scandinavia. It was a typical Friday night you would see all over Europe. A man in a motorised wheelchair led a can-can inside, a group of students shared a coke and some coke on the table next to us, whilst a very drunk girl dressed as a sailor bounced from table to table. When she heard we were English she was all over us. Correction, she was all over Andy. "Ooh, you smell very nice" she said, running her fingers through his Brylcreemed hair. Kevin Keegan wins the day. Again.

With the night getting late and with an early start to Lens the following morning, we started to finish off our beers. Our new friend wanted us to stay although her only real English sentence was "Do you think I'm pretty?". We soon realised that we could actually say anything to her and she would respond with a round of kisses on the cheek, thus a game was born.

"You look like Betty Turpin."

Kiss.

"You smell like a jockstrap."

Kiss.

"Your dress sense is worse than the Amiens SC goalkeeper."

Kiss.

Even a drunk, young French girl flirting with Huddo gets boring after a while, although to be fair that while did have a four in by the time we left and headed back to our hotel in the suburbs.

Fast-forward five hours and I was awoken by someone having a wee about three feet from my head. For some reason I had decided to sleep head first in the bathroom and was now looking up at a view of Andy Hudson that no one wants to see.

Who needs an alarm clock when you can have an alarm cock.

We had a schedule to keep as we headed eastwards on our journey that would ultimately see us take on one of the greatest challenges known to man – the Belgian Beer XI. But for now we were still in the suburbs of Amiens and the Stuart Fuller Taxis (no fare too small, no run too big) team were a little fragile to say the least.

Our first venture out of the hotel saw us quickly retreat back inside. It was hammering down with rain – the kind of rain that means you can only see a few yards in front of your nose. Perfect weather for negotiating unknown roads in a new country with a thumping headache. I kept repeating the mantra "drive on the right, drive on the right" to myself, but my brain just kept saying "I'm trying to sleep". A quick sing-song of our favourite football tunes soon had us in the mood for the day and slowly but surely things were improving.

We had skipped breakfast in favour of grabbing a bite to eat on the road and as soon as we had finished the third verse of Blaydon Races we pulled into France's most depressing service station somewhere on the A29. It seemed that the le monde et sa femme were also travelling to Lens based on the amount of cars trying to find a parking space. Finally I found a slot between a Dutch caravan moving rhythmically from side to side, and a group of hairy bikers who had their faces pressed up against said caravan's window. This is not the France you see advertised in Country Life.

Twenty-three minutes later Danny and Andy re-emerged with a thimble of cold coffee and a Mars Bar. Of course a Mars Bar – the universal emergency food used by astronauts, mountain climbers and overweight, hung-over football fans. The boys had already eaten their breakfast in the queue to pay. It seems that the French join that long list of countries that are still to use the common international standards of queuing. Andy had used his three day old French stick as a weapon and caused an international incident, which diverted the attention of the mob long enough to pay for their items and make a run for it. Was the caravan rocking when we made our getaway? Yes. Yes it was.

France is a beautiful country and rightly a must-see for world tourists. Back in 2009 nearly 75 million visitors came to France, more than any country in the world. The vineyards of Bordeaux, the beaches of Nice, the luxury of St Tropez and the slag-heaps of Lens. Well, three out of four isn't bad. The town of Lens itself was going through a renaissance. Those ugly reminders of their industrial past were now being turned into things of beauty and a dry ski slope had for too long been the most popular tour-ist attraction in the town. That was about to change with the opening of the second branch of the world famous art museum, the Louvre. Like McDonalds they're now franchising so expect to see a Louvre in your town soon. The town was very excited about the arrival of some culture with billboards heralding the new arrival due in 2013 as we parked up and made our way to the Stade Félix Bollaert, a stadium that could hold the population of the town and their mistresses.

Again, I wasn't a stranger to these parts. I'd been here in 1998 for the World Cup game between Saudi Arabia and Denmark as well as the sell-out Rugby World Cup game between England and the USA in 2007. Add in between these dates a couple of Racing Club Lens games and I felt I had earned the right to wear my yellow and red RCL socks for this game. Whilst I was happy with my sock-related fill of club merchandise, Danny was looking longingly for that oh-so-special present for Mrs. Last for their wedding anniversary.

He was stood in the middle of the sizeable megastore, trying to remember his French O-Level skills. He was on the lookout for a snazzy pair of RC Lens slippers and his heart was thumping loudly through his chest with excitement. Thinking quickly, he grabbed a shop assistant as they passed by.

"Où sont les Lens pantoufles, s'il vous plaît?"

(Where are the Lens slippers, if you please?).

A beaming shop assistant pointed him in the right direction, next to the RC Lens alarm clocks obviously (no RC Lens alarm cocks to be seen, thank God). He skipped out €10 lighter in the wallet department but three inches wider in the cheesy grin department. At this point he would have happily said it was the best day of his life.

We weren't going to be alone for this game, as if you could be in a place like Lens where thirty thousand Racing Club fans were slapping us on our backs as we sang 'Allez les Lens' in the car park. We were meeting a trio of old friends from Belgium. They had already procured our €9 (nine!) tickets earlier in the day. Pat, who you may remember as our chauffer on our trip to Spakenburg (chapter 1), young Super Hans (more of him later...) and their friend Little Maarten, who was actually seven-feet tall proving those Belgians have a crazy sense of humour. Those long winter nights must just fly by in the lowlands of Europe.

So what do six men standing outside a football ground talk about? Well, beer mainly and where we can get one. "Do you sell beer inside?" we asked the steward on the gate. "Yes, we do." came the reply so we headed inside with over an hour to go until kick off. "Six beers please," we asked at the bar with our best Anglo-French smile beaming, "we don't sell beer," came the reply. Of course they didn't.

Inside, the Stade Félix Bollaert was already rocking. It may have only been 11.30am but the locals had come out in force, forsaking Samedi Cuisine on the TV. A chap with Lens trousers was standing in the middle of the pitch twirling a huge flag. I could see that Danny was green with envy. Not due to the flag but because of his trousers. He was now regretting buying those slippers without perusing the trouser aisle I could tell.

The ultras in the Tony Marek stand which runs the length of the pitch were in full voice and colour - Sang and Or obviously. They were relentless and Danny immediately awarded them a place in his coveted top five of European football fans. It was obvious as the national anthem rang out and we linked arms with our new Lens friends (an elderly couple wearing matching home-knitted jumpers who had once been to Sittingbourne on holiday no less) that we would have our eyes fixed on the fans rather than the actual game. As the final notes of La Marseillaise rang out, the red and yellow flares lit up the stadium. This was going to be good. Very, very good.

And what was all this? Works of art adding to the riot of colour? Yes sir. Giant canvases, the size of the proverbial bus, had been positioned inside the stadium. They looked like reproductions of famous masterpieces from The Louvre with an additional twist/theme in the famous club colours of blood and gold. This was all part of the Louvre-Lens project taking shape behind the North Stand. Football and Art had never held hands with such unease.

With a provisional playing budget of around €20 million compared to that of €8 million for the opposition, Espérance Sportive Troyes Aube Champagne, you'd have expected Lens to dominate. And that they (sort of) did. They edged a fairly nervy first half, which passed us by as we watched the ultras launch into song after scarf twirling after synchronised flag waving. Life hasn't been too rosy for Lens in recent years. They won the title in 1998 and came a close second three years later. But since then they have been one of the many clubs who had to sit in the shadow of the Olympique Lyonnais millions. Relegation, promotion and then relegation again dominated the first decade of the 21st century, the final curtain call being presided over by legendary goal poacher Jean-Pierre Papin.

But this season (in that fashion that all football fans know and love) was all supposed to be so different. Under Jean-Louis Garcia the club were favourites to bounce back to Ligue 1, although it would be one of the toughest campaigns for many years with recent champions Monaco and Nantes both playing at this level.

We stood around twiddling our thumbs during the break. With no beer we became very dull, trotting out the usual 'random' trivia questions that we all knew the answer to.

Men + Football – Beer = Sober Football Trivia Questions.

Fortunately it was only fifteen minutes of pain and soon enough we were back in business. Lens brought on David Pollet, which raised a titter from us English fans as we in unison shouted "David Chicken!". It seemed that none of the locals found it funny. For a country that finds mime the funniest thing on earth, how could they not find that funny? Michael McIntyre would go down a storm here.

Pollet didn't waste any time before he made his impact, slotting home the opening goal not long after the break. It was disappointing that he didn't do a Kevin Nolan-style chicken dance as he ran towards us to celebrate. Self-deprecation is an endearing asset in a man, so the Current Mrs. Fuller once told me. Pierre Ducasse added a second in very similar fashion, before Troyes pulled one back almost immediately, through Benjamin Psaume to set up a nail-biting finish. After two opening defeats, Lens were finally able to climb up the table on the final whistle.

In France, there is a €15,000 fine, up to a year in prison and a five-year stadium ban for entering the field of play. That's harsher than inciting a Facebook riot or threatening to blow up an airport on Twitter, so we decided to forego our usual group hug on the pitch. Neither Danny nor Andy fancied the five-year stadium ban, although the fact that some prisons in France are mixed-sex did raise a Roger Moore-style eyebrow in the eyes of our Geordie Romeo. Our chat on the way back to the car focused on which English team Racing Club de Lens were most like. There could only be one; Leeds United, a slightly fallen giant with tremendous fans and splendid old school ground. With that debate concluded we went, ahem, marching on together across the border into Belgium for the second game of the day in Gent.

Good old life.

Chapter Seven

A Scholar and a Gent
Doing a Souness- a half here and a half there

13th August 2011
KAA Gent 3 Standard Liège 1
Jules Ottenstadion

14th August 2011
OMS Ingelmunster 0 Woluwe Zaventem 1
Ingelmunster Stadion

Sint-Eloois-Winkel 1 Union SG 1
Sint-Eloois-Winkel Stadion

> "...our new guest was a big Newcastle fan, so big that he
> carried a bag filled with Newcastle memorabilia..."

Previously on Le European Football Weekend, we left our heroes in the car park at Racing Club Lens having just seen Les Sang et Or beat Troyes. Our threesome had become a foursome as Hans had joined us for the journey back into Belgium. Our destination was Gent, a city of a quarter of a million people in the middle of East Flanders. Coming from Belgium, Hans was sure to know the way, right? Well, we needed his help to navigate us direct to the Jules Ottenstadion in time for the big match.

We ran into our first problem just a few miles outside of Lens. As I was slowly learning this weekend, the French like to have a little joke at the expense of everyone from 'abroad' that chooses to drive on their roads. From the outskirts of Lens you hang a left past slag-heap number three onto the E17 and carry straight on for a long way. All I needed to do was to find the signs for Lille, Kortrijk and Gent.

Despite the fact the whole of the Western world knowing the city as Gent, or sometimes the still highly recognisable 'Ghent', those loveable French like to call it Gand. Three of us in the car didn't know that, but one did. Hans told us the error of our ways after I had missed the first major interchange on the motorway near Lille. Never mind I thought, as long as we are heading for Kortrijk we would be OK. Wrong again, Kortrijk is called Court-rai of course, as Hans told us as we sailed past that exit as well. There is nothing better than being told to "Turn right now!" as you are doing about 80 miles per hour in the outside lane of a busy foreign motorway.

Eventually we found a road that took us east and passed through the Belgium border. "OK, top 10 Belgian footballers, go!" and so a variation on a classic that we play every time we come here, and a game we can never complete. Even with Hans on board we only managed to get to seven all-time great Belgians (current players still have it to all to do in our eyes, number one? Enzo Scifo of course), still it did break our previous record of four which included my new found fact that Bradley Wiggins was born not only in Belgium, but in the city of Gent. I know what you're thinking, he's a cyclist and not a footballer but I will offer only this in reply – when you are desperate, you are desperate.

We made good time, cruising across the relatively empty roads and admiring the flat landscape. At one point Danny thought he saw a hill in the distance, but it turned out to be a billboard poster for some soap powder. Hans's directions were by now perfect, and by perfect I mean he managed to read exactly what was on the road signs as we passed them.

"In 500 metres take a right for Gent Industrial Zone."

What would we do without you...

We approached Gent with thirty minutes to spare, looking like we could actually make kick off. "Hans, where's the ground?" I asked after he bigged up his last visit here with Royal Antwerp. He didn't know of course, although worryingly he could quite easily point out the exact location of the red light district as we drove round and round in circles looking for a sign. We needed some sort of visual clue, a car-park instruction maybe, an illicit glimpse of floodlight, or even a giant pair of KCC Gent slippers (Danny's dream scenario, the man's obsessed).

Then we saw a definite sign that somewhere close by was a football game on. Someone overtook us on a bike with a big KAA Gent flag and "follow that bike!" was the shout from Mr Last in the back of the car. A great idea in principle but the taxi still hasn't developed powers to travel down narrow bike lanes, so we had to sit in a long line of traffic, albeit a promising one.

Time ticked down and we knew we were close to the ground when we saw the police water cannon parked up. Such are the resources of the Belgian police that they can roll this beauty out for games each weekend, ready to cleanse the streets of any football fans who have had a Leffe and a chocolate waffle too many, yet back in Blighty when civil unrest kicks off our Government thinks that a policeman armed with a small can of pepper spray is a deterrent. Surely someone in government could've sent someone over on the ferry to bring one back when we needed it during the London riots? Just think of all the duty free beer, tobacco and bangers you could've fitted in the boot on the trip – win/win.

The fans were out in numbers for the game. The visitors Standard Liège were back in form, finishing as runners up in the Jupiler League last season and snaring the Belgium Cup according to Super Hans who had just looked up that fact on Wikipedia. About half a mile from the stadium we stopped at some lights and a chap jumped in the car. "Hi I'm Roland. I am a friend of Joris's. He text me your car number plate and said you would give me a lift". If nothing else it was nice to know that Stuart Fuller's Taxis (no fare too small, no run too big) had become well known in East Flanders. Always nice to have something to fall back on if work goes quiet. Bit of a commute though.

Our new guest was a big Newcastle fan, so big in fact that he carried a bag with him filled with Newcastle United memorabilia.

"And here's one of me and Philippe Albert" (of course Philippe Albert) he said as he thrust a blurry photo under my nose just as I negotiated a Belgian roundabout. Fortunately Andy was also a Newcastle fan and was given the job of keeping his scrapbook out of my face until we had at least stopped at some traffic lights.

We parked up some distance from the stadium meaning we needed a brisk walk down Voetbalstraat ('Football Street' – no word of a lie) to get to the ground. The game had just started which considering Super Hans's 'directions' was somewhat of a miracle as at one point it looked like we may not make half-time. We still needed to pick up our tickets, but with just three people queuing in front of us that would be a simple job. Alas it seemed that the start of the match was also a cue for 80% of the ticket office staff to close their windows and go to watch the game. The chap at the front of the queue was buying tickets for every home game for the rest of the season, choosing a different seat for each one. He was the footballing equivalent of a man banking the year's takings from the penny arcade.

Finally we bagged our €25 tickets, which compared to most clubs outside the Premier League (and La Liga and Serie 1) were pricy. Not to worry, they would be VIP seats for that price I'm sure. Of course they weren't. We were in the only part of the ground that didn't have a roof, a bit added on the end of the main stand to fill in an ugly corner with the most bizarre rule in place I have ever seen at a football match.

'No Food or Drink can be taken into these seats.'

I can sort of understand the drink bit, it's pretty much common place in most English grounds putting on professional football these days, but what damage can you seriously do with a small sausage? This was a sentiment shared by various ex-girl-friends of Mr Hudson I was told. Our seats were in the back row, slap behind a couple who wore matching jumpers (twice in a day - must be some sort of record), badly dyed blonde hair and even spots in the same place. Apparently the couple were voted 'Mr and Mrs Buffalos Fans' (the Buffalos being the nickname of KAA Gent) in the previous match for their undying love for the club and these seats were their prize.

Next to them sat Alan Biley. For those of you old enough to remember the '80s, Biley was your classic nomadic centre-forward, briefly terrorising defences in stints at clubs such as Cambridge United and Portsmouth. He was the man who brought the mullet into English football and here he was, hounded out of

England to find a home where such fashion disasters were still accepted as on-trend. On his shirt he had his telephone number for bookings for birthdays, weddings and bar-mitzvahs. We nearly booked him for the drive home.

The ground was rocking as our attention turned to the game. This was a proper old school stadium, four very different looking stands, built at various stages in the club's history when money had been available. The club had outgrown it and with a capacity of just 12,000 it simply wasn't able to produce the kind of match day income the club needed. This was to be the last season the club would play here, in theory, before a move to a new stadium called the Arteveldstadion on the outskirts of the city. Both sets of fans were making a fair noise, although there was a disappointing lack of flag waving, scarf twirling and general flare firing.

On the pitch there appeared to be no love lost between the two sets of players, with the referee having every single decision called into question (not just a Premier League disease after all). After 18 minutes he had his first big one to make when a Gent player was clearly fouled as he ran into the area. Faced with a wall of noise from the away fans just a few yards away he changed his initial decision of a penalty into a goal kick and brandished a yellow card to the Gent player for his misdemeanour of being scythed down.

We didn't have to wait too long for the first goal of the game after that incident. After the relatively sterile games in France this one was turning out to be a cracker. A Gent corner wasn't cleared well enough and Jesper Jørgensen's tame shot trickled into the corner of the net through a sea of bodies. Who cares how they go in as long as they do eh? Alan Biley-a-like went mad, showing the crowd his two-fisted pumping salute before breaking into some impressive air-guitar to AC/DC's Thunderstruck as it blared out of the PA system. This was more like it. Just in front of him another fan raised a huge umbrella in celebration and did a little dance in the aisle. The heavens answered his rain dance and opened accordingly.

One became two a few minutes later, and this time it was a strike that had us purring in delight. Ilombe Mboyo's run and cross from the right-hand side was brilliantly met by the Dane Jørgensen again for his, and Gent's, second goal. The Liège fans were stunned. This wasn't in the script and they let their back four and keeper know that in no uncertain terms.

Without alcohol for nearly twelve hours now the goal was enough to send Danny, Andy and Hans down to the bar, leaving me with Roland. Apparently the goal reminded him of Peter Beardsley's against Carlisle United back in 1985 and wouldn't you just know it, he had a photo of that in his man-bag along with a drawing he had made showing Beardsley's run. My self-imposed rule of forsaking alcohol until 7pm went straight out of the window and I joined the others in the Maes-fest on the concourse for the driver's requisite small beer.

Slowly but surely city and town centres in England are being invaded by plastic portal pissoires as public toilets are difficult to clean and police. These strange pods are very practical and have been common in Europe for decades. On the plus side they offer quick relief for us beer-laden chaps, but on the down side you are very exposed to everyone around you in more ways than one. The one on the concourse was positioned in such a way that any women who needed to use the ladies would queue on a raised platform above the portal pee-holes, offering them a birds-eye view of Gent's finest. Lots of giggling, pointing and one huge belly-laugh suggested that they weren't impressed with what was on display. However, one chap did cause a combined intake of breath from the audience so he was immediately nicknamed Tripod (of course Tripod, imagination is not our strong point).

Back to the action and whilst the first few minutes were taken up with a discussion about whether we could actually make a third game of the day at Kortrijk, Gent continued to press for a third goal. Super Hans was as useful as ever when we asked him about how long it would take us to drive there, what the ground was like, and how much it would be to get in.

"I don't know."

"The ground's alright."

"Can't remember how much the tickets are."

"I can show you the red-light district if you'd like?"

Of course you can Hans.

Twenty minutes into the second half and Kanu, no relation to Nwanko Kanu or Robson Kanu as it turns out, scored for the visitors and for a few minutes there were signs the home team were wobbling. The home fans turned the noise up a notch and as if by magic Tim Smolders hit a smouldering volley into the corner of the net to restore the two goal lead. If we'd had a roof over our heads, that would be the moment it came off.

To our left Gent's number one fan, a man dressed in what can only be described as a superhero costume you put together at the last minute from items of clothing at the back of the wardrobe, went mad. He deserved a special award, not for the silk blue pantaloons nor the white gloves worn over his blue silk shirt, not even for the blue and white cape or bandana, but for the crisp white Y-fronts he wore outside his trousers in true Superman style. Who said the Belgians had no sense of humour? Ah yes, that would be us.

The last few minutes of the game passed without incident, apart from a second yellow for Gent's Zlatan Ljubiankic who stomped his feet like a spoilt child before being escorted from the pitch by the home-team's physio. The full-time whistle brought most of the 10,739 in attendance to their feet in celebration and the players were joined on the pitch by the club's mascot, a Red Indian Chief complete with squaw and, of course, an umbrella.

We headed back to the car, still with our new friend in tow. There wasn't one piece of Newcastle memorabilia that Roland didn't have in his bag and he took delight in showing us everything. Over and over again. Perhaps we did play on his Belgian humour a bit too far by suggesting he wasn't a real fan as he didn't have Glenn Roeder's autograph, but it was simply far too easy in the circumstances.

As the home fans headed home for a bowl of garlic mussels, waffles smothered with chocolate and some Tin Tin on the TV, the night was still young for us. We eventually found our hotel via a route that ran us twice through the red-light district (no prizes for guessing who was navigating). At some point during the drive from Lens we had come up with one of our less sensible ideas for the evening's entertainment. Obviously being in the heart of Belgian brewing we wanted to experience the true meaning of being Flemish.

And what better way than trying to drink 11 different beers...

But not just any old beers of course, and not just drink either. Our plan was to choose a different beer in each round, trying to match its character, look and taste with a footballer in history. Each of us would throw a suggestion in for a particular position on the field, we would drink, debate the options and in theory come to a consensus by the time we had finished the beer. A sensible idea at 9pm, but after a gallon of Trappist ales your Carlos Alberto Parreira and Ray Stewart's do seem to blend into one. At some point in the wee small hours we had a nine-man side containing Gerry Gow, Ralph Coates and of course Bruno

Cheyrou. Hans had left in disgust to get a train back to Antwerp after he was outvoted on having Mido as his false-nine.

Events over the rest of evening are a bit blurry. At one point there was a clown, or possibly Danny in a clown-mask, I have no idea. Someone gave us some firewater – literally. We left the bar having finished off their whole stock of vintage Chimay and staggered to an all-night cafe where we ordered waffles and chips, and at some point we must have had another beer as when I awoke at 8am I was clutching a large bottle of Delirium ale. We also decided that the best ever football song was Sheffield United's version of 'Annie's Song', but still Danny kept singing "like a gallon of Magners". Then I remembered that we had had some news that reduced Danny to tears at one point. We were told that our Sunday afternoon game at Harelbeke, just down the E17 on our route back to the ferry, had actually kicked off at 7.30pm on the Saturday.

Bugger.

A week's worth of preparation pouring over maps and planning our timings to the last second had just gone out of the window. It was back to the drawing board, but with beers such as Kwerk, Primus and my personal favourite Floris Apple, our decision-making had been, as some would say, 'flawed'.

Sunday morning was as cloudy as the marvellous White Mystic wheat beer we'd drunk the night before, but after some breakfast in the romantic square (completely lost on us Englishmen) the realism that we couldn't take in Harelbeke hit. We narrowed it down to two venues, both just north of Kortrijk - Ingelmunster and Sint Eloois Winkel. Both ticked the boxes, both were essentially on the way home but which one to choose? Andy had a brainwave.

"Let's do a Souness!"

A what? Buy a grey curly wig and manage a number of teams badly but actually be a very good pundit? Seemed long-winded.

"No," he slurred on through breakfast and a hangover, "let's do a half at Ingelmunster and then off to Sint Eloois Winkel for the second." Uncle Google told me it was 11km between the two grounds, so that immediately became the plan.

But first to Kortrijk and then to Harelbeke 'just in case' they had left a door/gate open so we could have a wander around. And what do you know, they had. Sort of. I mean a 6-foot high fence with no barbed wire on top surely counts as an open door, right?

And it's not technically trespassing if all we are doing is running around the pitch? After all, we are sort of promoting the club by taking pictures of our adventures.

Boxes ticked we headed off to the small West Flanders town of Ingelmunster. The ground was overlooked by the Bacchus brewery that brews the world famous Kriek fruit beer as well as being home to the Kasteel brewing house. Of course it would have been rude not to sample some of their famous products (those that weren't driving anyway). The place was packed this Sunday lunchtime, people were queuing for tables and there seemed to be little in the way of order. If you cannot organise a piss up here then, well, you must be an idiot so we headed across the road to the ground instead.

Six Euros later and we were inside. The home side, Olympic Mill Sports Ingelmunster (OMS to you and I) were a relatively new club, formed in 2003 after the former side of the town KSV had got fed up with a diet of Cherry Beer so upped sticks and moved down the road to Harelbeke. In the eight years since restarting at the bottom of the pyramid in Belgium, OMS had managed to reach the fifth tier and had high hopes that this season would see them progress even further after finishing up runners up in the league a few months ago. The cup was an early season distraction for them, having already seen off Knokke FC on penalties in round one and then beating Sassport Boezinge just a few days previously in round two.

Their opponents were the little known KV Woluwe-Zaventem, who were plying their trade in the division above. Zaventem, as all good European travellers know, is where Brussels airport is based, but that is not the town's only claim to fame. Back in 1986 the place was cock-a-hoop after local Sandra Kim won the Eurovision Song Contest with that legendary song "J'aime la vie". Kim wasn't her real name. In fact she changed her name from Caldarone to Kim in honour of her hero Kim Wilde and to hide the fact she was actually just thirteen, pretending instead to be nearly sixteen. Her triumph remains to this day Belgium's greatest international victory, and Sandra was honoured with a statute made of chocolate in the town square. Probably.

The Municipal stadium was traditional, four different covered terraces and a double decker clubhouse that contained a fantastic bar. Benelux (BEgium-NEtherlands and LUXembourg - see what they did there) love their tokens. Despite the fact we were the only people in the bar you cannot simply order a beer and pay

cash for it. You have to go and buy your, you guessed it, Munts
from an old chap at the end of the bar then exchange them for the
treasures of the top shelf. It would have been rude not to (again,
apart from those of us driving *sigh*), and we had a perfect
vantage point to sup and watch the game.

Instead of your traditional fanfare and a slow walk out onto
the pitch, both teams sprinted out of the tunnel before lining up
on the halfway line. The visitors sported the dullest kit in the
world. Plain blue Nike shorts and socks, an orange shirt and that
was it. No club badge, no sponsor's logo, nothing. We immediately felt pity on them and vowed to raise the funds to sponsor
them. We always have the greatest ideas when the majority of
the group have had a few strong Belgian beers.

In truth the away side were the better team. Faced with two or
three of the oldest looking players I have ever seen since I came
out of retirement for a charity game a few weeks before, the
home side offered little in the way of pace, attacking flair or even
heartbeat. The away side ripped into them from the first whistle
yet simply couldn't score. If they had a banjo and took a trip to
a donkey sanctuary they would have had a fruitless afternoon.
Somehow they managed to fail to score in the opening forty-five
minutes, although a second half penalty from Gert Hermans was
eventually enough to see them through (according to the Belgian
equivalent of TalkSport anyway).

As soon as the whistle blew for the end of the first period we
were off for the short trip across Flanders to Sint Eloois Winkel,
population 3,500, where the home side were taking on one of
the fallen giants of Belgium football, Royale Union Saint Gillo-
ise, eleven times winners of the National Championship no less.
Think of them like a Huddersfield Town if you will, a club with a
more impressive history than many think. A massive cup upset
was on the cards here as they took on fourth division Winkel.

During the course of the afternoon we had seen a number of
nightclubs on the edge of the road, in really strange places. Neon
lights, shutters down, and very small car parks if you wanted a
big crowd in. Of course we eventually figured it out as we saw
a shifty old bloke coming out of one on the edge of Ingelmunster - they were the local brothels. It seemed big business in this
region as within the space of a mile or so on the way to Sint
Eloois Winkel we saw a dozen. Now that would have made for an
interesting night out. Instead of trying to match Belgium beers
with famous footballers what about if we tried...no, on second

thoughts let's leave it at a happily married that. Andy's suggestion of trying to find the "magic door" into one of these also raised a Danny Last eyebrow, but we were on a tight schedule and the Belgian Cup waited for neither man nor tide so we headed stoically onwards.

Ten minutes later and we were pulling up outside the Sportpark Terschueren in the village. The gates were wide open and we wandered in, the smell of liniment, sausages and beer encouraging us as if we needed it. Royale Union Saint-Gilloise had brought a fair size following from Brussels, packing out the Main (only) Stand, so we headed for the bar. Apparently it was 1-0 to the visitors and should have been more. Looks like we weren't going to see any shocks in the cup today.

We resisted the charms of a local variety of cuppa-soup (four flavours, all tasted of 'grey') and took our places next to the away fans, complete with a dog wearing a yellow and blue dog-sized football shirt, dog-sized bobble hat and dog-sized scarf. We were soon joined by a couple of the 'nightclub' workers who shouted encouragement at the home players, knowing them by first name, as well as flashing a bit of thigh to the officials when they ventured over to our side of the pitch.

"Oi Lino, that was a shocking offside call, you shudda gan to Specsavers!" shouted Andy as the assistant referee failed to raise a blatant offside flag. The problem was he clearly already had been to Specsavers as he was wearing glasses that would have made Olive from On The Buses look like she had perfect sight. It looked all over for the home side when they had a player sent off for a second yellow with a few minutes to go, but just to prove how crazy this whole game can be they then went up the other end of the pitch and scored a stunning equaliser.

Full time and it was 1-1. We had a decision to make. Time was ticking and we had a ferry to catch some eighty miles away. We could stretch to another 15 minutes of action but risked a traffic delay and missing our boat. Sensible Stuart reappeared for the first time since putting those headlight converters on at Dover and I ushered the others to the car. The appearance of another 'nightclub' worker wearing something that would make Borat blush couldn't keep us in the ground, and even the big cheer we heard as we got in the car wasn't going to pull us back. I mean it was only a corner or something surely?

An hour later and we had made it back to the port of Calais in time. A customs official stopped us and asked where we'd been.

"We've been to Amiens, Lens, Gent, Ingelmunster and Sint Eloois Winkel."

"Of course you have lads, now out of the car."

He asked us a few more questions to try and trick us.

"What colour do Lens play in?"

"What was the name of the ground in Amiens?"

"Which famous blonde ex-Portsmouth centre-forward now supports Gent?"

"Why did you leave Sint Eloois Winkel before the penalties?"

The last one stumped us as we had no idea the game finished level after extra time. But it didn't. Apparently they don't have extra time in the cup so it goes straight to penalties, and the cheer we heard on leaving was for Saint-Gilloise's first successful spot kick. He soon let us on our way and we were reluctantly homeward bound.

So after 650 miles, five games, two magic doors, over twenty different beers and a number of belly-aching laughs, our first European Football Weekend of the season was at an end. We grabbed a final drink and sat on the deck of the ship to watch the sun set on France. Another superb weekend at an end, we could do little but reminisce and laugh at what had transpired over the last two-and-a-bit days. As season openers go, this had been one of the very best.

Chapter Eight

Bailing Out the Euro Zone
Welcome to Oktoberfest

20th October 2011
Slovan Bratislava 0 Paris Saint Germain 0
Pasiensky Stadium

21st October 2011
Slovan Liberec 3 Banik Ostrava 2
Liberec Stadion

"...a mascot dressed up as a Slovan badge with white tights
on, busily high-fiving us all..."

Life, sometimes, just isn't fair.

You all know what I mean. That moment when the lottery numbers come up and you know that you would have picked those exact numbers if only you had a spare pound, or when the deposed Crown Prince of Nigeria can't send you half of his fortune unless you send him $500 and there's another week till pay day. I'm sure that Alanis Morrissette would call it ironic but to me being in a plane crash is not ironic, it's bloody tragic. And inconvenient. That whole song is rubbish to be honest, ten-thousand spoons when all you need is a knife? Improvise woman. Oh, and when you do "meet the man of your dreams" and then "meet his beautiful wife", you could just offer him a threesome. Trust me, men are awful, he would definitely be up for it - if you don't ask you don't get.

Anyway, back to the hero of this tale and for me life wasn't fair because I had to spend another ten days away from home travelling, from one side of Europe to the other, living out of my suitcase with nothing to keep me company at night other than my iPad and some stuff on my 'Bookmarks' list that was there when I bought it, honestly.

Oh, and a few football matches along the way.

A few?

Well, ten to be precise but I don't want you to feel sorry for me. I would be taking in five countries on my travels, meeting up with numerous old friends and drinking pints (and litres in some places) of beer ranking from €1 pilsners in Prague to €12 Amstels in Zurich. Sometimes life throws you lemons, when that happens you have to stand up like a man and make yourself some lemonade.

The third weekend in October is traditionally the 'European Football Weekend Oktoberfest' – an annual pilgrimage to some far-flung corner of Europe for three days of football, friends and acting like a teenager again. It's a collection of like-minded people indulging in their passion. After our previous successful jaunts in Holland, Germany, Hungary (well apart from the dysentery I suffered there) it was the turn of the Czech Republic this year. Travel booked, we looked forward to visits to some of the places that normal beer can't reach.

But then came the spanner in the works.

Not a nasty, oily spanner I'll grant you, but one of those nice ones from a box of chocolate tools at the sweet shop. For once UEFA had dealt us an ace – Slovan Bratislava versus Paris Saint

Germain in the Europa League on the Thursday prior to our arrival in Prague.

Could we?

Should we?

Dare we?

I need a wee?

Well, we referred to the European Football Weekends charter,
which clearly states in paragraph 3, sub-section 2:-

'If a game in a city/stadium is being played whereby transport is
freely available and journey time is less than 4 hours and there
are no other alternative destinations, you have to at least spend
an hour finding mitigating reasons not to go. If none are found,
get on it you lily-livered sap.'

I wrote it knowing I'd be reading it the most so I have no idea
why I was so mean.

And so that is why I found myself enduring the torture of a
6.30am Ryanair flight from London Stansted. Nobody should
ever willingly have to be put through the misery of the constant
adverts over the PA system, the crew that can hardly speak
English and seem to object to any passengers being on the
plane, and the insistence on playing that ridiculous jingle when
they land 'ahead of schedule' (which of course they achieve by
allowing 20% longer for the flight than the real flight time). In
true Ryanair style we weren't actually heading for Bratislava at
all, rather their interpretation of Vienna. Different country but
within 100 kilometres so it counted. Why let hundreds of years
of diplomacy get in the way of border agreements eh Ryanair?

Despite their attempts at changing European borders,
Ryanair flight FR2314 touched down on the tarmac at Milan Ras-
tisla Štefánika airport at 9.15am local time. Known as Pressburg
until 1919, Bratislava today is home to hundreds of stag and
hen weekends every week and as I decamped from the plane and
waited for the bus into the city, I was handed a leaflet offering
me 'Pussy Galore' at a club in the Old Town opening at 10am. I
asked the spotty young girl whether it was the name of a person,
since the capitalisation of the words suggested it was in homage
to the character played by Honor Blackman in Goldfinger, but she
simply said "...girls, boobs, fanny, sexy time..." and turned the
charm on a group of 'Lads On Tour' who all had wacky t-shirts
with names on their backs such as 'Milf-Hunter' - (Oi!), 'Lezza-

Converter' - (Oi Oi!) and 'Tit-Examiner' - (Oi Oi Oi!). They were far more interested in her wares, the simply awful Tit-Examiner even living up to his name with one ill-advised grope. It wasn't all just groups of desperate young chaps on the flight looking for their fill of cheap beer, cheap food and cheap adult entertainment. Among the pack heading through security were the Barnet Boys who had also managed to survive the Ryanair experience. We'd block-booked a dozen rooms at a hotel close to Pasienky, the ground that would be hosting the Europa League match and so headed straight there. The rest of the group had flown into Prague and would be joining us later in the day when they arrived across the border by train.

One group coming through border control by taxi and minibus, another already stationed there, another coming by train and another stationed in Prague permanently (well in terms of our jolly-up anyway) – this is as close to being secret-agents as it will ever get for us.

The situation of who plays where in Bratislava is as confusing as trying to work out who hasn't slept with whom on Eastenders. Based on the fact there are only really three teams and three stadiums in Bratislava you would think it would be quite easy to work out who plays where, and what time.

Wrong.

The situation is like a bad version of Celebrity Squares (random trivia fact – in the first ever episode of the game show in 1975 Vincent Price was one of the celebrities, why do I know this? Because I spend far too much time on Wikipedia travelling to random football grounds around Europe). It used to be so simple. Slovan Bratislava played at Tehelné Pole, literally across the road Inter played at the Pasienky, and young upstarts Artmedia, named after the owner's favourite subjects at school, played south of the Danube at the Petrzalka Štadión.

Slovan were the traditional powerhouses in the region, winning the Czechoslovakian league on eight occasions as well as having a European Cup Winners Cup title to their name from when they beat Barcelona in the 1969 final, also having overcome the mighty Dunfermline Athletic in the semi-finals. Since the Velvet Revolution, the Belasi have won a further six Slovakian titles, although they have also had to endure a two-year period in the second tier of Slovakian football after financial issues forced the club to sell almost all of their first team squad.

If Slovan's recent history has been traumatic, twice Corgo Liga winners SK Inter Bratislava's has been nothing short of a disaster.After winning the double in 2001 the club gambled on making a splash in the Champions League. They were within 90 minutes of reaching the Promised Land but a 4-0 defeat in Norway to Rosenborg saw them return back to Slovakia with just a huge bar tab from the most expensive country in Europe. Since then they struggled to hold their position at the top of the Slovakian football tree, initially losing their dominance to Art-Media and now to Slovan. It went from bad to worse for the Žlto-ierni who were forced into a merger with FC Sernica in 2009 and now play in the 4th level of Slovakian football.

The fall from grace for both Slovan and Inter meant that Artmedia could claim the spot as the top team in the city, and actually for a while the top team in Slovakia after winning the league in 2005 and 2008. In 2006 they famously beat Celtic 5-0 in the Champions League to qualify for the group stages. Unfortunately nobody had remembered to buy any floodlights at the Petrzalka so games had to be played at the national stadium, the Tehelné Pole, or Brickfield to you and me. At the time the stadium was also home to Slovan but since then it has all changed, and not for the better.

The local government decided that they needed a new national stadium, to be built where the Tehelné Pole was standing and so the ground hosted its last game in 2010, forcing Slovan to move next door to the Pasienky, home of FK Inter, who had of course by now merged with FC Senica and were playing in the fifth tier of Slovakian football. Confused yet? Well, you will be when I also add that Artmedia are no longer called Artmedia but FC Petrzal-ka. That's handy I hear you say, playing in a stadium the same as their new name. Er no. They moved to Štadión Rapid in 2009 on the north bank of the Danube.

So when UEFA got those warm balls out and drew Slovan Bratislava against relative big guns Bilbao and Paris Saint Germain, the debate opened up as to where the games would be played. It appeared that the Pasienky didn't tick all the UEFA boxes for gratuitous fine wine, food and dancing girls. The national team had been using the Štadión pod Dub om in Žilina for a few games and there was a nasty rumour going around that the game against Paris Saint Germain would be moved there, 200 kilometres northeast. Fortunately, UEFA agreed to bring in their own Cristal, fois gras and Pans People for the night so we were saved and happy. Our hotel rooms offered us a view of four sets of floodlights, two for the Pasienky and two for the demolished Tehelné Pole.

Well, demolished according to Wikipedia but actually not 'demolished' at all, more 'abandoned' if anything.

It would have been rude not to see what state the once mighty Tehelné Pole was in, so we wandered over. The gates were wide open but the condition of this great stadium almost made you weep. Here was a ground steeped in history, one of the biggest in Czechoslovakia and yet it had been pillaged and left to suffer a slow and agonising death. Where history demanded a lethal injection and swift removal for the rebirth, what had actually occurred was a death by a thousand cuts.

What could have been broken had been, the goal nets still hung down limply from the posts, and the huge weeds growing from the terraces and the remnants of the light blue seats just made you shake your head in sadness. I felt a bit wary walking around the stadium too much, remembering the 'Charlie says' videos of my youth seeing the exposed electric cables and holes in the concrete floor around the ground. Game-a-day-John found a ball and took it on the pitch and in the process became the last person to take a penalty in the stadium (for now), mirroring his hero, Chris Waddle, by ballooning it over the bar.

Nostalgia thick in the air and sadness all around, we headed into the old town and sampled some local cuisine before meeting up with the rest of the advance party who arrived by train from Prague. Our pre-match home for the evening was the Arena Bar, just next to the hotel which was convenient but they did have the cheek to try to diddle us by serving pints (well, half a litre) of fine Slovakian beer for €1.50! Outraged by these scandalous prices, we moved to a pub around the corner that only wanted a far more reasonable €1 for a beer. Amazing how quickly you acclimatise to these things once abroad. That'll teach the hotel for trying to make us buy a delicious beer for just over a pound, when round the corner we can get one for just under 80 pence.

You may scoff but you have to cut your cloth accordingly on these weekends.

Our host for the evening was Dan Richardson, a west-country lad familiar to readers of chapter one of this very tome. He lived in Bratislava, supported Slovan and ADO Den Haag, and worked on a rig in the North Sea. He was a season-ticket holder at Slovan and proudly showed us his 'Season Card' which cost him just €41. Tickets for this game? €20. And who says clubs try to rip off fans these days? No surprise there really – after all which clubs wouldn't try and maximise the revenue they can earn from a European adventure. They weren't the first nor would they be the last to whack the prices up for these games.

But at the same time let's put it into perspective. For our €20 we also got a Slovan t-shirt and a nice shiny flag to wave, which is more than the travelling PSG fans got. As they (apparently) approached the gates of the stadium they were told they weren't welcome, despite having purchased their tickets through the proper channels, and were relocated by the police to a local pub to watch the game on TV.

Despite a major renovation of the Pasienky in recent years to bring it up to UEFA 3 star standards so it can host games like these, it is still basically an open-air athletics stadium with huge Soviet-style floodlights and the biggest scoreboard known to man. The lack of a roof didn't stop the home fans whipping up an atmosphere to try to spur on their team against PSG who had won the lottery in recent months thanks to the take-over by the Qatar Investment Authority. The Middle Eastern money had allowed the club to start to bringing in players of the calibre of the Brazilian Nenê, Uruguayan Lugano and Argentinian Pastore.

Without a point from their opening two games in the Europa League few gave the home team a chance against the French side. Despite the flag-waving of the home fans it was the French who did all the early running, with Slovan's Lukás Hrosso by far the busier of the two goalies.

However, the home side seemed content to try to frustrate the French whenever they could and the first half ended with few chances and no goals. Still, we found amusement at the littlest things, as we always do on these trips.

An old-fashioned fire-engine (think the '60s here) ready to douse the potential fires of Slovan ambition?

Check.

A mascot dressed up as a Slovan badge with white tights on, busily high-fiving us all?

Check.

Big Deaksy falling off his seat and then noisily tumbling down the terraces?

Check.

Just a normal night out for us really. The only disappointing factor was that the scoreboard, which along with the Great Wall of China was the only man-made thing visible from outer space,

failed to spark into life. It would have been perfect to relay rousing messages of support, almost Soviet-style, to the fans but
instead it simply sat blankly high above the terrace.

It was much of the same in the opening exchanges of the
second half. The first talking point came on the hour as PSG's
Clèment Chantôme was sent off for a second yellow card. That
sparked Slovan into life, both on and off the pitch. Coach Vladimir Weiss, the third such Vladimir Weiss to play or manage the
club, prowled his technical area, making sure all of his team
knew exactly what he expected of them.

The night got even worse for the visitors in the 80th minute
when Siaka Tiéné was sent off for a late challenge. We were
standing in the 'Ultra' section of the home fans and as the player
walked off sections around us broke out into a chorus of monkey
chants. It was a shock to hear it to be truthful and Andy Hudson
walked out making his own one-man protest. Slovakian football
has had problems with this sort of behaviour before, famously
when England visited in 2002 Emile Heskey and Ashley Cole
were subject to terrible (is there any other kind?) racial abuse in
the Tehelné Pole. UEFA fined the Slovakian FA a measly £18,000
for the offence. With UEFA observers in the crowd it would be
hard for them not to ignore the noise, or would it?

With PSG down to nine men Slovan smelled victory. Only the
timely intervention of Zoumana Camara prevented Karim Guédé
slotting the ball into the net and taking all three points for the
home side. They couldn't find a way through and had to settle
for a nil-nil draw, both sides thankful in their own way for the
point each.

It would have been rude to simply ignore the hospitality on
offer in this fine city, so we went back to the Arena bar and
contributed significantly to the hole in the Slovakian economy.
Despite the 4am start most of us had to endure to get here,
we carried on until the wee small hours, donning our Slovan
Bratislava t-shirts, waving our shiny flags and re-enacting the
various tactical subtleties of the game using shot glasses.

Of course we would regret this period of extra-time in the
morning as we headed across the country to Prague on an 8am
train, but at that very moment, high on ridiculously cheap delicious beer and life itself, it was the best day ever (number 143).

As the Spice Girls once famously sang "Two Become One", which
if you didn't know was written in reference to Posh and Becks

first getting it on. Today was the day that the two Oktoberfest groups became one for a full twenty-four hours, and ticked another country off the list. The eyes were tired, the head thick, but my very own 7am alarm call from the human snoring clock Stoffers rudely interrupted my dream featuring Holly Willoughby in a Lewes kit. Still, it was a world away from Huddo's alarm cock in France. Time to rise, shine and cross the border.

The first casualty of the day was Hudson, spotted smoking on the station platform and issued with a fine. Seems it is OK in Bratislava to smoke in any confined space, but wander outside and you face the wrath of the fun police. The decent thing to do would be to have a whip round to cover the fine but deep down we are "selfish, thoughtless people, who are only interested in our own gratification" (© several ex-girlfriends) and so we simply pointed at him and laughed as he was being reprimanded by the police.

The four-hour journey across fields, mountains, rivers and grey industrial estates (heavy on the latter) was enlightened by the wit and wisdom of boys who thought that drinking beer at 8am was a great idea. Well, we were on holiday. The Slovakian countryside was a heavy feature in the torture-porn film series Hostel, and we debated for quite a while whether such horror in the world exists. Gary Lomas, the man with a watch bigger than Big Ben, then provided the amusement with his tale of his trip to Moscow to watch the Champions League final where we hid under the skirt of a large lady in a bar to avoid getting a beating from some Russian hooligans. The time just flew by and before you knew it we were alighting in Prague, home of Tomas Repka.

We wanted to enjoy the 'real' Prague so asked a very attractive young lady at the information desk where we could go for lunch. She pulled out a map and was poised with a pen.

"OK – McDonalds here, KFC here, O'Reilly's here and Pussy Galore here."

Oh good, there was a chain of them, Honor Blackman must be coining it in. We rephrased the question, "Where can we go to get Czech Dumplings and a creamy sauce?" Probably not the words I would have chosen but Stoffers seemed confident that he could speak her language, adding a cheeky German wink at the end of his request.

"I am not that sort of girl!" she replied, "although I do finish in 20 minutes, 100 Euro and you can all watch."

As we all stood there mouths agape for a good minute, it took

Danny to finally step up for his turn trying to ask a woman to not do unspeakable things and just point us to a local for lunch and a few beers. Within three minutes we were seated in one of the finest little restaurants known to man, ordering a steaming bowl of Bacon Dumplings and a litre of Pivo each. "So when does she get her tits out then?" asked Andy as our order was taken. You can take the man out of Newcastle, but never the Newcastle out of the man.

Now fully functional after food and beer, we traversed the old town to find our new hotel. Technically it wasn't a hotel but a botel, a clever play on words for our accommodation that was moored off the quayside just round the corner from the Charles Bridge. After enduring the longest check-in process known to man where we had to fill in a questionnaire ("Have you ever had scurvy?" "Have you ever been convicted of any incidents of Piracy?" "Who scored the winning goal in the 1986 Screen Sports Super Cup Final?") we finally met the Prague-based group and Two had indeed, become One.

This group, made up of virtually every Forest Green Rovers and Royal Antwerp fan known to man, arrived yesterday. They had spent their day in the Old Town. "Stu – we found a great bar" Super Hans greeted me with a wide beam, "it's called Pussy Galore but it has nothing to do with Honor Blackman, trust me."

Of course Super Hans found Pussy Galore, he did after all know every red-light district in Belgium as we had already established and was now in paradise.

They had also had a wander over to the Toyota Arena, home of Sparta Prague, and wouldn't you just know it, they had found another magic door. Inside the first team was training. We took this with a pinch of West Country salt until Shep (remember Shep is the most pessimistic man in the world from chapter one's adventures in Spakenburg) produced a picture of the FGR boys with Tomas Repka. That hit me harder than Super Hans's covert pictures of the girls from Pussy Galore doing their greengrocer act. Tomas bloody Repka. One of my West Ham heroes.

Repka came to West Ham in 2001 from Fiorentina with a reputation as a no-nonsense full back with an international pedigree. He was sent off on his debut versus Middlesborough and followed that up with a red card against Blackburn Rovers two games later. He was a fan favourite, devoid of personalities to worship since the retirement of Julian Dicks. The fact he never, ever gave interviews added to the mystery of the man. He was quite simply a legend, and here he was standing next to bloody Forest Green Rovers fans.

There was time for a round or two of local brew before we headed across the river and into our carriage for the night. Most Englishmen (and a smattering of other nations I'm sure) would have planned a night in the beer halls and 'adult specialist entertainment' venues in Prague. But not us. Oh no. We were getting on a chartered bus that was last used in that episode of Heartbeat when Nick Berry disappeared, and heading north-east to the town of Liberec, via a number of service stations for comfort breaks, for the biggest game in Czech football. Well, on this particular Friday night anyway.

We had rung ahead, letting them know that 39 football fans from six different countries would be arriving on a charabanc. They laughed and put the phone down. We rang again, and this time they were convinced by us paying for 39 tickets over the phone. As a thank you they agreed to open the bar at the ground an hour earlier than normal. These are the details that make these trips to far-flung footballing destinations so good.

The bus deposited us at the ground and Andy Hudson disappeared off with our cash, returning with an envelope stuffed-full of tickets. The pub at the stadium, usually pretty empty, celebrated Christmas and their birthday together that evening as the doors were flung open with the cry of "dev tat icet pivo". One of our group, a chap that neither Danny nor I knew, proclaimed that he was having a far better time than if he had remained in Prague with his mates. He had never heard of the trip and was on the flight over to join a stag weekend. He was simply in the wrong place at the right time, sitting next to Scouse Andy on the plane from Liverpool. "You should come on our European Football Weekend instead," Andy casually said, and before you could utter Accrington Stanley he promptly signed up and instead of strippers and beers in the capital, he was up near the German and Polish border supping pre-match ales.

After raiding the shop for any item of football memorabilia (read tacky shit) that we could cherish in the future, we headed into the stadium. It seemed that the must have item this Christmas in Liberec was some Slovan bunting and we bought strings of plastic Liberec flags in abundance. Current Mrs. Fuller would be over the moon that I had remembered to bring her back a gift I was quite sure.

We took our places on the wooden benches. To our left in the corner were the Slovan Ultras, belting out rock music as cheer-leaders danced up and down the aisles. To our right the away fans from Banik Ostrava were making themselves heard. The main stand opposite appeared to have been carved out of solid rock. Already through beery eyes, this had become the best stadium in the world. All we needed now was some fireworks, a fat man with a flag and some more beer. Tick, tick and tick as Super Hans arrived with a crate full of more lovely local brew.

The first half passed by quickly as both teams displayed some attractive attacking football. Banik Ostrava, a club famous for being where the great Ludek Miklosko came from, had travelled a distance of 400 km for this televised Friday night match and their fans displayed their worth on a banner saying: "Monday or Friday: you'll never get rid of us". With top-flight games being moved for television, as is the case across the world, it was thumbs-up to the Ostrava fans for making the long trip at quite short notice.

Liberec went in at half-time with a 2-1 lead after taking the lead through a Vojtech Hadaščok header. Václav Sverkoš replied for the visitors with a great strike from the edge of the box before Jan Nezmar scored with a back post header that just dropped beyond the line before being cleared. That's enough about the first period isn't it? You don't really need to know any more than that other than we were having a great time.

In the corner of the ground the 'Slovan Death Boys' had kept up the chanting throughout the first period. Their most catchy number, "Libe, Libe, Liberec", had us all hooked. We had man-aged to befriend a local fan and we asked him how we could get in there with the Ultras. He pondered the question, disappeared for a moment before reappearing on the other side of the fence and producing the keys to a magic gate that allowed us entry. From that point on the beers flowed and the songs ran from our throats. In a short interview that Andy did with one of the Ultra' leaders, he explained that "Liberec are apolitical as politics causes many problems at football, and so we stand with neither the right nor the left; we only stand with football".

And there were more cheerleaders.

Don't forget the cheerleaders.

The second-half continued at the same pace as the first, with both teams committed to putting on a good show for the watching thousands on TV. Banik equalised midway through the second period when Sverkoš lobbed the Slovan 'keeper. The home team, spurred on by the support of the Ultras (and us) never let their heads fall and they got their reward in injury time when Nezmar reacted first to a defensive header that went backwards and poked the winner in for Liberec from six yards out. We all ended up in various group hugs with complete strangers, although Super Hans's deliberate run down the terraces to jump on a cheerleader was a bit too obvious.

As the Ultras continued their celebrations in the bar, we sneaked into the empty stadium and struck various poses in the goal-mouth. Alas there was no time to join our new best friends in a beer or two. The cheerleaders disappeared into a minibus, sponsored of course by 'Pussy Galore, Liberec Branch', and out of Super Hans's life. All back on board our fun bus we pulled off into the night. The local police, confusing us for the Banik Ostrava coach, started to give us a police escort but when we took a right instead of the left as directed they gave up.

The singing on the bus was loud; the Spice Girls could never, ever, hold a candle to us. They would simply be Wannabes on this trip. We had the customary whip-round for the driver, handing it to him in a sanitary bag that one of the Forest Green lads had in his pocket (don't ask). The night was still young when we arrived back into Prague, well, ok it was just about 11pm but that is still early in this heaven of carnal pleasure. Some of the group (I will mention no names for legal reasons) headed off for the thrill of the naked flesh, whilst the more sensible ones like myself and Danny who have seen it all before, twice, made do with a pub around the corner from our floating palace. It was another late night and as "Libe, Libe, Liberec" played in our heads and our hearts, we looked forward to doing it all again in just six hours time.

Chapter Nine

Sex, Drugs and 80p Beer
Five games, two days and the value of adaptability

22nd October 2011
Sparta Praha B 2 Zbrojovka Brno 2
Zizkov Training Ground

No idea 6 Someone Else 0
Deep in the Suburbs

Dukla Prague 1 Jablonec 3
Strahov Stadion

23rd October 2011
Admira Prague 4 Turnov Pencin 3
Admira Stadion

Slavia Prague 2 C Budejonic 0
Synot Tip Arena

"...we turned up on the side of a pitch, in the middle of a
farmer's field somewhere in the backwaters of Prague..."

I was jolted awake by a distinct rocking motion. My whole room seemed to be rhythmically moving from side to side. That weird and distinct movement of people having sex in the same bed as you, and as you are not being involved you're acutely aware of the rhythm. Not that I make a habit of such an activity you understand, but we've all been to 'those parties' when we were younger, right?

Oh.

Well I will start again then.

I was jolted awake by a distinct rocking motion. My whole room seemed to be rhythmically moving from side to side. That distinct movement of being on a boat.

Better?

Good, then I'll continue.

But I was in a hotel, right? Actually, no. I was in a botel, an ingenious cross between a boat and a hotel (what will they think of next?). The movement was caused by a huge barge passing slowly very close to my port-hole, shaking the whole room. I started to remember the previous night's antics. The sing-song on the coach trip back from Liberec, the good intentions of a quiet drink before an early night. But this was Prague – it is illegal to be in bed in the city on a Friday night before midnight and so our quick drink had turned into a very noisy debate about the best corner flags in Europe over a few (read dozen) Pilsners. So 8am on a Saturday morning wasn't exactly a welcome friend but we were on a mission from God, if you could call taking in three games in the city such.

Over breakfast the 40-strong group of football tourists discussed our options, as well as hearing stories from the 'other' night out. The younger section of the group had shunned our suggestion of a quiet pub last night and headed for the flesh-pots of Prague. Led by Super Hans, of course Super Hans, they had taken in a number of establishments that catered for all wishes. It had been a struggle to remove some of them from these bars at 4am and consequently those who had lived life to the excess a few hours previously chose option A, which was simply to stay in bed. Option B was to take in a Czech Fourth Division game at a ground that had a big hedge, and Option C was to go to see Sparta Prague B take on Zbrojovka Brno in the Druha Liga. Andy Hudson had done his homework and updated us on Brno's last away game in Znojmo, where the away fans had been naughty boys, leading to the game being abandoned.

The majority of us, unsurprisingly, took option C and headed off into the early morning mist for Praha 9, a nice residential area, and home to Viktoria Žižkov's training ground. The reality of having 'B' teams in the league pyramid is that with one relegation you can find yourself playing your main rival's reserve team. This was exactly the case for Zbrojovka Brno on this chilly Saturday morning.

Brno is the second biggest city in the Czech Republic, with Zbrojovka historically a regular fixture in the top division. Last season, the travelling support would have been on a civilised mid-morning train departing to the capital for a sensible kick-off time in one of the city's main stadiums. This season, it is 'Druha Liga' and the ignominy of travelling to an outer city suburb for a 10:15 am kick-off against Sparta B.

Twenty men, walking four abreast in their finest Stone Island, Henri Lloyd and Helly Hansen isn't exactly the most inconspicuous look, and with the local riot police looking forward to welcoming the travelling Brno fans, their interest was roused as we arrived at the ground. The parking area at the back of the stadium was lined with a riot van, three police mini-buses and a team of stewards bigger than the Sparta Prague's entire squad. Once they realised that we were English, their interest waned and within minutes they had all left, realising that there would be no overtime for dealing with any football hooligans.

Despite the small hand only just touching ten o'clock, the bar was open. It would have been rude not to partake, and the first of many slipped down as the two teams took to the pitch with no more than a few dozen in the stands. A club anthem blared out of the ancient speaker system and after a quick salute to all four sides of the stadium (of which only one was occupied), the game finally started.

Winter seemed to have come early in Prague based on the number of players who sported gloves. Despite their precarious position at the bottom of the league, Brno started the brighter of the two teams and drew first blood when midfielder Jan Hromek took advantage of some defensive indecision and fired home. Fifteen minutes later it was one-all as Miroslav Mares scored for the home side, Sparta B.

As half-time approached there was only one place to be. In the bar. Warm and welcoming, with random sporting memorabilia on the walls it was the best bar in the world. Well, at 11am on a cold Saturday morning with a hangover it was. Some of the group fancied watching the game from another angle. The plan had been to segregate the Brno fans in the covered end behind the goal. A host of stewards were still on standby just in case there was a late rush from away fans but it wasn't going to happen. Andy Hudson, his bravado returning with every sip of Pils, suggested a new plan. "Let's take the away end."

So off he went, accompanied by Danny and Dan Richardson, down the street and back into the ground via the official away entrance. They reluctantly subjected themselves to a thorough body search (twice) by a young female steward, who Andy was insistent had appeared in a film he recently saw on the Internet.

Bottom of the table Sparta started the second half strongly and just past the hour mark they got a fortunate penalty decision that Mares slotted away for his second goal of the game. If the stay-away Brno fans would have been here they would have surely walked out in disgust or at least set fire to a few seats. A few minutes later, the referee obviously realising what a mistake he made for Sparta's penalty, evened things up. Sparta Prague defender pulls out of tackle, attacker runs a few steps further so he is just in the area, and then with a dramatic shriek, hits the deck. The crowd is literally laughing as the ref points to the spot. Having taken up position behind the goal, the adopted away fans from our party had a perfect vantage point to see Petr Švancara emphatically draw Brno level and earn themselves a point to take back to down the E65.

Not a bad start to a Saturday morning. By the time most people back in Blighty were waking up, we had already consumed four goals for our breakfast. In typical European Football Weekend style we invaded the pitch at the end of the game for photo opportunities. Even some of the away players tried to get in on the act. Formalities done we adjourned to the bar where we boosted the club's annual revenue by 20% in an hour before it was time to head to game two of the day.

I can't really tell you much about the next few hours. Sometimes there is a limit to what you should consider is worth watching. In England I have seen games at County League Three, which is step eight in the football pyramid. Even at that level clubs tend to have floodlights, a stand and even a clubhouse. But when someone suggests the same level in Czech Republic, just say NO. Our guide for the afternoon, Ian, somehow managed to convince a dozen of us that football at this level would be (and I quote directly) a "laugh."

Oh how we were rolling around on the floor when we turned up on the side of a pitch, in the middle of a farmer's field somewhere in the backwaters of Prague. An occasional tram passed by the ground reminding us that civilization (food, warmth, beverages) wasn't far away. We had no idea who was playing or what the score was when we arrived. The centre-forward for one team was a body double for Chris Moyles after eating the whole of Krispy Kreme's monthly produce; one of the goalkeepers only had one arm and the referee had a pair of binoculars.

We lasted an hour, which was fifty five minutes longer than most sane people would have waited before heading back into the centre of the city to regroup, redress and prepare for the final game of the day – a small matter of a trip to see Dukla Prague. Back in 1987 Dukla Prague were a run of the mill Czechoslovakian team, their golden days long behind them. And then along came Birkenhead-based Indie Group Half Man Half Biscuit with their album Back Again In The DHSS. Track no.9 became a cult classic – 'All I Want For Christmas Is A Dukla Prague Away Kit':

So he sent his doting mother
Up the stairs with the stepladders
To get the Subbuteo out of the loft
It had all the accessories
Required for that big-match atmosphere.
The crowd and the dugout
And the floodlights, too.
And you'd always get palmed off
With a headless centre-forward
And a goal-keeper with no arms
And a face like his.
And he'd managed to get hold of a Dukla Prague Away Kit
Cos his uncle owned a sport shop
And he'd kept it to one side

Danny was exceptionally excited about this game. A trip to see them at home has been on his bucket list ever since he was a teenager and he had genuinely only ever wanted a Dukla Prague away kit for each and every Christmas since. And now, twenty-four years later, here was the opportunity to lay his hands on an original shirt. Or was it...

Sadly, there was a hole in this particular bucket list. It became more of a fuck-it list as news filtered through that due to the installation of under-soil heating at the Juliska Stadium, Dukla's game was to be switched to another ground in Prague. On the plus side, it might save Danny £100 or more by not visiting the megastore and buying every item on offer. On the flip side, it would be a conversation starter for years to come. "I went to see Dukla Prague play once," Danny would say, before striking the person he was speaking to when they undoubtedly asked if he had bought an away kit.

So game three of the day saw us head across the river, and up the steepest hill in the city to the Evžena Rošického Stadium, which as all of you football trivia buffs will know is next door to the Strahov Stadium - one of the biggest stadiums in the world at a mere 220,000 capacity although it hasn't been used for sporting events since way back in the day. The Evžena Rošického Stadium used to be the National Stadium, as well as hosting matches for just about every team in Czech Republic over time when for various reasons their grounds haven't been available. Tonight it would be hosting Dukla's game in the Gambrinus Liga against Jablonec.

As we approached the ground we saw a small temporary yellow marquee that was the official club shop. I walked with Danny, trying to calm him down. This was his big moment, twenty-four years of hurt were about to be healed.

"Do you speak English?" Danny politely asked.

"Yes, of course." Danny's smile could not be any wider.

"I'd like a Dukla Prague away kit please!" the words he had waited to utter for nearly a quarter of a century.

"I'm sorry, we only have one shirt for sale, and it's the home kit in size small."

He looked like his beloved Brighton & Hove Albion had just announced a merger with Crystal Palace.

"OK - not to worry."

Exit Danny in tears.

I cheered him up by saying I would pay for him to get into the game. What I didn't tell him was that tickets were free. Because Dukla Prague cared about their fans and were worried about the inconvenience a trip across the city may cause to their supporters for this game, they decided that everyone making the short journey should be rewarded with free entry to the match. Not only that, they were knocking out scarves at half price so I treated him to one of those as friends would do. He cheered up and was soon clutching a wooden Dukla Prague yo-yo, showing off to the locals his skills learnt in the playground all those wasted years ago.

It had been at least an hour since we had a beer so we showed faith in our support for the club by getting a couple of rounds in. "Forty beers please!" became a familiar cry from our party who had been re-united after a day of various footballing and more primitive activities around the city. We mingled with the local fans, teaching them a song or two from our various European vocabularies. Dukla Prague has the oldest ultras in the Czech Republic. They were hastily nicknamed the 'Oldtras', and we got on famously save for the distorted noise of their vuvuzelas. Traditionally, Dukla play on Friday nights and the gates are low, but this match had been switched to a Saturday for television and they had twice the normal attendance. Modern football? Or simply because admission was free instead of the normal (I kid you not) £1.20?

We helped swell the gate to four figures which was 6% of the stadiums capacity. The visitors Jablonec for their part had brought with them four skinny indie kids and their parents for support. Eleven fans in total. Welcome to the premier footballing competition in Czech Republic.

The game sort of passed us by. Whether it was the beer, the company or even watching the attempts of the Forest Green boys to move in on the Czech WAGS, our attention didn't really stay focused on the pitch despite the Gambrinus Liga's top scorer, David Lafata, being on show. Stalemate at half-time wasn't a surprise, but three goals in a twenty-minute period from the visitors was enough to see them back on their way with all three points. Our work here was done and so we departed back down the hill, onto the waiting trams and headed for the bright lights of Pivnice U Sadu.

What do you mean "where?"

When all the tourists come to Prague, they head to the Staré Mesto. When that happens, the locals move out to Pivnice U Sadu. I mean who wants to pay £1 for a pint when you can get it for 80 pence. Honestly, tourists. Our choice of bar couldn't have been better. A dozen Czech beers to chose from, all served by wannabe supermodels and our own jukebox to boot.

But not just any old jukebox.

This one was free.

This was a video jukebox and it appeared to only play 1970s porn. Even eBay doesn't have any of those for sale, not that I have checked more than a dozen times since. There were rumours that these existed somewhere in the underground but here was one in the flesh, so to speak. You can never get bored of seeing a girl with more hair 'down there' than looked healthy (honestly it was like she was sitting on Don King's shoulders), being rogered by a man who looks like a young Ron Jeremy. Actually, that was a very young Ron Jeremy.

As it was our last night in this wonderful city we decided to check out a few locations from famous films. Great idea at 2pm, but 2am it probably isn't the most sensible. And perhaps we should've researched the topic first as between us we could only remember Mission Impossible. So that is why we found ourselves wandering across the Charles Bridge, admiring the ghost-like statues and the squatting women. Oh yes, we weren't alone. Two English girls decided that the 15th Century crossing over the Vltava was a perfect place to have a pee. They were obviously classy girls as they didn't have any tissue paper so used a crisp packet instead. Paprika flavor. I'll let you make your own joke here and believe me, there are a million. Which one you chose says a lot about you.

Five hours later we were up again at the break of dawn. The great thing about going to Prague for a weekend is that beer is cheap and plentiful. The downside about going to Prague for a weekend of beer and football is that they like their very early kick offs, meaning that once again we would be watching the action with thousands of stamping feet in our heads.

We could have stayed in bed but when do opportunities to watch Czech League Four ever present themselves? Exactly, so with that thought in our minds we set off for the northern suburbs for Admira Prague versus Pencín Turnov.

There were few locals around when we finally hopped off the bus "somewhere in Siberia" as Big Deaks put it. It certainly wasn't one of those beautiful, cold and crisp Prague mornings. Instead we had fog and drizzle. The grey communist-bloc buildings looked even more depressing as we tried to find the Stadion v Kobylisísch. We could hear what sounded like players warming up, and every so often we saw a ball hoofed into the air above the rooftops, but an entrance or failing that, a spectator was proving difficult to track down. Eventually, Google Maps on my phone came to life and showed us the entrance was a 2-minute walk from the bus stop where we had got off some 10 minutes previously and down the steep hill we had climbed.

Once inside (just the £1.25 for admission) it was hard not to fall in love with the club. From their massive club badge on the wall of the clubhouse, which Kenny Legg summed up as looking like "a pair of suspicious inter-racial Siamese-twin horses", to the walls that were adorned with annual squad photos from back in the Sixties. These were all relatively bland until around four years ago when someone got a copy of Photoshop for Christmas and therein afterwards the team photos weren't taken in front of the run down Main Stand of the Kobylisísch, but at Stamford Bridge, the San Siro and the Nou Camp.

The one element that appealed most to the younger generation of our group (aka Kenny, Olympic Spencer Webb and Super Hans) was the playground. It is always a problem when we men need to go to the bar and have to worry what to do with that trio. Admira had the forethought to solve that dilemma and in a roundabout way, it did swing in our favour.

Apologies, I am not proud of that last sentence but I couldn't let it slide.

Despite it being only 10:15am, the bar was open of course. Some of the group technically hadn't stopped drinking from the night before and had come straight from the delightfully named establishment Pussy Galore (yep, you've guessed it, it's part of the same chain from Slovakia) where they had been entertained by a female table tennis match played by naked players and not using bats - a delightful thought on a Sunday morning. We left the kids in the playground and started our morning as any good Praguian would.

About 125 or so (well exactly 125 if you believe Kenny who had moved on from the swings and was now demanding jelly and ice cream) fans had bothered to turn up for this fourth tier game. The fog made it difficult to see our hands, let alone the goal at the far end, but nevertheless we kicked off bang on 10:15am. We formed a "mob" on the terraces to try and give some vocal support to the home side. The terracing had once been concrete but was now just weeds, meaning it was slippery and we didn't have to wait long for our first casualty.

One lone fan had brought his own deck chair which he plonked down right behind a pillar then spent the rest of the half moving from side to side to see the game. He could have had the VIP area all to himself, mind. A flat roof of the toilets had been lovingly decorated in a Blue Peter make-it-at-home sort of way with some plastic grass you find in green grocers and a park bench.

The remaining Admira fans, including the obligatory one in huge amounts of khaki and shorts, despite the freezing weather, were also not shy about the presence of an open bar. It's not just for us Johnny Foreigners you know. They were armed with a big drum and an old school rattle that we all loved after our 12 pints of Plop last night. Next to us arrived the away fans. A decent turnout of all 19 of them, or 15.2% of the total attendance as Kenny quickly computed, complete with home-made banners, one quite clearly a blue sheet and a white sheet stitched together and the word 'Fans' felt tipped across the middle. Someone's mum wouldn't be best pleased when she saw that one. The Admira fans were welcoming to their guests and the club website reported afterwards that "..both groups showed how to cheer for - well, no insults and provocations. And after the game to fans of both clubs unison promised - in the spring and again in Turnov!"

At least that's what Google Translate informed me it said.

So to the game. What a humdinger it was too. Turnov drew first blood on the fifteen-minute mark only for Admira to go straight up the other end and score. The fog lifted revealing the tower blocks overlooking the ground like a crap David Blaine trick, and so surprised were the home side by the appearance of the round fiery object in the sky that they conceded two goals within three minutes. But back they came again, reducing the deficit to 3-2 just before half-time. It was exhausting stuff just watching and we needed some fuel to help us through the second period.

Kenny and Spencer came skipping back from the outdoor grill. "Chaps, they have food and it's not just sausages." After four days surviving on bread, sausage and mustard we eagerly tucked into something we couldn't pronounce or describe as anything other than 'mush'. We couldn't place the smell either but not being sausage we tucked in regardless. Whatever it was, there were unconfirmed reports that it contained potato, although on closer inspection that turned out to be a big piece of (at a guess - a hopeful one at that) pork fat.

Whatever the home team consumed at half time seemed to do the trick because within a few minutes they had drawn level. For the first time in the game Admira looked like they could win it. The sun was now shining and one or two of the away fans ripped their tops off. Super Hans got very excited by this and suggested we all did the same. We encouraged him to lead the way and then once he had whipped his top off revealing a bigger pair of breast than Kate Moss, we all took pictures of him and uploaded them to Facebook (as you do).

The sight of a semi-naked man jumping up and down on the terrace must have been an awful distraction for the away side because from a corner, with Super Hans's torso reflecting the sunshine into the Turnov keeper's eyes, Admira's Misko headed home to put the home side into the lead for the first time in the match. The away team was incensed, arguing with the referee that Super Hans's partial-strip had caused them to concede. Such were the protests that their skipper was dismissed.

Admira held out to take the three points and celebrated with a mass high-five session along the edge of the pitch with the youngsters and a few of our group who had grown bored of the slide. Could this weekend get any better that being high-fived by an actual player?

Alas no.

After the Admira game the group split into factions. One party headed off to the Viktoria derby as Plzen hosted Žižkov in the home of Czech beer. Unfortunately my early evening flight meant I couldn't join the fun train so I headed across town to the brand new(ish) Eden Arena to watch the storied Slavia Prague take on Ceské Budějovice.

The new home of Slavia is a different world from the ramshackle stadiums of Admira and Sparta B. It wouldn't look out of place in an unnamed nondescript industrial estate somewhere in England, complete with a Tesco superstore and McDonalds next door. I didn't fancy having to take my bag through the normal turnstiles with security guards inspecting my underwear and socks, so I tried the Media plan.

"Excuse me, you should have my name down for a media pass? Stuart Fuller, GTC Media from London, England."

Cue confused look as very pretty young lady on media desk looks through the lists. "I'm sorry Mr...er...Filler. I no have your name on paper."

I gave her my best smile, pulled out my International Press card and explained that my secretary should've sent a fax on Friday. I went on to add I have no issue buying a ticket but because I need to file a report with the News Agency I'd need to use a Wi-Fi connection. Smile again.

"Of course Stuart," now we were on first name terms as she fingered my card. "Here is your press pass, a Wi-Fi code and free Slavia USB stick."

For the third time I smiled, adding a small wink now we were the very best of friends.

I took my seat at the top of the uninspiring, yet modern stadium. A small crowd had taken up space at either end of the stadium, although I couldn't actually see any away fans that had made the trip from the south of the country. To be fair, if I lived in a city that made Budvar I doubt I would leave very often.

Slavia had gone through some financial turmoil in recent years that had threatened their very existence. Traditionally the only real rivals to Sparta's domestic dominance, Czech football needed them to stop the Rudi (the nickname for Sparta) from getting richer. The opening of the Eden in 2008, strangely against an Oxford University XI, had given the club hope that they could compete off the pitch as well as on it.

The game wasn't the best. Or perhaps it was because this was my sixth game in nearly 72 hours and I was simply footballed out. It was feisty opening period, with six yellow cards and one red (the away team centre-half David Horejs) but lacking in any attacking intent.

The second period was better, with Slavia realising that it was actually easier to play against ten men than eleven because you had an extra man, contrary to so-called expert opinion. Goals from Petr Janda and Martin Hurka secured the points for the home side, and then it was time to leave. The press lady handed me her card on the way out, suggesting that in my next visit I should "fax her", or at least that's what I think she said. One tram, one metro and one bus journey later and I was at Vaclav Havel airport. I headed to the bar for 'One Last Beer'.

Bratislava and Prague are Meccas for stag and hen parties every weekend due to their hedonistic entertainment and cheap beer. But there's another side featuring culture, architecture and history. Oh sod it, there's no way I can pull that off, it's all about the cheap and delicious beer and of course, football, football, football and more football.

This is how it must feel to be away with an international squad. Everyone comes from different teams with their set allegiances but as one, common purpose takes over for a short period of time. That's how I view these trips. One minute I could be sharing a room with Stoffers, the next a seat on a coach with Shep. The fans who survive aren't the strongest or most intelligent, it's the ones who can adapt the best – Charles Darwin said that, or something similar, and you can't disagree with him.

Chapter Ten

On a (Swiss) Roll
A letter from ITV's Brian Moore

26th October 2011
Grasshoppers 1 FC Servette 4
The Letzigrund

20th March 2012
FC Luzern 3 Grasshoppers 0
Swisspor Arena

"...I was one of the most feared goal-poachers in the North
Kent Sunday Leagues during the '70s and '80s..."

Take a seat.

I won't keep you long, but this is complicated and important stuff if you want to understand the footballing dynamics in one of Europe's richest countries. It involves two clubs, two grounds, one regional government and a series of broken promises. Let me take you back to 2005 when we thought Facebook was a pocket mirror and Arsenal were still considered title challengers.

UEFA had announced that Switzerland and Austria would co-host the 2008 European Championships, and one of the host cities would be Zürich. No real surprise there as big cities with the facilities to host one of the world's five largest sporting events are thin on the ground in Switzerland. The only question would be which stadium would be used? The city had two medium-sized stadiums being used regularly - the Letzigrund was the home of nine times Swiss Champions FC Zürich, as well as one of the most famous athletics tracks in the world and part of the annual IAAF Diamond League programme we all used to watch on Sportsnight. Across the railway tracks to the west was the Hardturm, home of Grasshoppers, the most successful team in Switzerland with 17 titles and 18 Swiss cups to their name.

Initially a decision was made to build a new ground, named the Stadion Zürich on the site of the Hardturm. Both teams would share this football-only stadium, leaving the Letzigrund as a multi-purpose arena. Grasshoppers would have to move out whilst it was being built and an agreement was made for them to travel the two miles or so across the railway line to the Letzigrund and share with their greatest rivals, FCZ for a couple of years. Following so far? Good.

Then the legal issues kicked in and a decision was made that instead of the Hardturm becoming the new European Championship stadium, it would be the Letzigrund that would be redeveloped as a multi-use state of the art stadium. Not to worry, Grasshoppers, the authorities said, we will build you a new stadium too so that after Euro2008 you can move into the new Stadion Zürich anyway. Well here we are years after the very successful European Championships and both clubs are indeed sharing a stadium, although not the one set out in the original plan. Stadion Zürich is about as finished as that symphony by Massive Attack, or Gaudi's cathedral in Barcelona. Instead they have to call the Letzigrund their home.

How do Grasshoppers feel about it? Well they are 'hopping' mad (too, too easy) to be truthful. They feel utterly shafted. They are the homeless ones, having to rely on the spare room of their bitterest rivals. They do not even have the crumbs of comfort of on-the-field success either. No stadium of their own for over five years now means no sustainable commercial revenue, which translates to little investment in the squad. Whilst FC Basel have been able to maximise the Euro2008 legacy on and off the pitch, Grasshoppers' last major honour was the Swiss title back in 2003. This season a fight against relegation was going to be more likely than a fight for a European place. Not that it was much rosier in the FCZ corner as their season had started poorly too.

Three weeks prior to my visit the two teams met in the first Zürich derby of the season. The game was finely poised with Grasshoppers holding a 2-1 lead thanks to a contentious penalty from Frank Feltscher with just fifteen minutes to go. Then trouble broke out between the two sets of fans and with flares being aimed at each other and the referee abandoned the game, sending shock waves through the Swiss game. Such open hostility to one another simply isn't Swiss.

So all was not well with football in Zürich. A perfect backdrop to take in a game or two with resident football finance expert Kieron O'Connor, known to thousands on the internet and beyond as 'Swiss Ramble'. Despite having seen a mere ten games in eight days, a visit to the den of discontent to watch Grasshoppers was a must as I was in the city anyway for work. You can never get enough football, just like you can never get enough beer. Well that was before I saw the price of a pint in the old town, in which case you can have enough beer when your Amex Platinum card is maxed out by a round.

Kieron said he would sort out the tickets for the game versus Servette. I have a theory that should be applied across the world when it comes to football ticket pricing. After extensive research in Slovakia and Czech Republic, I can launch to the world my new Beer/Ticket Ratio model for all football clubs to use from this point onwards. It is designed to be transparent, easy to implement and can be applied across borders. The theory simply goes:

'The price of your cheapest ticket should be no more than three times the price of a pint of local beer in the pub no more than half a mile down the road.'

In Prague this would mean ticket prices for the likes of Sparta and Slavia Prague should be no more than £3, in Slovakia £2.50 (not far off as Dan Richardson's season ticket at Slovan Bratislava was €41) and in Germany match tickets for most Bundesliga clubs start from around €15. England? Well unless The Boleyn next to Upton Park has started charging a tenner for a pint or a pub is actually opened near Emirates (which would undoubtedly charge £20 a pint), the Premier League would have to fall outside my model until countrywide changes were made. This should be the real basis for UEFA's Financial Fair Play rule.

But what about Switzerland? Well £21 for a Grasshoppers match ticket (30CHF) meant my beer shouldn't be more than £7...and lo and behold at 8.70CHF for a pint it damn well slotted right into my ratio theory. A Nobel Prize for Economic modeling won't go a miss for such insightful and thorough research if you fancy nominating me.

Now who to support? Well this was a tricky one. I had a long-term affinity with Grasshoppers as for over a decade I wore the famous blue and white stripes, like my brother before me. I scored something in the region of 350 goals for the club, including a still-record eleven in one game back in 1982. I refer of course to Grasshoppers New Ash Green rather than Grasshoppers Zürich, the less famous Swiss team.

I was one of the most feared goal-poachers in the North Kent Sunday Leagues (under 7s to Under 15s) during the late 1970s and 1980s. Grasshoppers of New Ash Green were legendary in the Gravesend area, regularly taking a clean sweep of all the age-group honours. We were named after the Swiss club for no other reason than it seems that club was first managed by a man who loved nothing better than some melted Gruyere. We adopted the kit, the club badge and even called our club house the Hardturm. One year we all got on a coach and came to see them play Sion at the Hardturm, marvelling at the battles off the pitch rather than the football on it. Hooligans 1, My Teenage Footballing Youth 0.

My parents have a box of mementos from my childhood that includes the famous blue and white shirt. I wanted to put it on for posterity but Kieron told me that walking round the suburbs of Zürich with a shirt that barely covered my 'extra padding' was probably illegal so I left it in the hotel.

After a beer or two we headed down to the ground by tram, passing one of my favourite signs in the city. I chuckle every time I see it, and so do literally thousands of visitors to my website, who are navigated there by searching for the term 'Glory Hole

Zürich'. I have no idea if this is just a translation-gone-wrong thing or if there really is a glory hole at that location, but the sign is still there and I wasn't stopping to find out tonight.

The visitors tonight, Servette, were also legends of mine hence my dilemma of who to support. In my early football watching years of the 1980s, strange football kits were always hard to come by (none of these sports warehouses selling off the Azerbaijan away shirt for £5 in those days). One day my brother came home with a new claret Umbro number. I had never seen it before, nor recognised the badge. I owned every issue of Match, Shoot and Football Weekly and could tell you every league club's kit just by an inch of colour, but this one was new on me. My curiosity got the better of me so I asked him whose shirt it was.

"Servette" he said.

"Gotcha" I said, with a knowing smile. I had no idea if he was just making that up. He did that a lot. In fact as most older brothers would testify, he spent most of his time trying to humiliate me. One day he put a dried puffer fish in my bed, the ones with the sharp spikes. His reason? To see if I would deflate it by lying on top of it.

The internet was still a wet dream in the geeky mind of the likes of Bill Gates and so there was no Wikipedia or the like, I had to find a way to verify it was who he said it was, and also find out who they actually were. So I wrote a letter to the only man who would know. Brian Moore. Presenter of ITV's The Big Match, and at the time my favourite commentator.

Three weeks later, he replied in person;

'Dear Stuart,

Servette are a team from Switzerland which if you have done Geography at school will know it is in the Alps. They play in a city called Geneva, which is close to the border with France and very pretty. Last season they won the National League in Switzerland and you can see them play in the European Cup this season, so perhaps your parents will let you stay up to see if they are on Sportsnight one week.'

He went on to give me some advice on how to get my own back on my brother but that is not for here. What a legend.

Servette were another once-great club that had fallen on hard times. After winning the national league in 1999 they then over-committed themselves financially and in 2005, with construction complete on their new stadium for Euro2008 they filed for bankruptcy, which saw them drop into the regional leagues. However, the fans didn't desert them and in May, five years of dedication paid off as the team won promotion from the Challenge League after winning the play offs and returned to their rightful place at the top table of Swiss football.

Kieron had procured seats in the family section - after all we were both fathers, which of course meant that they were slap bang in the middle of the hardcore Grasshoppers fans. Well, teach them early is my motto so what the heck.

The Letzigrund is certainly a stunning stadium from the outside at night. The ground is built down into the earth, meaning you enter the stadium at the highest point and walk down into your seat. The outside is built with 'distressed iron', the same look as the Angel of the North or just plain "rusty" as an FCZ fan in my Swiss office described it. The floodlights were mounted on spikes that penetrated the roof and high into the night sky. Impressive from the outside but the bloody athletics track on the inside means views were pants. The Grasshoppers fans could only watch on mournfully.

Does the score-line always reflect the performance? Probably not but in this case it definitely did. Going into the final few minutes Grasshoppers were on top after full-back Martin Lang had brought them back into the game at 2-1, but then two sucker punches from the visitors, coming either side of them hitting the post, left most of the crowd shaking their head in disbelief.

Servette came into the game having not scored a goal for 475 minutes. As a West Ham fan who had watched his team under master tactician Avram Grant bore us all to relegation, I know how the fans felt. This result was something of a coupon buster. The highlight of the first half was seeing a golf buggy come on to the pitch driven by the Servette physiotherapist; laziness of the tallest order.

Every so often a loud chime rang out around the stadium. At first I assumed this was some sort of 21st century cuckoo clock but all eyes diverted their gaze to the big screen where an advert for a clothes shop was playing. Strange stuff I thought. A few seconds later Kieron informed me that FCZ were winning away in Thun. The noise was to inform the crowd (and the players and the rest of Zürich no doubt) that there had been a goal somewhere else and if I diverted my gaze from the scantily-clad models in the advert, the latest scores were just to the left.

The second half saw more huff and puff from the home side without really creating much. It really was just like watching Avram's West Ham all over again. The home team's cause wasn't helped much when Lacopo La Rocca was sent off for a second yellow for aiming an elbow in the direction of a Servette player. The second goal was only a matter of minutes away, and sure enough more poor defending allowed Julian Esteban far too much space and he set up Matias Vitkieviez. You wait 485 minutes for a goal and then you get two in forty minutes. Grasshoppers threw caution to the wind and with the game entering the final ten minutes at last started creating chances. With the smell of class C drugs wafting in the air (not from us I hasten to add) the relaxing effects drifted across the athletics track and momentarily affected the Servette defence, thus allowing Lang to pull a goal back and renew the fan's hope accordingly.

But there wasn't to be any happy ending. With two of the allotted four minutes of injury-time up Francois Moubandje fired in a free kick from thirty yards, then just sixty seconds later and the stadium was quickly emptying as Antonio De Azevedo scored a fourth. Harsh, but you pay for not taking your chances.

With typical Swiss efficiency just twenty minutes after the final whistle we were back in the Lion pub in the centre of town. It was my round so I cashed in my pension and went to the bar. Grasshoppers still had a special place in my heart but I'm not sure they really cared for nostalgia at the moment. Three months into the season and any hopes of an assault on the top of the league was already over. There was still the Swiss Cup of course, and for that we need to fast forward a few months to where the struggling Grasshoppers had managed to reach the quarter-finals of the competition. Here they would face another team who play in blue and white, and once again I would be in the crowd.

Now here's a question for you - which city comes next in the following list?

Monte Carlo, Heidelberg, Salzburg, Florence.

Need a clue?

OK these are four of the top five destinations of choice in Europe according to Trip Advisor, where's the fifth?

Think Switzerland.

Think 14th-century bridge across a lake.

Think picture postcard pretty.

Think has a Swiss top division side.

Think anagram of Cruel Ne.

Still nothing?

You lot are rubbish. Of course the missing link is Lucerne. Or Luzern or Lucerna depending if you are feeling French, German or Romansh. Hundreds of thousands of visitors flock annually to the picturesque small city high in the Alps, on the crystal clear waters of Vierwaldstättersee, or Lake Lucerne for the uneducated.

The city straddles the Reuss River where it drains the lake, with a number of bridges linking the two banks. The most famous is the Chapel Bridge (Kapellbrücke), a 200 metre long wooden bridge originally built in 1333, although much of it has been replaced over the years in the same way that Trigger's broom from Only Fools and Horses is 25 years old but in that time has had 13 new handles and 17 new brushes. Part way across the bridge is the octagonal Water Tower (Wasserturm), a fortification from the 13th century and the city's most famous landmark. There are few more romantic spots for a moonlight walk in the world than across this bridge.

Ask The Current Mrs. Fuller about my romantic side and she will wax lyrical about some of my more inventive ideas in the past. It's not always been PSFs (petrol station flowers) and trips to football you know. Breakfast on a terrace overlooking the Ponte Vecchio, lunch in Monte-Carlo, tea at the Ritz and dinner in a private room at The Witchery in Edinburgh, but they couldn't hold a candle to midnight under the Wasserturm. Lucerne was a perfect romantic venue, strolling hand in hand along the Kapellbrücke under the moonlight. But of course you don't believe for a minute that is why I was in Lucerne.

And you'd be right.

CMF was 567 miles away at Fuller Towers and I was sharing that moonlight moment with a hundred or so Grasshoppers fans that were here for the Swiss Cup game against FC Luzern.

Well what did you expect?

The hosts, known as Die Leutchen in Switzerland, were domestic champions back in 1989 and were comfortably mid-table last season. They can be summed up in one word - Swiss. Predictable, conservative and solid. Their most exciting moment in recent years came when they were asked by the Brazilians to play them in a warm-up game prior to the 2006 World Cup about to take place in Germany. An 8-0 final score line probably wasn't a shock to many on the day.

Earlier in the season the club moved into the Swissporarena, the newest stadium in the country. The 16,800 capacity state of the art stadium has been built on the site of their old Stadion Allmend and was a combination of some of the best architectural elements of the new Letzigrund Stadion in Zürich on the outside, and the blandest of the new stadiums on the inside. Switzerland seemed to have the monopoly on new-build but dull stadiums. Functional is one word you can use to sum it up, although sitting nestled just under one of the Alpine peaks, with snow still covering the summit it certainly won some bonus points for location.

With CMF back in London I needed a companion to share the beauty and moonlight romance with. Of course it was going to be Kieron again and it was his job to handle logistics, beer and transport. I was in charge of bringing the Pringles.

We headed south from Zürich with the sun slowly falling across the water postcard style. You pay for beauty in Switzerland and so having paid £40 for the 45-minute return journey to Luzern I wanted a view and a half. As Basil Fawlty said to Mrs. Richards, "Well, may I ask what you expected to see out of a Torquay hotel bedroom window? Sydney Opera House, perhaps? The Hanging Gardens of Babylon? Herds of wildebeest sweeping majestically...?"

For my £40 I was expecting to see snowy alpine mountains, cows with bells on, St Bernard dogs with brandy bottles around their necks and Sepp Blatter. Three out of four wasn't a bad return I suppose without having to bother Herr Blatter.

All our talk on the way down was of the financial state of Swiss football. After visiting the impressive Stade de la Maladaire on the banks of Lake Neuchâtel in November to see Xamax take on FCZ they promptly went bankrupt and the Super Liga was reduced to 11 teams. Servette were now teetering on the brink of bankruptcy again despite having an almost brand spanking new stadium in Genève, built by the city for Euro2008. FC Sion have had a number of problems and of course, Grasshoppers themselves with their six-year old struggle of trying to have their own home in Zürich were in no better position than they had been when we saw them in October.

Buses had been laid on to the ground located on the edge of the city. We arrived with just over an hour to kick off. The stadium's alpine location meant there was a palpable nip in the air. The evening called for a few beers so we decided to head inside the Swisspor Arena but first we needed a 'club card' as this was a cashless stadium. Such technology has been in place in the Amsterdam ArenA and the Veltins Arena in Gelsenkirchen for some time (in fact I still have cards with cash on for both of them which will more than likely never be used again). The cards at Luzern at least have a good twist. Not only could they be used here in the stadium but also in a particular supermarket chain. Not particularly handy for the one time visitor like me but still a very good idea for the locals.

Fed, watered and our brains full of some interesting Eighties music playing on the concourses (remember Taco, The Maison-ettes and The Mobiles ? Neither did we, honest) we headed to our seats for the start of the 'Biggest game in Switzerland'. Certainly the biggest game being played on Tuesday 20th March 2012 as we contented ourselves.

Prior to the game the talk in the local papers was that if Grass-hoppers lost, manager Ciriaco Sforza would be sacked and the favourite to take his job would be the Luzern boss Murat Yakin. The manner of their defeat in this game will have done nothing to stop those rumours building momentum. Quite simply, they were very poor indeed. It wasn't until the 30th minute that they actually ventured into the Luzern penalty area, yet Sforza simply stood in his technical area, almost motionless, watching the last chance of glory for the season floating away over the Alps.

If only the Grasshoppers players showed just 1% of the passion their fans displayed. They were outstanding during the game, never giving up singing and supporting their club, even if the eleven on the pitch didn't deserve it. They welcomed the teams into the arena with a display of colour and fire, drenching the whole stadium in smoke which took nearly five minutes to clear, by which time Luzern should have taken the lead after they sprung the offside trap for the first of many occasions.

In the opening period the home side found their way through the Grasshoppers back line with ease but couldn't find an end product. Time and time again they threatened but didn't quite pressure the visitors goal, almost scared of Grasshoppers' repu-tation from twenty years previous. It was amazing that it took until the 42nd minute for the first goal to come, although it wasn't surprising which side scored. Luzern broke down the left and the winger sprinted into the area, reaching the byline and appearing to have taken it too far. Adrian Winter managed to pull it back, right into the path of the onrushing Dario Lezcano, and he slammed it home for a one-nil lead.

Half-time came and went with no material changes on either side. In fact the Luzern starting XI simply got stronger and stronger and it was no surprise that they doubled the lead when Nelson Ferreira, winning the award for the silliest hair on display as someone always must in todays football, found himself in space and debatably onside to slot home with ease. Even though there were still thirty minutes left on the clock Grasshoppers looked dead and buried. Despite the score their fans remained magnificent throughout.

The game was already effectively over but with ten minutes left Claudio Lustenburger nodded home a third. Instead of heading for the exits the away fans just lit flares. One was thrown onto the pitch and despite the presence of stewards and riot police in and around the away end, it was left to the referee to walk over to it and put it out. Finally the referee put Grasshoppers out of their misery and their season was over. For Luzern, second in the table and now in the semi-finals of the cup, things were looking up. "Tiré dans la matinée!" (Sacked in the morning) the home fans sang as they waved to a desolate looking Sforza, now a broken man with nothing left to cling on to.

We headed for the exits and within fifteen minutes we were on a train that was supposed to be travelling back to Zürich. Unfortunately, this particular train wasn't going anywhere fast. The Grasshoppers fans didn't fancy leaving the stadium or getting on the buses back to the station. With no more scheduled trains back to Zürich the local police weren't keen on have a few thousand angry Grasshopper fans rampaging across the Chapel Bridge at midnight. They used a bit of special encouragement in the form of water cannons, CS gas and rubber bullets. That'll do it. Finally they arrived at the station and we were on our way, complete with our own personal riot policeman for company.

So much for Swiss efficiency. Our train finally rolled into Zürich, thirty minutes late. It had been another top evening in the company of a modern-day football blogging legend, and of course a new ground for me. Whilst I hadn't exactly seen the beautiful side of one of the most popular tourist destinations in Europe, or got to walk arm-in-arm with Keiron across the Chapel Bridge, I had seen a decent game with a great atmosphere and in my book that beat a moonlight serenade hands down. If only CMF would agree.

Swiss football is at a real crossroads at the moment. Financial issues are crippling a number of the smaller clubs who have

Top: From left to right, Kenny Legg, Danny Last, Nenad (our guide and bodyguard in Belgrade), your author, and Andy Hudson.

Left: The ball is round and very, very chilly in Lodz.

Right: The magnificent seven, Real Betis striker Jonathan Pereira Rodríguez.

Top: Djurgarden fans can never be accused of not being colourful in response to the AIK welcome.

Bottom: The New Firm derby in Copenhagen. Brondby fans haven't had much to wave their flags about recently.

Top: Roma fans prepare for kick-off as the countdown nears an end.

Bottom: Danny and Kenny live out their Fireman Sam-related dreams.

Left: Who says the Belgians have no sense of humour? Gent's number one fan and resident superhero.

Bottom: Britain's worst ground? Central Park, Cowdenbeath gears up for some post-match banger racing

Top Left: The teams at Avarta emerge from an actual tunnel.

Top Right: Bring your own stand – Serbian second-tier football.

Bottom: Rhodes take the Island Games by storm with their tears, tantrums and tracksuits.

Top: The Black Army of AIK welcome the teams in the Stockholm derby.

Bottom: Your author, ready and waiting to answer any football travel-related questions at Red Star Belgrade.

gambled, and failed, to break the current big two monopoly on winning trophies. FC Basel are slowly becoming the Celtic of the league, winning the title before a ball is kicked and making progress in Europe. In a Catch 22 situation this means they get richer, they can afford to hoover up the talent in the domestic game, leaving a few crumbs for clubs like Servette, Lucerne and even Grasshoppers to fight over. Football in Switzerland is definitely worth a look, albeit an expensive one.

Chapter Eleven

Red Hot and Chilly
The new Germany?

10th December 2011
Legia Warsaw 0 KS Cracovia 0
Pepsi Arena

11th December 2011
ŁKS Łódz 1 Slask Wrocław 2
LKS Stadion

> "...I can't remember whose idea it was to come to Poland in
> December, one made by a drunkard or a madman..."

When people ask me what I'm up to at the weekend I sometimes lie. It's difficult to try and explain to someone you don't know why you'd be heading off to some strange town on the other side of Europe to watch football. I tend to say that I've got no plans - it's easier in the long run. Those who know me better still occasionally shake their head when I share my plans to go to Belgium, Slovakia or Norway for the Sandfjord derby, but when those who are closest to me suggest I am mad, then I question whether I do need help. And then I look into those brown eyes of Danny Last and he soothes my furrowed brow, reassuring me that visiting Poland in the sub-zero temperatures of December is perfectly normal.

So that's why we were standing in a long line of other miserable looking travellers at London Stansted as we prepared to board a Ryanair flight to Poznan, which unlike some of their other destinations is exactly where it is. I refer of course to the likes of Vienna (Bratislava), Oslo (Sandfjord) and Frankfurt (Hahn). Some passengers had tried to alleviate the impending pain on the senses by drinking heavily. At least two groups were sharing a bottle of vodka, a perfectly acceptable substitute for breakfast at 5am prior to experiencing some true old-fashion customer experience O'Leary style.

Two hours later and we were on a bus heading for the outskirts of Poznan, Poland's fifth largest city and the capital of Wielkopolska. Those who don't know us could be fooled to believe we were heading for the Basilica of Saint Peter, or even to pick up some local lace from the Christmas markets. But of course we weren't. This was the opening leg in our pioneering Polish footballing extravaganza.

Whilst the streets of Poznan were deathly quiet on this Saturday morning, the Polish FA would ensure that there were ladies dressed in traditional Polish folk costumes stood on every corner come June time and Euro2012's start. UEFA would also insist that the fans drink only Coca-Cola, Castrol or Carlsberg and that no food should exist outside of McDonalds. 'We care about Football' is the UEFA motto. Not when temperatures dip below freezing they don't. Michel Platini and Lennart Johansson had waived their free passes for this weekend leaving Danny and I dressed in more layers than a mille-feuille vanilla slice, to brave the cold and have a pre-Euros look at Polish football.

Unfortunately, due to the last minute change in fixtures for Polish TV there would be no game for us here. However, with our flights already booked it would have been rude not to at least drop by the new 43,000 all-seater Stadion Miejski which would be hosting three games in the European Championships in just a few months. The bad news was that try as we might there was no 'Magic Door' to facilitate our safe passage to pitch side. The good news was that the club shop had Lech Poznan socks. At least one of us was happy as we left to head into the city centre.

In June 2012 the city would be taken over by Irish fans. When England play away the less than cultured fans (some of us have read at least one page of The Guardian) always head for the nearest Irish Bar where they drink Guinness or Magners and stand on the tables singing No Surrender in between choruses of The Pogues or U2's It's A Beautiful Day. But does that mean that when the Irish arrive, they will seek out the nearest English pub and drink watered down Fosters, look at pictures of dogs playing snooker on the walls and watch episodes of Only Fools and Horses with their Roast Beef and two veg? A gap in the market for a world-wide chain I think, that is unless you go to Magaluf, Kavos, Malia, Benidorm, Tenerife etc where every bar offers such 'hospitality'.

Cultured out we headed for the railway station, bought our £8 First Class (First Class - £8!!!) tickets that included our own compartment (First Class Compartment, £8!!!) and access to the First Class Dining Carriage (beer, food, First Class £8!!!). It turned out we weren't alone in our compartment. A very smart-looking gentleman was already in situ. Of course when in a foreign country and you are thrust upon a situation that in England would be uncomfortable, you do the complete opposite to your normal behaviour. We greeted him like a long-lost uncle, warmly shaking him by the hand and introducing ourselves as "Sporting cultural ambassadors". What a coincidence! Our travel companion was an ambassador too, although slightly more important than our made up titles. Ladies and gentlemen may I present to you the Italian Ambassador for Poland no less. Cue polite chit-chat about football and what the protocol would be if a major Parmesan Cheese incident happened in Poland. We also discussed at length how many Ferrero Rocher you need to buy for the average ambassador's party to which, alas, he didn't know the answer or have a clue what we were on about.

Forty-five minutes on public transport in a strange land without alcohol has a funny effect on Danny so we bade our new friend goodbye and headed to our dining car for some much-needed refreshments. Borscht and Kiełbasa all round, washed down with a few Żywiecs for good measure made the rest of the journey across Poland very pleasant and before you could learn how to say dziewiecdziesieciokilkuletniemu, we were easing into Warsaw Central station.

Warsaw today has more five star hotels than Brussels, Valletta and Skopje put together and at bargain weekend rates too. When I happened to mention our trip they were literally falling over themselves to give us the best deal, well at least that's what Hotels.com led me to believe. We chose the Westin because it said it had a 24 hour bar - we are discerning consumers and not easily swayed by trivial boasts by hotel chains. So bags dropped off and the usual reassurances that we definitely required two beds and not one in the room confirmed, we headed off for a bit of culture and the odd museum or two.

What better place to start then than the Palace of Culture and Science. It is after all the tallest building in Poland and from its viewing terrace on the 30th floor we reckoned on being able to see at least two of the city's football stadiums. What we hadn't factored in was a giant display of Adidas Tango balls placed in front of the entrance of the building. After getting up close and personal with ten foot balls for fifteen minutes we took the lift to the top of the Palace. Our eyes lit up at the view that greeted us. "That's the best sight I've seen since I saw the current Mrs Fuller waltzing down the aisle" I proudly beamed as the new National Stadium had been lit up especially for our visit. We (well Danny was doing the reading whilst I was transfixed by the view) learned that the Palace was a gift from Russia; it was hated at first but now begrudgingly accepted, and that the Rolling Stones were the first major rock band from abroad to give the Poles some satisfaction by playing here in 1967.

To wrongly paraphrase a classic Stones number, time was not on our side as we had a game to get to. Just a small matter of Legia Warsaw v Cracovia. Rumour had it there was no love lost between fans from the capital and Poland's second largest city Krakow. I'd been to see Legia just a few weeks previously and was very impressed by the passion and intensity of their supporters. When the revised TV fixtures came out I had no hesitation in suggesting a quick revisit to the Polish Army Stadium for our Saturday entertainment.

Legia's base, Łazienkowska, lies just south of the city centre so we hopped on a bus that for less than 80p plonked us right outside the ground. Alas the football museum was shut and the queue for the pub we'd been recommended was enormous so we chose to head inside and soak up the atmosphere.

At a recent Europa League game, the Legia Warsaw fans unveiled a banner declaring the imposing legend 'We hate everyone'. Unless you're from or support Szczecin (MKS Pogon), Sosnowiec (Zagłebie) and Elblag (Olimpia). For some strange all-to-frequent-unwritten continental reason they're all actually friends of Legia along with ADO Den Haag whose colours we saw all around the stadium. Once again Danny had his finger on the pulse of Polish footballing history and told me that the hatred all steamed from some comedy match-fixing in the early nineties. Going into the last game of the season Legia and ŁKS Łódz topped the table and won their final games of the season by cricket scores against teams who'd possibly been slipped a few bob. The PZPN (Polish FA) were having none of it and awarded the title to the third placed team, Lech Poznan. Grudge matches and hooliganism have reared their head ever since.

The stadium had been transformed in recent years from the dilapidated Polish Army Stadium to the shiny Pepsi Arena. In recent taste tests, whilst the latter reflects the modern European image of the club, the former was more fun for the fans.

Inside there was of course a pulsating atmosphere complete with some textbook choreographed singing. It's like this all the time here. I can't think of a single ground in Britain where there's relentless noise for 9 minutes during a single game, let alone 90 minutes at every game. Away to our left in the Zyleta, the stand where the Ultras gather which translates to the 'razor blade', all dressed in white were the Legia hardcore. They all knew the score. The first rule of the Legia Club is don't wear black. 'The Black Shirts' is the nickname of their hated rivals in the city, Polonia. "We hate those bastards," said the chap to my right before noticing our black coats. A big faux pas on our part. The second rule of Legia Club is, as we now know, don't wear black.

Danny turned to me and said "It's impossible not to tap your foot along to the rhythm of the beat as anthemic brilliance pours from the lungs of every single fan." Well that's the literal translation of his "it's fucking mental!" I'm guessing. It was the loudest atmosphere I'd ever experienced in a football stadium and it was bloody brilliant. There are flags and banners everywhere you looked on the Zyleta. Once again Danny got out his notes and gave me the lowdown on the importance of the flags. Many of them date back over 30 years and are incredibly important to the fans. They represent the true identity to the club and thus are seen as major trophies for other club's 'fans' to try and steal. If they are able to steal a treasured flag of another club, they then hang it on the fence during the match against that team, upside down (naturally) and then burn it.

The game, which was fact fans, the 1000th to be played at this stadium in all of its various guises, finished 0-0. But the fans didn't seem to react to anything that occurred on the pitch. When a player was clean through on goal they didn't raise or lower their voice. It was just unwavering support throughout. If they'd have won 4-0 or lost 0-4 I'm guessing it wouldn't have made any difference. Could you imagine Old Trafford rocking to its very foundations during a bore draw at home to Wigan?

At one point a few Legia fans tried to break through into the away sector. And sort of half-heartedly a number of Cracovia fans tried to break out of their end, but security dealt with it swiftly and there wasn't any actual trouble that we noticed anyway. Considering they were second from bottom in the league, Cracovia were backed by an impressive following of around 1500. Bizarrely a lot of them didn't turn up until the second half prompting a cracking visual display of flag waving. There were definitely fans of Lech Poznan in amongst them (another fan friendship) and by all accounts a few supporters of Polonia Warsaw had also popped in to lend a verbal volley of hatred towards Legia.

Danny is the linguist out of the two of us and had been polishing up on his Polish all week in preparation for the post-match press conference. After all, we were actually here in a sort-of work capacity, doing some research for a guide for the Euros to be published on the website 'In Bed With Maradona', and thus wanted to get right at the heart of Polish football. So whilst mumbling away about a pretty dull scoreless match for twenty or so minutes, neither Legia gaffer Maciej Skorza nor Cracovia boss Dariusz Pasieka said "dwa piwa prosze," (two beers please) or "jestem z zespołem muzycznym," (I'm with the band). These were two of the three phrases Danny had learnt. The other one allowed him his big moment in this gathering when it came to his turn for asking a question. Slightly tentatively Danny leant into the microphone and asked "Czy ten pociag staje w Warszawa?" (translated to 'does this train stop in

Warsaw?'). Unsurprisingly, thirty-seconds later we were out on the streets and in need of a beer.

The night was young and we found ourselves surrounded by plastic English and American fans of Real Madrid and Barcelona, marvelling at the skill of Ronaldo and Messi, talking as if they had intimate knowledge of the pair. "I'd love to go to the Camp Nou one day," said one, before his mate corrected him "It's called the Nou Camp and it's awesome. It has a massive roof that opens and closes." There is nothing Danny and I, experts at European Football travel, hate more than people like this who are uneducated, lazy and like their football like they like their women - in a bar, alongside a beer. We moved on, finally deciding on a return to the hotel for a visit to the 24-hour bar, which of course was closed. Fortunately our receptionist knew a little bar called Pub Slusarna around the corner in ul Walicòw that was still open at 1am so we made tracks.

We arrived and were greeted like long-lost brothers. The good news was that there was a lock-in planned. The bad news was that it was a Polish Karaoke lock-in, hosted by Chris Evans (at 2am he could've been his twin brother anyway). In normal circumstances we would have said our goodnights and headed off, but Evans kept plying us with local beer Lech, with the mistaken belief that we were journalists and would write nice things about Pub Slusarna in our official (...ish) guide to Euro2012. Well, we couldn't be bought that easy! And if he thought we would be joining in in getting up on a table then he was grossly mistaken.

Of course two hours later it was all different. Peer pressure got to us, and to avoid a Polish girl grinding into my knee anymore (I wasn't giving up my bar stool for anyone!) we got involved. Danny lead the way by belted out an N-Dubz version of (White Man) in Hammersmith Palais, whilst I brought the house down with my slurred version of Summer of '69. "Encore, Encore!" they shouted and so we paired up for one last time on stage (well, a very small table) for a version of 'Islands in the Stream' that would have reduced Kenny and Dolly to tears. Our day couldn't get any better than this so we picked up the various items of underwear that had been thrown at us and headed back to the hotel, in preparation for another big day of footballing adventure.

Sunday morning saw us rise early from our five star luxury abode. Events of the previous day/night slowly started to unfold. Mobile phones tend to leave a history and looking at my call/text/Twitter log left me in no doubt I had had a few too many. All I will say is that no, I don't think we should do that, yes it was very hairy and Mum, I was only joking. The noise of the Legia fans was still ringing in our ears, and after a quick Poznan across our Westin hotel room we headed out into the freezing day trying to piece together the evening.

Our plan was to head southwest to Poland's third largest city, Wooge - well that is how I was told it was pronounced. The fact that the lady at the train station understood what I meant suggested I was right and we boarded the 9:49 'express' that would see us in the city by 11.15am. All was going well as we sped through the Polish countryside, spotting grounds left, right and centre. We pulled in just after 11am at Łódz Widzow station which was to the east of the city. We wanted the other station, which was to the west, Kalinka. But our train was going on to that one so we stayed on. Fifty minutes later we were still travelling at a speed that South-Eastern trains would have called slow, stopping every few hundred yards so the driver could have a chat with the locals on their allotments. It appeared we were the only passengers left in the train and we weren't going anywhere fast. Finally Danny got the driver's attention. One of his favourite films is the Railway Children so he improvised just like they did to draw attention to the train driver on the silver screen with a stick and his underwear. It wasn't a pretty sight but it was effective as the train started on its journey once again, the driver remembering that he is supposed to run to a timetable and stop in the right places.

"Ella, Ella, Under my Umbrella, Ella, Ella." Just five days prior to our arrival in Poland's third biggest city, those words has re-verberated across the Stadion ŁKS as one of the most famous and sought after artists in the world, Rihanna played in front of a sell out crowd in the adjacent Atlas Area. One hundred and fifteen hours later, Danny Last and I were wrapped up like Michelin men outside the football stadium, huddled under a canopy, waiting to pick up our press passes from ŁKS Łódz. Now don't get me wrong, I love Danny Last but he's no Rihanna and so when he uttered the chorus line for the umpteenth time I told him exactly where he could stick his bloody "Ella" and wandered off in a huff to find some football socks for my collection.

Łódz is the city that brought to the world the founder of Max Factor, coincidentally called Makysmillian Faktorowicz (and butt of one of my favourite jokes of all time - "Why did the make-up blush? Because Max Factor!" – admittedly that only really works in a cockney accent to be fair) and Roman Polanski. Martin Scorsese was also in town, doing the Łódz football double over the weekend no doubt as a guest of Rihanna.

We picked up our passes, which were as big as a pools coupon, and then headed to the bar (obviously), sharing a brief moment with the world famous Czech ground-hopper Christof who had endured a nine-hour bus trip for two days in Łódz. As you will have gathered, Rihanna, Christof - Łódz is the place to be.

We had been warned that Stadion ŁKS was 'quirky', what they had meant was that this was actually the worst ground in the top league of Polish football. The story as to why is a tale of woe, broken promises and general disappointment. With two top league sides in the city, there was some momentum behind a bid for one of the places in the Euro2012 host ground list.However, Łódz, along with Krakow missed out, although for a brief period there was a hope that the unprepared Ukraine would simply have their games taken away and then Łódz would have been in the frame. Alas, UEFA deemed that cities such as Donetsk and Lviv, where there were barely enough hotel rooms for the two domestic teams, let alone the concept of 40,000 international fans wanting to watch a game, were more than ready and so funding for a new stadium was never forthcoming. The kick in the teeth here for ŁKS was the construction in 2010 of the Atlas Arena next door, which took place at the expense of a new stadium. Still, at least Rihanna was happy.

We entered the ground via a magic blue door, following the club mascot as he seemed to know where he was going and we didn't. The gallant knight (for that was him forsooth), walked down some steps and into what appeared to be a school hall. It had that gym smell of sweaty socks and rubber mats, and the ropes hung forlornly down from the ceilings. We walked across the floor, assuming we were in the wrong place, then up the other side of the steps and into the main stand.

Our seats were front row and amongst the WAGS. What was good to see is that the full EU regulation was in place meaning that the WAGS were all the requisite orange in colour, wearing FMBs and generally showing disdain for everyone else around them and the game itself. Danny and I tried to strike up a conversation in Polish to impress them but after we'd asked each other if they were with the band, if they wanted a beer or if this was Warsaw Central Station, we were completely stuck. Best revert to plan B then, which was to watch the football.

This was a banker away win. Top of the table Wrocław could open up a four point gap at the top if they won thanks to Legia's goal less draw yesterday, whilst ŁKS had struggled all season and languished too close to the drop zone. Let's clear up one myth straight away without having to get those strange ginger Americans involved (from Mythbusters) - "Poland in December is cold."

It wasn't cold. It was ball-freezing, ice-breaking, cock-shrivelling cold. Even with our hats (yes, Danny and I both wore our silliest but in our minds stylish hats) and our EFW issued thermal gloves, we were freezing. So cold in fact that neither of us got our EFW issued iPads, or even the EFW issued scraps of paper to write any notes down on.

Whilst we were all wrapped up ready for the next Ice Age, only a few players were actually wearing long sleeve shirts, let alone gloves. These Poles are made of strong stuff. So strong that this season they are even playing on Christmas Day. Perhaps it's the numerous types of vodka that the locals consume (seventeen different varieties at the airport duty-free shop when we left) or the Zurek (Sour Rye soup) they quaff so much of but they are made of sterner stuff than Danny or I.

The Stadion ŁKS was certainly unusual in the fact that the main hard-core fans stood along the side of the pitch. The away fans unfurled a huge flag that covered the whole away end with almost precision dimensions. They kept it in place for the first ten minutes of the game, obviously sure in the knowledge that they would miss nothing. The home Ultras stood out like a sore thumb behind a big banner that just said "Troublemakers."

The match itself was fairly uneventful. The home goalkeeper, looking like a chap pulled in off the streets in his baggy tracksuit bottoms, didn't fancy taking goal kicks, and it was from one of the toe-pokes from the defender taking them in his place that the opening goal came. His kick sailed over the heads of the visitors defence and a cross found Antoni Lukasiewicz unmarked to head home against the run of play. The home fans, not used to seeing such events even stopped their singing and dancing for a minute in shock. Current form has only seen one point in the past five home games and goals are as rare as a spare hotel room in Kiev during the European Championships.

Slask didn't seem too bothered by the goal and they played as if they knew they would win in the remainder of the half. With the cold shrinking our bladders we set off in search of toilets. Back across the sports hall (which was now the scene of amusing incidents galore as the substitutes all tried to keep their balance on the shiny wooden surfaces in their boots) and up the steps and outside. However, the way was blocked. About fifty riot police were trying to keep some rogue home fans at bay and stop them reaching the away end. We didn't need the little boys' room that much all of a sudden and went back the way we came. And then a door opened up in front of us, as if the God of Football Stadiums himself had said "Let the lads in here to warm themselves up."

We walked into a room with hot soup (Zurek if you really want to know), pasta with meat (no idea what meat it was as the tin didn't have a label on) and beer. All free of charge. This was our reward for making the journey to the forgotten city of Polish football. Oh yes.

As we stumbled back out we found a port-a-loo. These are very common all over Poland these days. Toi-Toi's are the main brand, which apparently have extra base ballast to stop the age old toilet tipping japes. Very welcome it was too and as I came out I noticed a previously hidden passageway. This was literally the stair-way to heaven, a route now blocked off to the 'closed for safety reasons' upper tier. With my "I'm English," excuse ready if I was stopped, I climbed to the top to be rewarded with a view and a half across the stadium, with the sun setting in the distance. I returned to my seat with 'that smile' as Danny says, which means I've found something. It didn't disappoint either.

With twenty minutes to go the atmosphere in the ground changed. A flare was thrown/fired from the outside of the stadium into the away fans. It actually missed and ironically landed on the grill set up for the sausages, giving a new meaning to the word 'bangers', but it incensed the away following. They started taking down their banners, being their most treasured possessions, and began climbing the fences to get at the home fans, who in turn had taken theirs down as well and were gathering at the far end of the side terrace. A nervous stand-off took hold with both sets trying to show bravado, but not having the bottle to make the first move.

It was events on the pitch that broke the spell that had taken hold of the fans as firstly Przemsylaw Kazmierczak and then Marek Wasiluk scored for Slask to put them in the lead. The away fans went mental, putting up a set of new banners, suddenly forgetting about starting any aggro. The final whistle followed and

it was time to depart. We fought our way through the riot police now in place to keep the fans apart and hopped in a taxi.
"Airport, please," I said in my best Roger Moore voice, adding a
slight eyebrow raise. "Huh?" said the driver. Danny took over,
using the international language of gestures made a flapping bird
motion and the driver said "Ah English – Lublinka," and away we
went to the airport.

I still can't remember whose idea it was to come to Poland in
December. It was a ridiculous idea, one only made by a drunkard
or a madman so probably based on those two characteristics it
could have been either of us. If you want cheap tickets, a decent
atmosphere and some old school stadiums then Polska is for you.
Any Football Tourist worth their salt will tell you that this is the
place where it is all happening these days. They even have a Body
Shop, a universal sign of culture in anyone's book. One weekend,
two games, three goals, four dumplings, a five star hotel, six
taxis, seven buses and trams and about a million beers - all for
less than £150. Poland is officially the new Germany for cheap
football thrills.

Chapter Twelve

Roman Holiday
Stuart and Danny's magic box

4th March 2012
Lupa Frascati 4 San Cesareo 0
Stadio Comunale VIII Settembre

AS Roma 1 Lazio 2
Stadio Olimpico

"...we had our own Roma umbrella, Roma rucksack, strange
Roma headband thing and a Roma scarf..."

Match fixing, doping, prostitutes and Silvio Berlusconi. The view from afar that basically sums up an average week's headlines in the world of Calcio. There barely seems to be a week pass without some scandal breaking in Italian football. Whilst the northern cities of Turin, Milan, Genoa and Florence have grabbed the majority of the front as well as the back page headlines in recent years, for sheer intrigue, financial mismanagement and downright bad behavior, look no further than the Italian capital.

Rome is where the true essence of Italian spirit lies. In his excellent book 'The Dark Heart of Italy', Tobias Jones comments that the Italian words for history and story are the same, 'storia', meaning that sometimes the truth gets confused with the fable. So what was the storia at the current time at the heart of Italian football? That is what we aimed to find out as we boarded the Fuller private jet (aka British Airways, paid by Air Miles) bound for Leonardo Da Vinci airport, on the outskirts of Rome. Our story would be starting in the Eccellenza, the regional league of the province of Lazio, and end up in the modern-day Coliseum with the Derby della Capitale.

By we I mean of course Danny Last and I, but we also had another reason for flying to Italy for a slice of the Dolce Vita. That would be a legend by the name of Adam Lloyd. His rise from the control room at the Madejski Stadium to his villa overlooking the hills of Rome is pure 'Boys-Own' stuff. He'd followed the well-documented on the silver screen, yet highly mysterious path trod unsuccessfully by such luminaries as Ernst Stavro Blofeld, Paco Scaramanga and Auric Goldfinger. His quest for world domination, controlled from his villa high above Roma, was going well. So well in fact that he was personally able to welcome us at the airport with a selection of all the usual Italian cold meats and a chilled Peroni. Champione.

As we were whisked through the suburbs of the city, Adam pulled out the top secret file, codenamed 'Magic Box' for the weekend. The plan of action for Big Match Eve (BME) was a wander around Grottaferrata, known officially as the city of books and unofficially as the swinging capital of Rome, a glass of Frascati in Frascati and an afternoon of sightseeing around the capital with a splash of some retail therapy in the AS Roma store thrown in for good measure. We'd already had a browse at the online store and earmarked the Totti soap for Mrs. Last and Roma hand-cream for the Current Mrs. Fuller. We would be heroes in our respective ladies lives for bringing such fine gifts home for them.

As we tucked into one of the biggest salami sandwiches known to man in the town square, the temperature hit a balmy 20 degrees. It was short-sleeves all around yet just two weeks previously Rome had shivered as temperatures plummeted and snow had fallen in this very spot. This was a real rarity in the city and caused many a style-conscious Italian to stay at home for fear of people thinking it was dandruff settling on his shoulders rather than Mr. Frosty.

You can never get bored of wandering the alleyways and seeing the sights of Rome. There's history around every corner. So much so that we were forced to stop for a beer or two in the Campo d'Fiori. I'd been set a task from back home of photographing a number of items during the day. The more I managed the more of a treat I was promised on my return home. They started easily enough. An Italian lady riding a Vespa, feeding Danny some ice cream, posing next to a comedy knob on a statue and throwing an item of clothing instead of a coin into the Trevi Fountain. But we needed some rude vegetables and Campo d'Fiori was the place to go.

Rome's biggest open-air food market didn't disappoint and soon we had enough pictures to make Esther Rantzen blush. Never has a €10 beer been so richly deserved. After an afternoon of culture we needed to get our ying back in balance with our yang. What we needed was the biggest meal ever eaten by an Englishman in Rome, and Adam knew just the place back in Grottaferrata, down a small side street, up a blind alley and then in the back passage. Three special knocks on a plain white door and we were in. To add to the mystery Adam explained that the restaurant had no menu, with the owner and head chef simply cooking what he felt like (if at all) each day. The next few hours involved polishing off a mere five courses of outstanding food, four bottles of red and a Grappa to end it all off. Our host, the love child of Gareth Chilcott and Willie Thorne, wished us well at the end of the evening with a genial "Fuck Off!" (Adam had been teaching him some English phrases in preparation for a visit to London soon) and we went on our merry way back to Chez Lloyd (not to be confused with Cher Lloyd because, well, that would just be a horrible thought), peering in the windows of all the villas on the way to see if it really was the home of the Swingers Association, Rome branch. Alas, none of them were.

Match day dawned and in true Italian style Adam brought in

our presents. BME had given way to BMS (Big Match Sunday) and that was only marginally behind Christmas in terms of gift giving in the region of Lazio. Our presents were Roma Magic Boxes. Now we understood the code-word from yesterday. They don't do things by half here in style conscious Rome. Not only did we have some of the best seats in the house for the game, but we also now had our own Roma umbrella, Roma rucksack, strange Roma headband thing and a Roma scarf all washed down with access to the President's Lounge at half-time. We weren't sure if it was THE President's lounge that would surely have dusky Italian maidens liberally scattered around on chaise longues, but I was willing to find out if forced.

Before we could set off Adam brought us to attention in front of the blackboard to explain the big plan. Our plan (herewith called "The Plan") was to head out to the countryside and take in a regional game as l'antipasto before the AS Roma v SS Lazio primo. And could there be a better place in the world to have the starter than a place where some of the big Italian knobs hang out sipping white wine? Frascati, just a 15-minute stroll down the road is where everybody who wants to be an anybody will want to be seen on a Sunday morning.

A football team named after a nice wine has never won a major honour in football - FACT. Well, apart from Bordeaux. And Porto (but that's just punch gone wrong). And Lambrini United and Blue Nun Rovers. I may have just made them up. Lupa Frascati was hoping one day to break that duck. They had twice won the Eccellenza Group B, the most recent being in 2007 and gained promotion to Serie D, but their stay in the fourth level of Italian football had been brief. Last season they finished runners-up again in the regional league and coming into the game against rivals from just 3 miles down the road, San Cesareo, they were again in secondo posizione. Easy home win then? Not quite as the visitors were al primo posto meaning this was the game of the season, second versus first.

Frascati were a club on a mission. Taking their club colours from AS Roma, they had also added the Lupa name (meaning Wolf) to reflect their bond with i Lupi (AS Roma) after they bought the licence to play in the league from the defunct Cisco Calcio in 2004, who then reformed as AS Cisco Lodigiani, then Cisco Roma (where they signed Paolo Di Canio) and finally Atletico Roma before falling into that black hole of Italian Calcio licences in 2011. As with most things Italian, simple it ain't.

The Plan also had a liberal sprinkling of culture interwoven with the football. Danny wanted to see the Ethiopian Museum of Cardinal Guglielmo Massaia, whilst Adam wanted to visit the sights from Lord Byron's Childe Harold. Me, well you know me. I was happy as Larry just seeing the building where the Tokamak was housed. After all, if you are going to see a device which uses a magnetic field to confine plasma in the shape of a torus, then this was a Tokamak you don't want to miss.

ahem

Culture ticked off for another day we headed for the Stadio Comunale VIII Settembre, our destination for the festivities and part one of The Plan. We hoped that as the town was twinned with Maidenhead there would be, *cough*, gentlemen's entertainment provided. Maidenhead United's York Road is not just famous for being the world's oldest continuously used football ground, but it is also the only one I can think of (or visited) that has a strip club on its doorstep, called of course, The Honey Pot (correction - I've only ever visited the football ground and not said entertainment establishment).

First look at the pictures of the ground in Frascati showed a couple of impressive villas overlooking the arena that could have indeed hosted one or two of Silvio's legendary parties. We arrived at the gates of the ground with 30 minutes to kick off. The away fans from just down the road in San Cesareo were just arriving. Sunglasses - tick, scarves wrapped around faces - tick, banners – tick, tight jeans - tick. Your typical Italian football fans uniform. They all piled into the ground that was pumping out some of the loudest techno music known to man, quite out of character for this stunning location and as it sounded like a million car alarms going off at once, most unwelcome.

Despite some rallying banners around the town centre encouraging the locals to come to the arena and 'do battle', it was a surreal atmosphere. Middle age men with their impeccably dressed stunning lady friends and a few youngsters made up the home crowd, sitting high up on the terrace. A few policemen, obviously winding down towards retirement patrolled the sparse crowd, their waistlines fighting with their upper-middle age spread. The teams emerged into the sunshine and there was a small display of flag waving from the away fans, whilst some polite applause from the home supporters was 'enough'. Sleepy? On looks alone yes, but looks can be deceptive.

After a few minutes of tediously feeling each other out, the game exploded into life. A ball over the top of the San Cesareo defence reached a Frascati player who was clearly offside. Play continued and he was hauled to the ground. Clear penalty and an unavoidable red card for the defender. Just two minutes on the clock and all of a sudden the league leaders looked in tatters. It took a good five minutes for the offender to leave the pitch, slouching all the way to the dressing rooms, kicking a cone, an advertising board and then throwing his shirt to the ground on the way. Penalty dispatched, one nil. The crowd went mental. Well, as much as a dozen middle-aged, well groomed Italian men can go mental I suppose.

All of a sudden some of the previously placid away fans went ballistic. Clearly riled by the events on the pitch they charged at a section of home supporters, with the fence and a fat old policeman keeping them apart. You got the feeling that these were people who knew each other, perhaps worked together and this was an outpouring of emotion and frustration, similar to the scene in Football Factory when Danny Dyer and Tamar Hassan have a scrap at a kids Sunday League game. Police re-enforcements were called and a second officer arrived, wearing trousers far too big and fingering the trigger of his service pistol that probably last saw action a few decades ago. Calm was restored and a mobile phone was passed through the fence, who-ever was on the other end (bets were on someone's mum telling them to behave) put them back in order.

Whilst all of this was going on play still hadn't restarted. It had all kicked off on the touchline and both benches were now at each other's throats, physically contesting a decision with some violent finger pointing. Being in Italy there was lots of noise and gesticulating but there wasn't any real violence. Gladrags rather than handbags even. The result, however, was a sending off for the San Cesareo coach. Definitely not a good start for the day's league leaders.

It was hard to focus on the game with the sun shining, the picturesque setting and more importantly the fans goading each other. The crowd had calmed down and the extra policeman wandered back to his seat to continue his Sunday morning snooze. Then came the second goal as Frascati took advantage of some poor defending and the extra man, smashing the ball in from close range and almost getting stuck in the stanchion in a Brooking-esque moment. The man running the refreshments at the top of the terrace suddenly burst into life, galloping down the steps to join in the player celebrations at pitch side. Out of puff he slowly climbed back up and met our bewildered eyes. "Questo è il mio figlio!" which Siri on my iPhone translated as "That's my son". This explanation was far more likely than Adam's translation of "He's my lover!"

The second goal didn't bring any comfort to the away team and a second member of the bench was ordered off, but not before having a further row with the home team substitutes. Quite an extraordinary half of football. It would've been perfect to have stayed a bit longer, but we had a date with 60,000 Romans to keep unfortunately.

On the Fuller private jet on the way over to Rome, Danny and I tried to draw up the best derbies in the world. Always a difficult topic but we finally agreed on a top three. Outside of Istanbul, is the Rome derby the most atmospheric? We said 'yes' because otherwise we were heading off to the Stadio Olimpico for no real reason apart from an opportunity to be in the President's Lounge.

In the past the game has had drama, controversy, clowns and championships. It was first contested back in 1929 and since then AS Roma has led the way with 63 wins to Lazio's 46. In 1979 a Lazio fan was killed by a flare fired from the Roma section at the far end of the stadium and in 2004, the game had to be abandoned after the leaders of the Roma Ultras groups walked unopposed onto the pitch and approached Francesco Totti to tell him to walk off after a rumour spread that the riot police had killed a fan. Violence then escalated onto the streets outside the stadium. The power of the fans in Italian football should never be under-estimated.

Few players ever dare to make the move across the city with them either being sky-blue or claret for life. The rivalry comes from the moral right to be the one true team to represent the city, as well as how the club's were originally formed. To us mere English fans Roma means Totti, Cafu, Gabriel Batistuta and Christian Panucci. Lazio is Beppe Signori, Ravanelli, Alessandro Nesta, Gazza and Paolo Di Canio. But to Italians, or more importantly Romans, it goes much deeper than that.

Both teams have been through the mill in terms of off the field antics. Back in 1980 SS Lazio were relegated, along with AC Milan after being implicated in a betting scandal. Match-fixing also cost the club dear in 2006 when they were implicated in the Calciopoli scandal that saw Juventus relegated and Lazio excluded from all European competition. Long time club owner

Sergio Cragnotti arrived at the club in 1992 and initially funded some massive transfers (£18m for Veron, £19m for Vieri and £35m for Crespo). But when his Cirio food empire collapsed, so did the club's fortune.

AS Roma were also implicated in the 2006 scandal but have had a bit more of a stable time financially since, although like their cross-town rivals have had to play second fiddle to first the Old Lady of Turin and then the Milan clubs. Every season they've been one player away from a Scudetto-winning side, one decision away from beating their rivals, and one manager away from getting the balance right. Today it's the turn of the Spanish duo Luis Enrique and Ivan De La Pena to try and bring some Barca magic to the side. On the other side of the stadium all of the talk was of Gianfranco Zola arriving on a little white pony to save the club from the management of Edoardo Reja.

Danny was to say the very least, excited. He confessed to me on the way over that he had dreamed about the game all week. In his last vivid encounter we were in a corporate hospitality box at the Stadio Olimpico. He had been reading the small print on our Roma 'Magic Box' which apparently said 'Food is provided, but it's a lottery, please understand that the odd box will only contain a mere goose'. I had no idea what that meant. He had however by now gone Roma Magic Box crazy. We left our Roma umbrellas at home for fear of being immediately singled out as English (as well as our headbands, rucksacks and scarves). In fact we were armed just with our invite as we boarded the football special from Frascati to Roma Termini.

One thirty-minute train ride and we walked out into the Roman sunshine. Nothing screamed 'Derby-Day!' to us. No riot police, no sirens, no fans. Strange. If this was Manchester Piccadilly, Liverpool Lime Street or even Mile End in London on derby day two hours before kickoff there would be chaos. Here, in a country dominated by chaos, there was calm. We hopped in a taxi and went on a nice (but somehow unnecessary) drive through the Villa Borghese (think Hyde Park but with sunglasses and Vespas) before eventually being deposited at the Ponte Duca d'Aosta. This was the bridge that everyone we spoke to had gone out of their way to warn us about.

"Watch your arse on that bridge", "if they clock you're English they'll stab you in the bum," and "they'll throw you in the river if you look foreign" had been a few of the nuggets of info received before we arrived. Thanks for the words of comfort Mum. But all we saw were souvenir sellers and families wandering down towards the stadium. Granted some of the scarves said things like "die, Lazio, die" but even so it was a serene stroll. The reason? Ninety minutes prior to kick off the hardcore fans were already in position in the stadium.

We had to go and pick up our tickets, exchanging our Magic Box voucher (gold plated of course) and we entered the stadium, walked around a bit following a red carpet for VIPs like ourselves which took us back out of the stadium and finally to "Box One", a stall manned by a stunning Italian woman (there is a theme here - bear with me). She checked our ID, slapped each of us a plastic wristband on and ushered us through a gate, where we got to re-enter the stadium on another red carpet lined by stunning blondes in little black dresses. This then led to the same spot where we were standing five minutes previously but because we had our magic wristbands on we were somebodies and not nobodies and became of interest to the ladies who told us, in Italian of course, they would do anything to pleasure us. I'm not sure that was the literal translation but Adam is still learning. We didn't want to ruin our day before the game so we sensibly asked for a raincheck

Surprise number one was that they were serving beer in the stadium. But then again Italians tend to get their highs from caffeine rather than alcohol which probably explained the blanket ban on espresso within a two mile radius of the Stadio Olimpico on match days. The beer wasn't cheap at €8 a pint but it was the real deal so we indulged. There was still thirty-minutes to kick off and the noise was on a par with anywhere I've been in the world, perhaps bar Legia Warsaw. Both ends of the stadium were full and prepped for action. The teams warmed up to incessant whistling and our Magic Box area around us filled up with people wearing their Roma headbands, carrying their Roma rucksacks (undoubtedly with their Roma umbrellas in).

Disappointingly, the 'sell out' that the local papers talked about actually meant that for safety reasons some 15,000 seats would have to remain empty, most of them in the stand opposite us. Quite what the atmosphere would have been like with those extra seats taken was hard to imagine. The club hymn, "Roma, Roma, Roma", started and most of the stadium rose as one. The song was the cue for the pyrotechnics and banners from either side. At some point the teams came out but for us the focus was on the fans and not the players. The time for singing was over.

In our earlier game in Frascati one refereeing decision early in the game essentially decided the result. Across the city a few hours later you could argue the same point.

Just seven minutes were on the clock when the referee made himself the most unpopular man in the stadium (well, with 80% of them anyhow) by sending off Roma keeper Maarten Stekelenburg for a supposed professional foul. The Roma players reacted as if they had been told that hair bands had been banned by FIFA, clutching their faces and running through an impressive display of hand gestures. Off came the brilliant Argentine attacking midfielder Erik Lamela, on came sub keeper Bogdan Lobont to pick Hernanes' penalty out of the back of the net.

Back in 2006 West Ham lost the best ever FA Cup final against Liverpool basically due to one man's poor decision making. That man was on loan full back Lionel Scaloni. His decision to try to hoof a ball up field in the last-minute of injury time when West Ham were winning instead of whacking it into touch cost the Hammers the cup they fully deserved on the day. His clearance went straight to Steven Gerrard and the rest is history. Scaloni never played for the club again and ended up at Lazio, and now here he was fulfilling the role as my pantomime villain for the day. His first act was to get booked for a silly, caught-up-in-the-moment foul on Totti, and then a minute later he was a spectator as Roma's Fabio Borini equalised.

The game was not conforming to the Calcio stereotypes. It was fast-paced, open and chances were coming at both ends. The fans were distracted by the game for once and whilst the noise didn't really abate, the show did. Both sides should have scored again before the break and it was left to the referee to become the common enemy as he dished out four yellows as well as the one red in the opening period.

Half-time meant we had access to a much-anticipated President's Lounge for 'complimentary drinks and food'. After the ridiculous long route we had to take to get to the lounge we had just six minutes to enjoy all of the facilities. The lounge was surrounded by very glamorous hostesses, all dressed in black and all six-foot plus tall as I predicted, although they were upright rather than reclining on beds as I had imagined. They looked on as we tucked into the free wine and what seemed to be bowls of Angel Delight. One wasn't impressed when I asked if they had any Butterscotch flavour. Either that or she didn't understand my literal translation of Burro di Ecoste.

Four glasses of red and three mousses in six minutes is going some but we put on a fine display for Queen and Country before we went back to our seats. The second half seemed much better through a haze of vino rosso and was a genuinely good game. The yellow-card count started to creep up with Stefano Mauri and ex-Manchester United defender Gabriel Heinze going into the referee's book.

Any controversial moment in the game and the crowd reacted as if they had been personally affronted. One chap kept popping up and pointing his finger and thumb at the Lazio fans in a gun gesture, whilst someone behind him kept filming everything on an iPad. Yep, someone had brought their iPad, encased in a lovely Roma leather case of course. Modern football at work.

On the hour came the winning goal. A Lazio free-kick was floated into the area and Mauri sort of turned and stuck out a leg at the same time, diverting the ball home. It had come against the run of play for sure but that's footballing life. If the first eighty-five minutes had been dominated by a very un-Italian style game, then the last five conformed to what we had seen a thousand times on TV with time-wasting, play acting and cards being flashed galore. First was a second yellow for Scaloni (shame that), although Lazio did try to send on a sub at the same time to confuse the officials but referees never fall for that trick do they?

Four other players went into the notebook in the final few minutes including the legendary Totti for a desperate dive. Even his God-like powers didn't sway the officials who saw through his histrionics. The final whistle was greeted with fireworks in the Lazio end and boos all around the rest of the stadium. Two derby defeats to their bitter rivals in the season seem to have ended Roma's Champions League challenge as well.

We headed away from the stadium, disappointed that the ladies who had promised pleasure had now disappeared, again crossing the bridge of doom without any issue at all and back on a tram within ten minutes of the end of the game. For all of the bluster, the city centre was a quiet place as we sipped our €9 beers in Piazza Popolo as the sun set. We could get used to this lifestyle and we were soon 'ciao'-ing everyone who wandered past our table.

Back to the centre of swing in the countryside, we found time for a nightcap or three in the town square, and reflected on an excellent weekend of fine food, fine wine, fine football and above all, first class hospitality from Mr. Lloyd. Tomorrow would be a painful day in the office for many a Roma fan like Adam, but they would live to fight another day.

Sometimes Italy is hard to love, with the crazy politics, bureaucracy and above all the way they drive, but the history, the way of life and above all the football more than makes up for this. Any Football Tourist worth their salt should make at least one pilgrimage to the home of Calcio every few years.

There was only one topic for discussion on the plane home. Which derby would be next on our list?

Turin?

Moscow?

Belgrade?

Hmmmm, Belgrade...

Now that would be a trip and a half. If only we could get a team together and find someone who lived in Belgrade to act as our guide.

Chapter Thirteen

Slav to the Rhythm

Four games plus one Eternal Derby

4th May 2012
HD Zagreb 1 NK Radnik 1
Stadion NŠC Stjepan Spajic

Lokomotiv Zagreb 2 Lucko 2
Maksimir Park

5th May 2012
OFK Belgrade 2 Metalac GM 0
Stadion OFK

Partizan Belgrade 0 Red Star Belgrade 1
Partizan Stadium

6th May 2012
FK Belgrade 2 PBK 2
Stadion FK

"...we had no option but to seek refuge in the executive
boxes, within seconds the whole crowd had joined us..."

It's 1am and the train's grinding on the rough rails is keeping me awake. We are chugging along somewhere between Zagreb and Belgrade. We could be in Croatia, we could we be in Serbia. It's possible we may have popped over the border into Bosnia. But we actually have no idea at all where we are. Mobile phone coverage died a few hours ago and the windows steamed up long ago thanks to the hot air four slightly drunk Englishmen produce as well as the thermostat being stuck on a toasty 24 degrees. Conversations have moved on from how this train is like the one in the film Hostel, to how many tourists get robbed at gunpoint on these things according to Trip Advisor. Just the kind of conversations you want to have when you are in one of the remotest places in Europe with no mobile phone signal.

The single five-watt bulb is too dim for me to read so I'm forced to amuse myself by playing Angry Birds on my phone. Trying to sleep is pointless. The compartment is too hot, I am suffering from a chest infection, the bed is too high (sleeping on the top bunk suffering from vertigo isn't funny), and the room stinks like blokes who've been on the beer all day generally smell - pretty awful. Added to these issues is the fact that at any moment armed border guards will demand to see our passport for the fourth time, sleep is pointless.

Quite how and why we ended up on a train that would have put a British Rail football special after West Ham, Millwall and Chelsea had travelled on it in First Class is still unclear. As usual I blame Danny Last and as usual, I'm right to. It's normally his fault. He saw a YouTube video, and that is always how these things start/snowball.

"Stu, look at this video, it's the maddest local derby of all time. We HAVE to be at this one next season."

That's a fairly typical email from one junkie to another.

Before you know it there are more with links to flight times, hotels that are "just perfect" and suchlike. Then we're at Gatwick airport at 4am with a pint of Guinness for breakfast waiting for a 6am flight to a place some rational people had never heard of, let alone visited. Spakenburg, Łodz, Trnava, Coxyde, Amiens. You name a town in a European backwater with a football team and it is more than likely that we have turned up there at some point, or at the very least have plans to do so soon.

But this trip was different. Not one crazy derby but two. In two days. In two countries. Two plus two equals? Four sets of fanatical fans. In theory. As well as a third day to try and find another game(s) for. And to make it even more 'interesting' we were entering a land that had been torn apart by Europe's biggest civil war, acting as a 21st century football seeking squad of Peacekeepers (of sorts).

Earlier in the season the seeds had been sown by Andy Hudson, who had blagged his way into the Belgrade derby at the Red Star stadium. He enthused about the atmosphere, the fireworks and flares, the songs, the chanting, oh, and the football wasn't bad either. This man knows his football and after he said we HAD to be at the return game, we begrudgingly agreed. Begrudgingly in our vocabulary actually translates to "Yes of course we will come but have to find the right moment to ask our respective wives".

So after making another withdrawal from the PSF fund (Petrol Station Flowers), I had my visa for travel approved by the Current Mrs. Fuller. She was a bit worried about this one though. She too had seen Hostel and seen how easily led the three chaps were by scantily clad women. But I was able to reassure her about safety in numbers as well as learn the Serbian word for stranger that I would shout loudly whilst pointing if anyone like Serbian female tennis ace Ana Ivanovic started getting their kit off on the train to lure us anywhere.

As a further safety measure we recruited a fourth pair of hands. You have to do these trips in pairs you see. When you walk down the mean streets of Spakenburg you need the reassurance of a hand of a friend. So what if people think you are a couple? You know you aren't. Girls hold hands all the time, so why shouldn't us boys? You need a bit of reassurance that everything will be alright just as you see that big mob of Dynamo Dresden fans with sticks marching towards you. So along with Danny and Andy, Kenny Legg completed our foursome. Kenny Legg. A man who literally carries the hopes of tinpot adventures in Non League on his blog's shoulders. Belgrade's gain would be Weymouth's loss for a weekend as Mr. Legg took the place by metaphorical storm.

The plan for these trips always takes the same format. Let's go to game X...oh hang on, if we go a day earlier we can get to game Y...whoa, hold on. Just 100 miles away the following day is game Z. So our initial plan for a weekend of football in Belgrade took a turn for the better when it was discovered that 'just over the border' was another local derby. Zagreb. Capital of Croatia. Home of the famous "Bad Blue Boys" of Dinamo Zagreb, Antonija Mišura and Slavan Bilic, although there's only one of those three you'd fancy meeting down a dark alley. Sounds perfect you may say. Indeed but the main Zagreb derby between NK and Dinamo was of course moved from Friday to Saturday for broadcast live on Croatian TV when we'd already be in Belgrade.

Not to worry Danny reassured us, because the other derby, Lokomotiv Zagreb v Lucko, was still in the diary for Friday night and it was to be played in the 38,000 capacity national stadium (home of Dinamo) the Maksimir. Unfortunately, Lokomotiv aren't exactly a big draw in terms of attracting the locals with an average attendance of 259, meaning there would be more fans at Harrogate Railway Athletic v Wakefield being played 800 miles away in the Evostik Premier League at the same time. In fact, the average attendance in the Croatia's top division, Prva HNL, is currently less than 2,000 so it is more Blue Square than Premier League, except the winners of this get the chance to play in the Champions League.

This was not going to be my first visit to Zagreb. If you listen to the stories of the Current Mrs. Fuller she would have you believe that I nearly died the last time I was there back in October 2006. It was never an issue. I mean walking along the road, wearing full England kit (it's a long story that did involve my actually playing football and not just looking like a full kit wanker) towards a few hundred strong group of the most fanatic Croatian fans whilst saying things down the end of a phone like "Oh shit, we are going to die" and "The will is in the box under the bed", before I dropped my phone and it stopped working - who would really take that seriously? Granted, when I couldn't answer the phone for the next three hours and with the TV pictures of the crowd trouble prior to the game filtering through, it may have been a bit worrying, but surely an over-reaction on her part, no?

Danny, Kenny and Andy decided to head out to Croatia on Thursday to visit the zoo or something. So by the time I landed at teatime on Friday they had already immersed themselves in the local culture. It appeared that the Croatian Kuna had taken a bit of a tumble recently that meant we were literally beer millionaires. The chaps had laid on a car for me to be whisked straight from the airplane steps to the Stadion NŠC Stjepan Spajic where our first game of the weekend was being held. What's not to like about that. Unfortunately my request for a brunette driver with smouldering eyes must have got lost in translation as she was a he, the wrong side of 30 (by about

200%) and his eyes were pure evil. But he delivered me almost in one piece at the ground so I can thank my lucky stars for that, especially surviving his tactic of waiting until traffic lights had turned red before accelerating through them. Match one of the escapade was here.

I had pitched up in Zagreb that Friday afternoon, starry-eyed and looking for adventures. And beer. You have to remember that the only thing more important than the football on these trips is a beer. And of course we had won the beeromillion conversion rate lottery. Danny, Kenny and Andy were already in position at our first football game of the weekend, a cheeky little encounter between NK Hrvartski Dragovoljac and NK Radnik at the Stadion NŠC Stjepan Spajic. With the sun shining we raised a glass to our colleagues back in England, still working, still getting wet.

As we sat outside the clubhouse we got some funny looks from the locals. It seemed we had somehow been transported back to the Eighties with shell-suits all the rage. And with our logoed t-shirts, designer ripped jeans (we were too mean to replace them when they tore more like) and sunglasses we appeared to come from a different generation, which of course we did - it was called the present day.

But the main difference was that we didn't have a bum bag on. You know, what the Americans call a fanny pack (chuckle) and wonder why everyone laughs at them. It seemed they were fashion in these parts. All the trendy youngsters had them, whilst the older generation went for the washbag style of accessory, once made trendy by English goalkeepers such as Ray Clemence and Fraser Digby. Kenny loved them so much he vowed to set up a new business that would bring goalkeeper man-bags to the masses.

Obviously, being the type of men who looked like they had just stepped off the pages of GQ or Nuts (2012 not 1987 editions), we were getting quite a bit of attention from the Croatian WAGS. Obviously they were lured to the game by the huge floodlights, club branded popcorn and Andy Hudson. It's always about Andy Hudson, so he would have us believe. Or it simply could've been that they were waitresses, we had a thirst like there was no tomorrow and they saw us as one big tip.

This was third tier Croatian football, probably the equivalent in skill and resources to our step 6 or 7. The Stadion NŠC Stjepan Spajic had one stand plus a strange Meccano structure behind one goal. Around a hundred or so fans had come to watch this early evening game, a perfect start to a weekend in anyone's book. For some bizarre reason beer wasn't allowed through the main gate despite the game being visible through the chain fence from our table. So no great surprises where we watched most of the game from...

It finished one-all and whilst our waitresses Ana and Mija urged us to stay having seen what a winner they were on to in the tips department, we had a derby to get to. THE derby I should say. It's not every day a Zagreb derby is in town (apart from tomorrow of course). As we rode in our taxi we laughed at everyone back home, getting ready for a weekend of depressing rain, lots and lots of rain.

The taxi driver dropped us right outside the ground. There didn't seem to be many fans around. Correction, there didn't seem to be ANY fans around. Had we, and by we I mean Danny, got this all wrong? Apparently not. We spotted a ticket booth open and purchased our seats, numbered 3 to 6. The game was due to start in fifteen minutes. Do you get the idea yet that football in these parts isn't really a spectator sport at these levels? Perhaps if I explained a bit about the current state of football here you may understand why Premier League clubs like Lokomotiv average crowds of 581.

If you thought that Scottish or Portuguese football was dominated by just two or three teams, then welcome to Croatia and Serbia. Their leagues have been completely dominated by just two teams since the breakup of the Yugoslavian state in 1991. Hadjuk Split and Dinamo Zagreb in Croatia, Partizan and Red Star in Serbia. Those four have won every title bar two in the last twenty years and guess what? This season the titles had already gone to Dinamo and Partizan respectively, with several rounds still left to play.

But surely there was still some interest in the other games being played? Obviously not as we grabbed our beers and headed into the main stand in the Maksimir. Everything was very blue. We could tell that as only around 100 of the 38,000 seats in the stadium had a human bum on them. With the early evening sun still shining, thirty-pence beers in hand and some football about to start, what could be better? Coming into the game, Lucko were the form team yet Danny managed to gets odds of 6/1 on an away victory. What could possibly go wrong?

What indeed. Despite an early trade of goals by M Pejic (surely not Mike Pejic, the Everton, Stoke and Villa full back who would now be past 60 years old?) for Lucko and then Marcelo Brozovic for Lokomotiv, this wasn't the best of games. In fact I'd rather have been watching Stoke City, that's the measure of how bad it was. As the half progressed then the darkest cloud in the world slowly drifted over the stadium. Rain threatening? Nah. It would blow over surely. We were in the middle of a heat wave after all.

Fifteen minutes into the second half Lucko took the lead again. Nikola Rak turned the ball in and Danny was sitting on a pot of cash. In fact he could literally claim to be a Croatian billionaire as long as they held on for 30 more minutes. Once again Lokomotiv came back at them and ten minutes later Škvorc equalised. It was now anyone's game. That big black cloud had got bigger and blacker and was now right overhead. Just as Kenny and Andy had been dispatched on beer duty the rain started to fall. A downpour quickly turned into a deluge, which soon gave way to a torrent and then a monsoon. Bet those back at home were jealous now.

We had no option but to seek refuge in the empty executive boxes. In fact, within seconds the whole crowd had jumped into the VIP area. That was all except Kenny and Andy who came back into the stand and were greeted by thousands of rows of empty seats. Oh how we all laughed until we realised that it was our pints that were become more watered down than a Fosters at the Oval.

With the rain turning the pitch into a boating lake neither team could actually do anymore than hoof the ball up front. Danny thought he had sewn up his winnings when Lucko broke three-on-one and with the goal gaping in front of centre-forward, Rak the winger crossed the ball for him to tap home.

But the ball never reached him, sitting instead in a puddle on the penalty spot.

It was difficult to see who was angrier - Danny or the Lucko centre-forward. Full-time meant honours even but not for us band of explorers. The rain was still pouring down and the sky-line of Zagreb was being lit up with flashes of lightning. We didn't fancy moving on just yet, especially as we were dressed for the beach rather than the rainforest. We made our way down to the concourse and tried to find the Magic Door to get onto the pitch. We didn't have to look too hard and just a few minutes after the game ended we were cavorting around the Recaro seats in the dugout.

Finally the rain stopped and we were able to make our way back into the city centre, via a couple of local bars. The Belgrade train left at 23:53 so we stocked up on provisions for the journey. Six beers each and a Mars bar. What else could a man possibly need?

Fast-forward seven hours. Our carriage is bathed in sunshine, streaming through the window and lighting up Andy's arse like a beacon. We have arrived in Belgrade. At some point in the night we awoke to find two policemen with machine guns and dogs in our carriage but assumed that was something to do with the smell. If only the aroma could be bottled and sold on the markets of Essex we would be real millionaires.

Despite being one of the most uncomfortable nights I'd ever had, I was reluctant to get down from my bunk. There were two reasons for this. Firstly, I have a fear of heights and whilst I had got up into the roof space quite easy last night, I had the aid of six cans of Croatian beer. Now, hung-over, I wasn't moving. Add to that the fact at some point in the night I'd removed my pants and was stark-bollock naked under my sheet. Still, I'm sure the toga look would be perfect for a bright and sunny Serbian day.

Eventually I managed to get down after Kenny found a ladder in his bed (he had bitterly complained throughout the night that he was uncomfortable). I got dressed and prepared for the longest day of my life. It was 6.30am as we slowly pulled into Belgrade main station. As we emerged from our smelly compartment it seemed as if we were the male meat in an all-female sandwich, groups of young American girls filtering from the compartments either side of us. If only we'd have known.

Saying that, we'd have done nothing different.

Andy had been to Belgrade a few months previously and had met up with a fellow Newcastle United fan called Nenad. Now here was the Serbian Man Mountain giving up his Saturday to be our guide in this wonderful historic city. The man could easily body-double for Hagrid if they ever fancied doing a Serbian remake of Harry Potter and the Derby Tickets. He guided us through the essentials such as taking £80 out of the cash-point and not the £8 we had just withdrawn, how to avoid ticket inspectors on the trams and buses, and of course how to find magic doors in Serbian football grounds. The first stop on our beginner's tour of Belgrade was a ground just to wet our appetite. The home of FK Rad in the Belgrade suburbs to be pre-cise. Second stop, his house to sate that very appetite with a spread laid on by his mum that was just outstanding.

This was hospitality of the top order. His mother couldn't speak any English yet made sure we were fed watered and fed again before going out on the beers. Breakfast had more meat than you could shake a stick at, homemade grape brandy and something called 'Lazy Pie' which filled a hole the size of Greece's Euro debt. With only a few hours sleep and now a full stomach to work with, a nap was very much on the cards. But we had no time for such necessities, we had an itinerary to follow.

Everything you have heard about Belgrade is true. Yes, the women are stunning. Yes, the city still shows scars from the conflicts twenty years ago. Yes, beer is indeed £1.20 a bottle. We sat on the terrace of the Kalemegdan Citadel for a few hours discussing eighties music, life in Serbia and of course football, before Andy's pasty northern chest couldn't take it anymore and he went and sat in the shade. Culture and sightseeing is all very good but football is better, and a short cab ride later in a 20-year-old Lada saw us deposited at the OFK Stadion. 400 Serbian Dinar (£2.80) later and we were ready for our first slice of Serbian Super League action.

Mid-table v bottom in most top leagues in Europe may generate a few thousand fans but in Serbia there really is only Partizan and Red Star. Despite only being a few points off a Europa League space there were less than 100 fans in the crumbling 19,000 capacity Omladinski stadium here to watch OFK. The club actually played in the Europa League in 2010 in the stadium which shows the farcical nature of ground-grading in England. A stadium where there were no floodlights, no food facilities and unsafe weed-ridden terraces was deemed safe by UEFA who allowed Galatasaray to travel here in the 3rd qualifying round and win 5-1 in front of over 6,000 fans.

But today in the sunshine there was about 60 here, and apart from a dozen or so noisy home fans it seemed like the only atmosphere came from the toilet block in the corner that should have been condemned a long time ago. I have no idea how clubs can make money at this level. Gate receipts could not have topped £250, so who pays the players, the officials et al? There wasn't even a club shop selling OFK slippers.

We needed to get some food before the big game as there was little chance of anything being available in the Partizan Stadium. Fortunately Nenad knew just the spot, on a major roundabout just down the road from Stadion OFK. Whilst you could hardly call it appealing from the outside, the food was out of this world and we shared our tea with a couple of Serbian policemen who obviously knew a thing or two about where to eat.

Enough of the foreplay, it was time for the real action to start. One of the biggest and most volatile derbies in the world waits for no man. Another trusty Lada took us far as a sane man would go and then we were on our own. Andy and Nenad set off towards the away end, whilst Danny, Kenny and I followed the home fans along the motorway. The police cordon was set some distance from the ground and once we had passed through the lines of Robocops we were on our own. To our left the floodlights of Red Star's stadium peered down on the crowd as we hiked up the hill towards the chaos and madness ahead.

Let's face it, who wouldn't have wanted to be in the thick of thousands of fanatical fans holding up their flares and bouncing up and down on your seats? Well, having suffered with a chest infection for a week, it wasn't the wisest idea for me to be taking in huge lung-full's of acrid smoke, but that's why God created Amoxicillin right? Once you have experienced the atmosphere at one of these games you cannot wait for your next fix. It's like a drug and your dealer is Danny Last.

Partizan had won the league the previous week and had agreed to keep any celebrations low-key in such a tinderbox atmosphere. Fat chance of that with the fans organising their own celebration with banners mocking their opponents as well as more than a few digs at their own manager, the loveable, laugh-a-minute Avram Grant, and by digs I mean coins, lighters and kitchen sinks being thrown at him as he exited the pitch at half-time. Poor old Avram. How we miss your wonderful cheery personality and clueless tactics in East London. It is good to see your tactics are as popular overseas as they were back in England.

The game itself wasn't a classic. In fact in line with much of our football this weekend, it was a shocker. Neither team could improve their league position and so with Champions League qualification already sorted for the pair of them, it became a bit of a bore draw, only livened up by the antics of the fans at either end. In fact you could have quite easily suggested (as we did) that a 0-0 draw had been agreed beforehand just to keep all of the natives happy.

Just as the second-half started, an old chap to our left passed us a flare and lit it for us. If you have ever shot a gun (in a controlled environment I hasten to add) you will know the feeling of doing something very dangerous and very naughty. That's how it felt holding the firework aloft in your hand. It started burning down and then I started to panic - what do I do with it when it burns out? The pitch was too far away to safely throw it but it was starting to get hot. Very hot. I looked at Kenny and he just shrugged his shoulders. I threw it on the floor and stamped on it, getting some strange looks from the home fans around me who were launching theirs at the Red Star players.

The game was nowhere near as exciting as the antics surrounding it. The Red Star fans must have been getting chilly as they started a few fires, using the Partizan seats as kindling. We should have put our shirts on the goalless draw. But then just as we were looking forward to a quiet night in the city centre, Red Star's Cadu popped up and scored in the third minute of injury time. To say the place went mad is a bit of an understatement. All of a sudden the Red Star fans flowed onto the running track, mobbing the players. The brave referee tried to get them back to restart the game but after a few more seconds of play, he called time on proceedings and ran for cover.

Cue more celebrations from the Red Star players in front of their fans. It was as if they had won the league rather than just the bragging rights for the last meeting of the season. Players, some now almost stripped naked by the fans, sprinted for the tunnel and the away fans decided to set fire to a few more seats to celebrate for good measure.

Again, organisation outside the stadium was quietly efficient and we saw not a hint of any trouble as passionate fans were kept well apart. In fact within thirty minutes of the final whistle we were back in a bar in the city centre with Red Star's biggest fans, Nenad and of course Andy Hudson. A few more £2 beers (we were paying the premium for drinking in the Irish Bar by this point) and it was time to bid Belgrade a good night, ready for what tomorrow would throw at us. We could've headed for the flesh-pots of the city but once you've been to Cleopatra's in Huddersfield, you've seen everything there is to see in that department.

Day three of our Balkan adventure began after a welcome night's sleep in the hotel with a civilised breakfast of Serbian meats, Serbian cheese and Serbian beer. It was voting day in the Serbian elections and the chatter in the dining room was of power sharing, election rigging and ballot boxes. Our choice of candidate was chosen on looks alone, although we then discovered her husband was on trial at The Hague for war crimes so we quickly removed our rosettes and hoped that politics was the winner instead. For us it was more football (but of course it was), starting off with a field trip to watch FK Belgrade in the third division.

We hailed a taxi, of course a Lada, and handed the driver a scrap of paper with the address of where we believed FK Belgrade's home ground was. Twenty minutes later and we were deposited in the sunshine in a quiet residential street. A strange place for a football stadium but as we were quickly learning, Belgrade did things in its own way.

There are few grounds in the world where there is little point in charging people to get in. This is one. At either end of the ground were tall blocks of flats offering perfect views of the game to any residents. On one side was a grass bank where at the top, through a magic door of course, came fans in their droves for this Sunday morning game. This was level three in Serbian football and if I was going to have to compare it to anywhere in England, Whitehawk from the Ryman League would come to mind, although 'caravan park' doesn't really translate well in Serbian.

The officials led the teams out of a little house in the corner of the ground. Hang about, here was a first - a female referee and a linesman. The latter certainly pulled off the whole woman-in-football-kit look so desired by Sepp Blatter from our vantage point. All three officials (and let's big up Mr Linesman here too) allowed the game to flow and it was certainly an enjoyable Sunday morning run out.

Apart from a makeshift wooden structure that could seat three old chaps, everyone else stood up. I couldn't see the logic in this - the grass was dry, it was in the sunshine and soon enough those English fools were lolling around on the floor. Of course, they knew best. I went to stand up and all of a sudden my feet disappeared from beneath me and I slid on my arse down to the foot of the bank. Not only did the whole crowd circa of 40 people, but the players and officials turn to see what the commotion was. My five minutes of Serbian fame had arrived. Thanks to Kenny and Danny who helped me immensely by taking pictures of my predicament.

The game burst to life in the second-half as both sides decided that defending was optional. I could give you blow-by-blow details of who scored when and where but you don't really care, do you. Could we fit anther game in? Of course we could. The EFW handbook states that we had an obligation to try (section 15:2:3 covering visits to new cities), so before you could say 'this is madness' we were off, hailing down a taxi (going upmarket this time in a Skoda) to take us across the city, where somewhere in the suburbs third division Zârkovo were tantalisingly taking on Radnicki Obrenova.

So off we went, driving past the new bridges over the rivers that were destroyed by the NATO bombs in the early Nineties, waving a cheery 'hello' at the World Rowing Championships ("Go Team GB" or something) before the taxi driver turned to us with a confused look. He simply couldn't find the ground. "That's no problem - we can ask Google Maps". Oh how this one decision would bite me on the arse later.

I located the ground, paid the cab and went in search of game number six of our Balkan adventure. Except game number six wasn't there. Nothing was there. The ground was just empty. Uncle Google had let us down...or had he? There was another ground just 5 minutes away according to my phone and so we walked. And walked. Half an hour later we were no nearer seeing game six of the weekend. It seemed for the first time ever we would miss a game because we couldn't find the ground. Instead we headed for lunch and to formulate a plan B.

Over a fantastic Italian banquet we seriously discussed the viability of hiring a car and heading into Bosnia for the Sarajevo derby. It was 'only' 220 miles but looking at various websites such as 'the world's worst road', 'highways of death' and 'things to do to bring certain death', it seemed that the drive may be problematic. I wasn't keen, particularly being the only driver in the group, and I made sure I quickly downed a couple of beers so that my over the limit excuse would be valid. Not that would make much difference judging by the standard of driving I had seen since arriving.

Plan C was a visit to Red Star's Marakana stadium, the spiritual home of football in what used to be Yugoslavia. Once the stadium literally shook to the sound of over 100,000 fans on regular occasions, making it one of the most intimidating places for visiting teams to come to. The infamous Busby Babes team played their final game before the Munich Air Crash here in 1958, the 1973 European Cup final played here saw the legendary Ajax team beat Juventus and in 1976 it hosted the finals of the European Championship, won by Czechoslovakia.

But it was closed.

Closed is not a word in our vocabulary. Just ask the question is our mantra and finally we found a man to approach. Everyone and everything has a price in Belgrade and ours was 1,000 Dinars (£8.33) between us, and for that the door not only to the stadium, but also the press area and the Executive lounges swung wide open.

So what does one do when you have got into a ground? Try to get into another of course, and so we set off down and then up the hill to Partizan's stadium. The two stadiums are separated by about 500 yards in one of the closest top-level rivalries in European football, alongside Afan Lido/Port Talbot Town, Dundee/Dundee United and Shortwood United/Forest Green Rovers. The clean-up operation was in full effect from the night before and so we decided it was beer o'clock and headed into the courtyard adjoining the ground. Hello, what's this? Of course another magic door, and even a guide to boot who didn't need a top up on his pension and let us in.

As we left the stadium we saw a troop of players leaving the changing rooms all kitted up. Partizan Under 18s, no less, off to play a game in the Military Stadion just down the road. Well, it would be rude not to drop in on that one, although we have no idea who they were playing and what the score was, although we saw them score seven goals in little more than forty-five minutes so I'm guessing they won.

The rest of the day was spent wandering the sites of the city, beer, some Serbian food, beer, a little rest, beer and so on until that 4am airport wake-up call drew us back to the hotel for that over-rated sleep thing. To see buildings that had been destroyed by NATO's bombing raids twenty years ago standing (just) side-by-side with five-star hotels and famous name retail outlets is a surreal but sobering sight. Serbia had been a fantastic experience, with hospitable people, prices to make you rub your eyes and a derby day experience that is up there with the best in the world. More please. Belgrade is now officially the new footballing Munich.

Chapter Fourteen

The Boys From Brazil
Original and blue

26th July 2012
Honduras 2 Morocco 2

Japan 1 v 0 Spain
Hampden Park

28th July 2012
Cowdenbeath 1* Alloa Athletic 1
Central Park

29th July 2012
Egypt 1 New Zealand 1

Belarus 1 Brazil 3
Old Trafford

"...due to safety precautions for motor sports, high fences
and a track separated the paying fans from the pitch..."

And so just 7 years and 3 weeks since London were awarded the XXX Summer Olympiad at the IOC conference in Singapore, the Olympics were upon us. After years of debate about whether the venues would be ready, whether any tourists could actually afford a hugely inflated hotel room, whether anyone actually had tickets and whether our already over-stressed transport system could cope, the time for talking was over. While the moaners still had plenty of ammo to do what moaners do, one overriding feeling had swept the country - how could anyone in Great Britain not be excited by eighteen days featuring the world's greatest athletes, competing in some of the world's greatest sporting venues?

My family was among the lucky ones. We had tickets for a number of events, including some for the opening day of the men's competition. Whisper it quietly, but the London Olympics didn't actually start with the multi-million pound Danny Boyle directed opening ceremony in the new Olympic Stadium in Stratford, but actually some fifty hours earlier in Wales. At 4pm on Wednesday 25th July 2012 in the Millennium Stadium, Cardiff, Team GB ladies football team took on New Zealand in the first event of the XXX Olympiad. Even the official Olympic website suggested the games start on the 27th July, as if someone was embarrassed by the fact that football even existed in the games or perhaps more presciently, that to some football was still thought of as an outsider.

It was hardly a surprise that virtually every game in the Olympic football tournament not featuring Team GB had struggled to sell tickets. I argued on my website in the year prior to the games about the logic in using such big stadiums in the far flung areas of the United Kingdom. In fact I actually felt that this was the London Olympics and so with plenty of stadiums in the capital that had more than enough seats, it was pointless to use these stadiums in other cities, and in the case of Glasgow and Cardiff, different countries. Upton Park (35,000), The Valley (27,000), White Hart Lane (36,000), The Emirates (60,000), The New Den (20,000) and, of course, The Matchroom Stadium (9,000) are all first class football grounds within a twenty-minute Boris-bike cyle ride of the Olympic Park.

The romantic minority told me that the residents of Newcastle, Glasgow and Cardiff would flock to watch the likes of Honduras, Morocco, Belarus and Gabon because it was the Olympics. But just two weeks before the Games were due to start the

London Olympic Games Organising Committee took the decision to remove over 500,000 unsold tickets for the football tournament from sale and simply close down parts of the stadiums, obviously making sure that the TV-facing seats were full. It was too late to argue the merits of using smaller grounds in or closer to London for the football (Reading, Southampton, Brighton for instance in addition to the ones already mentioned), but it still leaves a bad taste in the mouth that such a logical outcome was ignored.

But hang on.

There was a massive up side to the flawed logic. At least for me anyway. By playing the games in the four corners of the United Kingdom (and Coventry), public interest was limited. This meant, happily, tickets were easy to come by so I of course indulged. A double header in Glasgow as part of a Fuller Family jolly to Scotland, and a game at Wembley seemed just the very things. At least prior to the draw being made there was some mystery as to what games I would be going to see, so there was the added lure of lucking into one of the big boys.

I had also secured Press Accreditation for the Games. The process had been arduous but I felt very pleased on the day I went to LOGOC and picked up my ID and free pink 'Access All Areas' Oyster card. Just one problem - I had been accredited for football at Old Trafford only. Hardly a short hop away on the DLR, or anywhere my new Oyster card was valid for. If nothing else it was a talking point, especially when it appeared on the UK Border force screens when I had my passport scanned on re- entering the UK a few months prior to the Games. I could tell the Border guard was impressed as he raised half an eyebrow. Visible signs of emotion with these guys is a sign of weakness and who knows what chaos could ensue if they drop their guard for just one second and smile.

The football draw almost passed me by until I saw a byline on the BBC website saying that Team GB was a nailed on cert to meet Brazil in the final after an easy Group Stage draw. Already having tickets for football before finding out that you will be seeing that at the end of the tournament (as that is what would definitely happen) is like Christmas Day in Fuller Towers. Our other presents had also now been unwrapped and I was going to be ringside for Morocco v Honduras and Spain v Japan in Glasgow. Not too shabby, although the game at Wembley was a real potential stinker in Gabon v South Korea. Nobody would want to see that even caught up in the full throws of heady Olympic excess, would they?

A chance to see Spain wasn't to be scoffed at. As well as seeing the World and (twice) European Champions I'd also be seeing Brazil when I headed to Old Trafford for my press assignment. Perhaps football wasn't such a bad idea at the Games after all, I may not be the average punter but few would be disappointed with what lay ahead, at least in theory.

Despite my frequent trips north of the border, Hampden Park had never featured on the radar for a match (great tour and even better museum as I had previously discovered) so when it was announced that games would be held in the Scottish National Stadium it was too good an opportunity to miss, especially as tickets to any events in the proper Olympic venues were impossible to get. One thing you could not complain about was value for money. Four tickets for a double-header of international football cost just £61. Hotel rooms in Edinburgh were offering special deals and to top it all off, the weekend would see the opening round of the Scottish League Cup, sponsored by Ramsden's the Pawnbrokers (the glamour). There was an endless choice of games within an hour of Edinburgh but one tie stood out. As I was heading to see the boys from Brazil at Old Trafford on Sunday, it would be poetic to see the Blue Brazil the day before. Cowdenbeath it was then.

So come the last week of July when everyone else left London for the beaches of the Med, we swapped a mini-heat wave in the South East for a dreary grey mist of Edinburgh. Welcome to the Scottish Summer. We headed to our home for the next few days at Edinburgh Park before getting into our Olympic clobber and catching the train to Glasgow. There didn't seem to be much Olympic spirit on display around the centre of Glasgow apart from one of the mascots in a kilt. Even the signs pointed the way to the '2012 Summer Games', not the Olympics. But as we arrived at the bus station for our free shuttle service to Hampden Park, it seemed like the locals were getting into it. The buses were full of people dressed up for the football and some excellent organisation ensured that they left every ten minutes. However, traffic management in the city hadn't been properly thought through and soon enough the lines of buses were sitting stuck in the city centre traffic. No sign of an Olympic Lane here.

Eventually we reached the drop-off point close to Hampden. For all of the fuss of the branding police out in force in London, it seemed as if they couldn't find their way north of the border as numerous unofficial outlets were selling Olympic branded items as well as more traditional football tat. Ubiquitous 'See You Jimmy' wigs with fake ginger hair seemed to be selling like hot cakes among the Japanese fans whilst one stall had an array of scarves for those random Mauritius, Serbian and Taiwan football fans that had strayed down to Hampden.

So, to the good bit. Sense had prevailed and despite originally saying that there would be no ticket sales on the day of the games, the local organising committee had released seats that were being sold on the gates (well, next to the gates) for £20. The bad bit came after you bought a ticket and tried to head into the stadium. It was a nightmare. We had arrived after kick-off in the first game, Honduras v Morocco, so there were no queues at the turnstiles. Fifteen minutes later we finally entered the stadium. A ridiculous system was in place where you had to empty all of your pockets into huge plastic bags, and then go through a manual search and examination of the contents in your bag, before having to empty the bags again the other side. Once you had done this, in a space just big enough to swing a cat, you could enter the stadium. Trying to pick odd coins out of a bag that's four foot deep is not the easiest job in the world, but to have a child trying to do it and then falling into their bag isn't exactly health and safety compliant. Still, once in we had finally made it to the XXX Olympiad. So how to celebrate? What about four pies and two Cokes? Sure, no problem, that will be just the £17.50 please sir.

sigh

As international matches go, this was an absolute cracker. It is fair to say that most of the 36,000 (or marginally less as people were still trying to get into the stadium) were in their seats ready for the Spain v Japan game. But this was a great hors d'oeuvre. Two attack-minded teams, a couple of cracking goals and one of those absolutely ridiculous red cards that we all cry out about but secretly love.

Morocco were already one goal to the good when we finally sat down. The atmosphere was unusual to say the least. There was an undercurrent of chatter, an expectant buzz. It was still hard to feel you were part of the Olympic Games but there was a markedly different feeling to a normal football match. At half time there were some half-hearted attempts to get us in the Olympic spirit, but it didn't really work for us (never been a huge

Mexican waver). Unfortunately all the talk was still of the 'Opening Ceremony' tomorrow, whilst we were sitting here secretly already part of the greatest show on earth.

The second half saw Honduras attack our end of the stadium. Soon after the break they overturned the one goal deficit with two goals from New England Revolution's recently announced Designated Player Jerry Bengtson, the first with an assist by Wigan Athletic's Maynor Figueroa and the second from the penalty spot after an off-the-ball incident had been seen by the linesman. The Hondurans had endured a torrid time in Beijing four years ago, losing all of their games but had bounced back to qualify by beating arch political rivals El Salvador, Panama and Trinidad & Tobago on their way to Glasgow. The Moroccans didn't stay behind for long though as Zakaria Labyad somehow managed to get the ball out of his tangled feet and find the perfect chip over the Honduran keeper from the edge of the box. It was a goal that would have been talked about for weeks in the Premier League, yet here it barely got a replay on the big screen before another 'shout' went out over the speakers to start a Mexican wave.

Five minutes later Morocco's other Zakaria, Racing Club Lens's Bergdich, was given a straight red for reacting to a late challenge and completely over-reacting by pushing a Honduran player in the face, who of course himself over-reacted by going down quicker than a working girl in Amsterdam. The game lost some of its momentum after Bergdich's departure with neither side prepared to risk losing their point, although Morocco's star man, Al-Arabi's Houssine Kharja, continued to look capable of winning the game right up until the last kick.

So honours even after game one and time for the hyped 'interval show', which involved a Scottish pipe band, some big Olympic footballs being thrown into the crowd and Muse blaring out on the PA. Personally, my highlight was watching the groundsmen expertly mow the grass, putting a different pattern in from the first match, which based on some of the rubbish sports already in the Games, would be a highly competitive, very watchable and skilful new Olympic sport.

With nothing else going on, our attention was drawn to the flags hanging from the roof. After the faux-pas at the previous evening's Olympic football games over the wrong Korean flag being used, it appeared that the US flag was hanging the wrong way round. Or so we all thought. We put the question out on Twitter and the debate raged for quite a while. It turned out that the US one was correctly hung despite looking quite odd, but the Uruguayan, Canadian and United Kingdom ones weren't. Oops. And before we knew it, it was time for the main course.

When the final whistle blew in Hampden there was certainly one person from the Spanish camp who was living up to the nickname of the side. La Furia Roja (the furious red) was an apt title for Coach Luis Milla who had seen his team show all the attacking intent of a sloth. Whilst we have come to expect the slow, patient build up play of the Spanish, the young side demonstrated none of the killer instinct that the seniors had done in the final of Euro2012 against Italy just a few weeks previously. To say the crowd was stunned was an understatement. They had come to be entertained by the young masters and instead had seen them out-passed by the Samurai Blue.

Despite starting in typical Spanish patient passing style they simply failed to move the ball into the danger areas. Japan slowly started to push forward, realising this wasn't the European Champions Spain but a mere shadow of their namesakes. They demonstrated willful abandonment at set pieces and it was no surprise that Japan took the lead through this route when Yuki Otsu had the simplest of tasks to score after being left unmarked at a corner.

Spain rarely troubled the Japanese goal in the remainder of the first half. In fact the Samurai Blue could have scored three or four if they had had their shooting boots on. This was a Spain side featuring De Gea, Juan Mata and Jordi Alba, and one that should have given any country a run for their money. Spain's back four looked very shaky and towards the end of the half Inigo Martinez made a hash of controlling a pass, gave possession away to a Japanese forward and then pulled him down. A harsh red card was brandished by the referee giving Spain a mountain to climb in the second half.

The home crowd had come to get behind the Spanish, with more sporting red shirts than anything else, but it was the Japanese fans who kept the noise levels up. They even tried to whip the crowd up into a hand clapping frenzy, with two chaps running up and down the aisles waving flags, until the fun police arrived and told them to sit down. The second period saw the inevitable Mexican Wave start as well as a few people nodding off in their seats. Despite being behind, the Spanish failed to move the ball forward at all. It seemed that they believed some miraculous divine intervention would save them. However, Japan stuck to their job and recorded a famous and highly unlikely victory.

One odd final thought for the day struck me. The official attendance for game one was 23,000, game two was 37,000. How do they differentiate? After our experience trying to get in, would we be classed as game one or game two spectators? Perhaps the 14,000 difference in attendees was simply down to delays in getting into the stadium?

Friday saw the Fuller family at leisure in Edinburgh, seeing all the sights before heading to the big screen for the opening ceremony of the Olympics. It was a magical night where the whole country suddenly woke up and showed we had passion for the magic of the Games. With a late flight home on Saturday I had plenty of time to sneak in a game in the afternoon. After all, how could I resist the lure of the Ramsden's Cup? Cowdenbeath had won my vote, not just because the promise of South American style football from the Blue Brazil, but a visit to Britain's only top-flight ground that also doubles up as a Stock Car racing track in its spare time.

Central Park, home to the club since 1917, has hosted greyhound and speedway racing over the years but it has been the hosting of stock car racing since 1970 that has made it famous the world over. Cowdenbeath is whispered in hushed tones in destructive motor sports the same way that Wimbledon is for Tennis, Hickstead is for Show Jumping and Lewes is for Toad In The Hole (yes there is such a game). The home of the Blue Brazil has even hosted four World Championships, such has been its importance in the sport. However, it is primarily a football ground, albeit one with an average attendance of less than 500.

This season the club will be playing in the second tier of Scottish football, the highest level they have ever played at, after promotion as Second Division Champions under the stewardship of player/manager Colin Cameron. The previous season they were the second worst supported team in the league, with an average attendance less than some Ryman Premier teams. The problem is that within an hour of the delights of Cowdenbeath you can be watching a game at Celtic Park, Tynecastle, Easter Road or Ibrox, not to mention that last season Premier League football was being played just 10 minutes down the road at Dunfermline's East End Park.

I'm no stranger to Scottish Football League grounds having been to a few up and down the country in the past decade but

Central Park was to be a rare new experience to me. The train from Waverley started across the Firth of Forth in bright sunshine and ended in torrential rain. As we pulled into Cowdenbeath the rain stepped up a gear to biblical proportions. Despite the ground being no more than a five minute walk away I needed some shelter. I ran from the platform heading into the nearest open doorway, which as luck would have it was a pub. A pub on my wavelength it seemed as it blared out 'Gimme Shelter' by The Rolling Stones. At least it wasn't the infamous Goth pub, voted by many as the Roughest Pub in the UK. Of course it wasn't. This was the New Goth, described on one forum to 'avoid like the plague'. The 'For Sale' signs outside added to the aesthetic pleasure of the establishment, although the old woman outside sitting on the curb with no shoes on and a big bottle of Panther Cider in the pouring rain was obviously putting off potential buyers at that very moment.

Fortunately the rain eased before the surly looking woman behind the bar had a chance to ask me what my pleasure was and I headed across the road, under the bridge and into the car park of Central Park. Unbelievably the club were asking £14 for this Ramsdens Cup game against the mighty Alloa (your local, friendly pawnbroker sponsoring a cup competition with high ticket prices – the irony Alanis, oh the irony) which considering the surroundings was excessive to say the least and only six pounds more than the double header Olympic tickets we had from two days previous at Hampden Park. Perhaps that's another reason why no more than a few hundred come to watch football here. It did, however, give me free entry to the banger racing taking place at 6pm. Football and motor sport in one ticket? Let me think about that for a moment.

My first view of the ground was through an eight-foot high fence. On one side of the ground was a steep bank of terracing that offered a better view although the driving rain soon had me diving for cover in the main stand, and a view of the Scottish League Two trophy proudly on display. A cup of tea and a Scottish pie in hand I prepared myself for the action.

In the end it took a penalty shoot out to settle the Fife derby, although by that stage with the impatient banger racing enthusiasts tapping their fingers on their steering wheels by the edge of the track I was on a train back to Edinburgh. The game was played in a mix of hot sunshine and violent rain showers, hardly aiding the players, let alone the few hundred fans who were running back and forth between the open terrace and the covered main stand throughout the game.

After the excitement of Cowdenbeath's own Olympic Torch relay, handled by a cow mascot (called Den Beath no less) and accompanied by the ball boys, the game started with a bang as the home side wasted no time in opening their account for the season. Just ninety seconds were on the clock when Lewis Coult danced around the Alloa keeper and slotted into an empty net. He seemed confused as to where to run to celebrate. He did think about leaping the huge painted tyres that surrounded the pitch, but fearful of a Gordon Strachan-style incident from Mexico 1986, he simply 'did a Shearer', raising his arm and running along the touchline.

One should have been two a few minutes later when Coult was put through again but he let the ball run too far ahead when he was bearing down on goal. Alloa, Clackmannanshire's finest, were promoted themselves last season from the third tier of Scottish Football but never looked at the races until the twentieth minute when Ben Gordon stabbed home an equaliser from an apparent offside position. The travelling fans came alive on the terrace, revelling in the inclement conditions. As one of them said to me, "if ne wan the rainbow ne havva the rain". I think that's a Dolly Parton quote but he could've been threatening me.

One-each at the break and after the half-time scores from the other Ramsden Cup ties came out over the PA, a kids 'shoot-out' took place with Cowdenbeath v Alloa represented by youths sort of dressed for the occasion. I say sort of, as the home team's players had full kit on with boots, whilst the Alloa ones looked like the children who had forgotten their PE kit and been made to do it in their vest, pants and school shoes. Each player was given ten seconds to run from the half way line and score, although the countdown did seem to slow down for the home side's players. Corruption in modern football in action? Possibly as the Blue Brazil did secure a highly suspect home-halftime-kids-shoot-out-win. I've informed FIFA accordingly.

After a pretty dull second half honours were still even. There was certainly no samba beat accompanying the home side's play unlike their namesakes in yellow. Extra time failed to produce any further action and with the revving of engines from the impatient banger racers, penalties would decide the fate of the two teams. With only two trains available and it being an hour back to Edinburgh and then an 8pm flight back to London, I had to forego the most exciting ten minutes in the game. The home side triumphed in the end to progress to the next round where they would meet East Fife in a battle of Fiefdom.

I sat on the train back through the lowlands of Fife with the Ochil Hills in the distance and contemplated what I had just seen. If Cowdenbeath was a reflection of the modern state of Scottish League football then it was in terminal decline. Central Park is not a venue where a spectator can feel part of the game. Due to the safety precautions required for motor sports, high fences and a track separated the paying fans from the pitch, whilst amenities were firmly filed under the heading 'basic'. The Blue Brazil's samba beat was almost silent. Could the real deal lift my spirits?

After the excitement in Scotland it was time for the second part of the Boys from Brazil weekend bonanza. A late night flight to Gatwick on Saturday night, followed by a crack-of-dawn flight back up the country to Manchester (I have planted a tree in my garden to make up for such air mile fuelled extravagance) was taken and act two was about to begin.

The main event was obviously Brazil v Belarus, the odds-on favourites to take the men's gold medal after the certain elimination of the Spanish following their defeat to Japan, but before that we had a packed agenda. Not only was there a small matter of Egypt versus New Zealand but we had also planned a trip to the National Football Museum at Urbis in the city-centre as first port of call. You could spend hours wandering around the museum with its interactive displays, brilliant pictures and all sorts of mementos from around the world.

Did I mention the photos? I should have done as I had a personal interest in them because a couple of mine (well, OK, five) had been included in a section called 'Fields of Dreams'. Those little snippets of life at Crawley Down (now with a Gatwick at the end), Hucknall Town, Ilkeston, Beckenham Town and Chipstead all bring back great memories for me and will hopefully provoke a tear or two in other people's eyes. Alas, I am no Stuart Roy Clarke (genuinely 'the Daddy' of football photography) and it is only good and proper that the exhibition features a collection of his work, but I can say to a (very) small extent that I have made it as a football photographer, and that feels good.

After the issues getting into Hampden Park on Thursday today's transportation arrangements couldn't have been better.

Well, almost. As I arrived at Manchester Piccadilly numerous signs and the information sheets supplied to the Games Makers informed us that Brazil v Belarus and not Egypt v New Zealand was the first game of the day, kicking off at 12pm (which may have explained why the stadium was so full by 12.15pm when I arrived...). Shuttle buses were once again laid on, leaving every five minutes for the short trip down to the drop off point opposite Legends Fish and Chip Bar, which had been disappointingly renamed from the original 'Lou Macari's Chippy'. On the walk down to the ground the Games Makers were on hand giving out the clear bags and urging people to stash their swag long before they reached the turnstiles. The result? No queues, no fuss and plenty of happy football fans already in their seats watching the first game.

Of course most people were here to see the Brazilians, but there were a fair few Kiwis and Egyptian fans around to see which of their sides could make it through to the quarter-finals. Egypt had been battered by Brazil in 45 minutes of pure footballing rhythm on Thursday, shipping three goals but then only to put in an excellent second period performance and pull it back to 3-2. New Zealand, on the other hand, had one last chance to record a win after the defeat in their first game to Belarus. This, on face value, was one of those goat's cheese and aubergine bakes you see on starter menus before you can move onto the fillet steak. It may be absolutely delicious but there's an equal chance it's just going to taste of oily cheese and grey.

I arrived at my seat in the press box via a strange route that seemed to take in my own private tour of the Theatre of Dreams, getting to my chair just as Mohamed Salah equalised Chris Wood's earlier strike for the All Whites. As seats go, you cannot get much better in English football then at Old Trafford with a decent view of the lower two tiers of the Sir Alex Ferguson Stand.

Like the Honduras v Morocco game on Thursday, people arrived expecting two minnows trying to string a pass together, and like Thursday what they saw was a great game of attacking football. British interest was in the form of referee Mark Clattenburg, although the majority of the male proportion of the crowd's eyes were on the dancing semi-clad Brazilian girls in he front section of the Stretford End. With temperatures barely breaking 12 degrees the word 'fripples' sprang to mind.

What's a fripple?

It's the condition incurred from wearing a tight top on a cold day that makes it look like you've got a Smartie lodged in each cup of your bra. See also 'smuggling peanuts' and 'they're like two chapel hat pegs'.

Both teams wanted to attack, and moved the ball forward quickly, finding gaps in each other's defensive lines with ease. Egypt should have been long out of sight by the hour mark. Time and time again the ball flashed across the goal-mouth but they simply could not get anyone on the end of it. The impressive part of the Egyptian performance was not the attacking flair they showed throughout the second half, but the fact that all bar one of the squad was home grown and still played their football in Egypt. Only Mohamed Salah played outside the country, plying his trade in Switzerland. New Zealand could boast (or 'unboast' – is that a word? Probably not) only six of their squad who played in their national league, with four playing in England (Ryan Nelsen, Tim Payne, Chris Wood and Cameron Howieson) as well as their coach being former Tonbridge Angel and Wolverhampton Wanderers midfielder, Neil Emblen.

With the game deep into injury time, Egypt attacked for the last time. The ball found its way to the goal scorer Mohamed Salah who jinked past one defender, sold the keeper a dummy and with the goal laid open before him, blazed the ball over the bar. There was still time for both teams to have another go before Clattenburg blew full time and virtually every man, woman, girl and boy in the stadium rose to applaud both teams off the pitch in one of the best international matches many will have seen for years. The draw probably favoured the Egyptians more, who were now firm favourites to beat Belarus on Tuesday and grab a quarter-final spot.

I ventured down through the press area to find the mixed zone, which was in a tent in the car park, to speak to the New Zealand team. I bumped into Emblen, reminding him of the coaching course we took together some 18 years ago (needless to say he didn't remember it, but was polite enough not to show it) and he was positive despite the fact the All Whites now had to go and beat Brazil. I tried to find my way back to my seat in the stadium. I went down a staircase, along a long corridor with pictures of United legends lining the walls and through a door into a dark-ened room. For the second time in a little over an hour I found myself lost in the bowels of Old Trafford, randomly trying doors to eventually find myself almost back where I started in the car park. I went cap in hand to a member of security and explained

I had just arrived and needed to know which way to go so I could get to my seat in time for the Brazil game. He couldn't be bothered describing the route back so he tapped the side of his nose, opened a magic door and down the tunnel we walked into the sunshine. 60,000 football fans mistook me for the Brazilian striker Hulk based only on the strength of us both being 'big-boned'. Finally I was back at my desk with a cup of tea and the fillet steak had arrived.

It seemed everyone wanted to be a Brazilian in Manchester. Some United fans had come, red shirt on but covered with a Brazilian cape to support Rafael, others simply wore the famous yellow shirts seduced by thoughts of sunshine, beaches, neatly trimmed under-carriage hair, carnivals and stylish football. The reality of their own day-to-day lives were more on the side of drizzle, dark satanic mills and Amazonian bushes, this was a welcome splash of colour.

Football is the glue that binds society together and there can be no better example of that than in Brazil where the rich and poor support one single cause - the fortunes of the national side. To say there was pressure on coach Mano Menezes to bring home the gold medal was an understatement. Having seen the Argentinians win recent Olympic tournaments, and even Uruguay pipe up that every time they had played in the Olympic football tournament they had come away with a gold medal, there was a huge expectation that this year had to be their year.

In the countdown to kick-off the stadium announcer seemed to be getting a bit confused. Number 1, Gabriel, Number 4, James Tomkins, Number 7, Lucas....

Hold up a minute.

James Tomkins?

How can you confuse a middle of the road Championship player who was playing for Team GB with a Brazilian footballer?

And whilst we are on the subject of mistakes, DJ Spoony on the roaming mic? Really? At least use someone that has some credibility in football. Presenting 606 once in a while does not qualify you as an expert on football despite what David Mellor, Robbie Savage and Mike Parry may have you believe.

The Brazilian starting XI featured talent from Fiorentina, Manchester United, Paris Saint-Germain, Internazionale, Real Madrid, AC Milan and Porto, European giants one and all. All eyes though would be on Neymar who was still playing for Santos despite those "envious eyes" from Europe on him, as H G Wells once remarked. This was seen as his stage, with the transfer window due to swing open in just three days (does the transfer window 'swing open'? Certainly 'slams shut' so I'm guessing yes).

Apart from the upper tier of the Sir Alex Ferguson Stand, Old Trafford was almost bursting at the seams. The official attendance was just over 66,000 which was an outstanding effort. Had people come to experience the London 2012 Olympics? Of course not. They were here to watch Brazil and with most seats costing less than £40 (including that fantastic earlier game) they'd bagged a bargain.

Seven minutes in and the Samba beat suddenly stopped. Belarus's Ilya Aleksievich threw a hopeful cross into the penalty box and Renan Bardini Bressan sneaked in between two Brazilian defenders to head home.

Blimey.

Apart from a small pocket of Belarussian fans in the upper tier of the North Stand, the ground was silent. Brazil were shaken, this was definitely not in the plan. Hulk then showed all the right attributes of the Olympic spirit by throwing himself to the ground, over the on-rushing Belarusian keeper Aleksandor Gutor, but the Japanese referee was having none of it. He resisted brandishing a yellow card, opting instead to award the Porto striker a 7.3 for technical merit.

Five minutes later and the Brazilians were on level terms with a very similar move to the opening Belarussian goal. A long cross from the left hand side saw Milan's Alexandre Pato dive in between the defenders to head the ball home and lift the roof off the stadium. You just got the feeling this was now going to be a long afternoon for the Belarussians. Even so they held firm, resistant to Brazil's frequent incursions to the byline where the ball always ended up flying over the heads of the forwards who had run to the near post. Half an hour in and you had to say that Aleksandr Gutor had been the quieter of the two keepers.

On the hour mark Belarus almost took the lead when Bardini Bressan saw Neto off his line and tried his luck from twenty-five yards only for the Brazilian keeper to get a hand to the ball and tip it over. Finally we saw some Brazilian magic. Neymar jinked his way past two defenders and was brought down on the edge of the box, although replays suggested he simply fell over the prone body of Belarussian captain Stanislav Dragun. From the free-kick he curled the ball into the corner of the net, running off to celebrate with his team mates by pretending to suck on a dummy that was always there if he needed to spit one out at any point.

Two could have so easily have been three as Oscar curled an-other free-kick around the wall but it was tipped over the bar by Gutor. Belarus's spirit had evaporated like cheap Minsk potato vodka in the last quarter of the game (that stuff is lethal – long story...) and in truth Brazil were happy to simply keep the ball without really pressing forward. Dare I say it but the game be-came quite dull. In injury time they scored a third with one of the few bits of utter class we saw from the South Americans. Neymar led two defenders on a merry dance on the edge of the area be-fore back-heeling it to Oscar who had the easiest job to roll it in.

So no real surprises in the end as Brazil coasted to a 3-1 win which put them into the quarter-finals, and in doing so sent the majority of the sixty-odd thousand fans home happy. The sup-porters had come to get their slice of samba and overall that is what they had got, although perhaps not as big a slice as they would have liked.

In previous tournaments the Brazilians had flattered to de-ceive, coming unstuck against more organised and disciplined opposition. However, in this competition there didn't seem to be an obvious candidate to do that. Gold medals all round for sure in my opinion and I'm rarely wrong. I was certain they would smash their way to the final (probably against Team GB) and without a shadow of a doubt they would then win that comfortably. Oh yes, the organisers may as well have engraved the medals then as far as I was concerned, although they shouldn't use the same list as the stadium announcer as James Tomkins had contributed very little to the Brazilian cause in truth.

That final was, of course, played just twelve days later on August the 11th.

The score?

Mexico 2 Brazil 1.

Chapter Fifteen

Yankee Doodle Dandy
"Let's Go Red Bulls!"

24th June 2012
New York Red Bulls 3 DC United 2
Red Bull Arena

19th September 2012
New York Red Bulls 0 Sporting Kansas City 2
Red Bull Arena

"...the parking lots were empty, the scalpers were desperate
to off-load their tickets and the stewards looked bored..."

It seemed like an eternity since my spectating season had ended watching Dartford lift the Blue Square Bet South Play Off Final trophy back in May. In actual fact it was only six weeks ago, but that was my last game of the season and I was starting to get withdrawal symptoms. It had been game number 104 attended of the 2011/12 campaign, my first ever century of games in one season. Since then I had tried to amuse myself with cricket, rugby (league and union) and motor racing. Damn, I even went to Harry Potter World for some Quidditch. At last I had an opportunity for another game, the 105th and final one of what I could class as my football season.

I am not saying I was desperate for a game but I had traveled 3,461 miles to North America for just ninety minutes of the beautiful game. My destination? The Garden State, home of 'Jersey Shore', the programme that spawned English versions in the form of 'The Only Way is Essex', 'Geordie Shore' and all of those other crap TV shows whose only contribution to the world is encouraging young girls to stick fake diamonds around their twats. Oh, sorry, I forgot, 'twat' is a very rude word in America. I have been warned before not to say or especially write the word twat when in the USA. Apparently it can really cause offense so I won't say twat anymore. Ironically I can say 'fanny' as that just means arse over there and not, as Keith from the Office once said, "...your minge".

It shouldn't have taken much detective work on your behalf to work out I was heading for New Jersey (or as the the locals call it 'Noo Jerr-zee'), home of such musical stars as Count Basie, Frank Sinatra, Jon Bon Jovi and Whitney Houston. All of these are now dead (I've not seen Bon Jovi for ages so it's a fair assumption, only joking Jon) but all contributed massively to the musical history of the USA. When I'm in these parts I never travel alone. My good friend and Englishman in New York Luge Pravda was with me, and just to make sure we didn't get too distracted, diverted or delayed, so was his patient, understanding and thoroughly enchanting wife Katie.

It was a gloriously hot weekend when I arrived in The Big Apple, and I had two days of culture US-style before the serious hard work was due to start on Monday in the office. After watching some of Euro2012 in a very deserted Wall Street on Saturday followed by a few Blue Moon's (local brew), I'd managed an early (...ish) night. Unfortunately, so overcome with emotion at my arrival, Luge had failed to make it to bed when he returned home to Brooklyn, falling asleep on the living room floor of his apartment. Katie made me promise I wouldn't tell anyone he was comatose on the rug, thumb in mouth. This may have been alcohol but I'm sure he would claim it was down to a completely unrelated virus. Bless.

In an amazing stroke of coincidence, my old travelling companion Football Jo (See Passport to Football for some of her antics abroad) was also in town and so we arranged to meet for breakfast on Sunday morning. She was on a whistle-stop tour of various East Coast cities for work but had a spare hour to meet up. It had been a good few months since we had last seen each other, as finally she had found a toy-boy and was enjoying a more conventional life instead of trailing round Europe with me watching obscure football matches and buying DVDs that were illegal in most European cultures (her not me I hasten to add). Breakfast ticked off it was time to think about lunch as all good Americans do - when in Rome and all that. Finally I was going to follow in the footsteps of one of my non-football true heroes, Mr. Adam Richman.

'Man versus Food' is a phrase that is equally well known on both sides of the Atlantic. It's a television programme based on the simple concept of one man touring America's finest diners taking on their food challenges. Whether it's the biggest or the hottest, Adam Richman takes it on in exuberant style and has created a hugely popular concept and a very watchable half-an-hour of television. Football-loving Richman (he's a big Tottenham Hotspur fan don't you know) is a regular in these parts, and it was to one of his locals where Luge and I headed on the hottest day I had ever sweated through.

Our destination was a place well known to me by name certainly. Gravesend. I was schooled there, courted there, and as my parents would say, arres...actually, let's just leave it there. Suffice to say I had happy memories of Gravesend, Kent, so I was sure that Gravesend, Brooklyn, would do me proud. Our destination was the legendary Brennan and Carr diner where the Man versus Food specialty was Roast Beef sandwiches, dipped in a beef broth. Oh yes my friend, double dipping. Brennan and Carr has been serving these beauties for decades.

After lunch we had originally planned a visit to the American Hungarian Museum, where North America's biggest collection of lace tablecloths can be found as well as the Sam Azeez Museum of Woodbine Heritage, but Katie was having none of that. "I want football boys!" she cried over her bun, floating in rich and salty beef gravy. Who were we to disappoint? These American girls can get very feisty if they don't have their own way. So with In-ger-laaaand due to play Italy in the inevitable painful Euro2012 defeat in just a few hours, we donned our traditional national dress of knotted hankies, string vests and sandals (with socks on of course) and headed back across the East River to Lower Manhattan.

We did try and find a bar that would be showing the England game in Little Italy. Despite its reputation as a multi-cultural hub, New York still hasn't given us Brits our own little slice of the city. Little Italy, China Town, Koreaville - where's Albert Square for our afternoon watching Roy's Boys? Never mind, what could be better than watching a game in a small Italian 'family' bar around Lower Manhattan chatting about Catenaccio with made men? Well it seemed that Luge valued his life more than me, so we headed for Becketts in the shadow of Wall Street instead.

Three hours later, with the all too familiar feeling of pain in our hearts, we walked out of the darkness of the bar. Bleary-eyed with emotion and several pints of fizzy pop American beer sloshing around our stomachs, we headed due west for the PATH train that would take us not only into a different state, but a different world. Allegedly, 53% of Americans have never left their birth state, yet here I was barely in Frank Sinatra's Noo York, Noo York for less than 24 hours before I was going inter-state. As per, England beaten and that game out the way, our day was just getting started. Katie wanted football with a side order of silky skills, dubious decisions and a dollop of US sporting razzmatazz, and that's what we were going to give her. Half an hour later and we were in the metropolis of Harrison, just across the water from Newark in New Jersey. This isn't the prettiest part of the US; in fact it looks like Stockton-on-Tees on a bad day. However, right in the middle of the deserted factories, scrap yards and container depots is the relatively new Red Bull Arena, glistening in the ridiculously hot sunshine. It may have been getting on for 6.30pm but the mercury had not fallen below 30 degrees all day.

The stadium, which for those who know their Euro-pean grounds, looks identical to the Wörthersee Arena in Klagenfurt, Austria (and for those who don't, well it still looks like the Wörthersee Arena but you will just have to take our word for it). A smart, purpose-built home for footba...sorry, soccer, that houses the New York Red Bulls. Yes I know we aren't in New

York State anymore, but there's no denying it sounds sexier than the New Jersey Red Bulls.

It's hard to not write a long monologue about Red Bull and their plan to franchise football. Currently they own football clubs in Germany (Red Bull Leipzig), Austria (Red Bull Salzburg), Brazil (Red Bull Brasil) and Ghana (Red Bull Ghana). Whilst they have invested big money into the game, their methodology of taking over a club, stripping it of its history (including badge, club colours and in some cases fans as the Salzburg supporters will tell you at length) does leave a bad taste in the mouth. However, in the US where franchise sport is all the rage, they have been welcomed by the local residents of Harrison, New Jersey and have made a decent fist of marketing themselves to the Tri-State area, especially at the MetLife stadium, the nearby home of the New York Jets and Giants.

This was to be my first MLS game in seven years. Back in 2005 some bright spark came up with the idea of hosting a double-header of an MLS game featuring the then New York/New Jersey Metrostars and an England v Columbia game at the old Meadowlands. Great idea to get some new faces along to a MLS game, except they put it on after a Michael Owen hat-trick had seen off the South Americans, and thus most of the crowd were too pissed or sunburnt to stay like I did for the second game.

Seven years later I was back, and what a game to choose. It promised to be a decent match judging by league positions. The visitors, DC United, came up the East Coast sitting on top of the league with 30 points from 16 games, but the Red Bulls had a game in hand in third place. They were the league's leading scorers, with New York's marquee player Thierry Henry having scored nine goals so far. Local derbies are very few and very far between in the MLS, only one city hosts two clubs - The LA Galaxy and Chivas calling The Home Depot Stadium in Carson City, Los Angeles home. But these two had something to prove and a sizeable away support (a rarity in any US sport) was expected.

As any set of fans will tell you at the start of the season, 'this is our year'. They have been saying that in these parts since the club's inception back in 1995 when they started life as the Empire Soccer Club before they became the New York/New Jersey Metrostars, ready to take a place in the newly created Major League Soccer competition. Since then and despite a playing roster that has included Tim Howard, Branco, Youri Djourkaeff, Roberto Donadoni, Luke Rodgers (what do you mean who?) and Lothar Matthäus, they have basically won nothing. In fact they are the only original franchise team that hasn't won the Division or the Play Offs, although in 2010 they did win the Walt Disney Pro Soccer Classic (eat your heart out Man City and Chelsea, one trophy you cannot buy your way to). This year was going to be different though, Swedish coach Hans Backe, once assistant to Sven-Göran Eriksson at Manchester City, Mexico and Notts County, had assembled a multi-national squad featuring players from twelve different countries. We all know that such an approach, once dubbed the Redknapp United Nations theory, is a sure-fire recipe for success...

Football fever had grasped the Eastern Seaboard as we walked from the station. Huge 'SOLD OUT' signs welcomed us as we arrived, an almost unheard of situation in these parts. Fortunately we had used the services of StubHub to secure our tickets. This is one of the best little secrets in the US, although it will soon hit our Premier League. It is at heart a ticket exchange but you hardly ever end up paying more than face value as they are all paper tickets, sold at the last minute by people who simply want rid of their seats. Last November on the website I picked up court-side tickets for the New Jersey Nets for $10 and for this game we paid $20 for $27 tickets. Tickets are then emailed to you by StubHub within seconds of paying. Top service that puts certain other ticket companies, mentioning no names, to shame. Watching football in a foreign country can be a daunting business; it's the little touches like these prove it's far easier than you may think.

The big team news was that Henry had been managed to shake off a hamstring injury, brought on by too much va-va-vooming around New York no doubt, although he would start on the bench - hardly a popular move considering the number of fans we saw with 'Henry 14' shirts on or brandishing big foam hands saying similar. The atmosphere was building nicely inside the ground as kick off time approached. This being America a kick off time of seven actually means nothing. A countdown clock in the corner reached 00:00 at 7pm and still the players were in the pre-match warm up on the pitch.

With our Coors Lite in one hand (long story but it was the only beer we could get with cash) and a hotdog in the other we took our seats, impatiently waiting for kick off. Why say seven if it clearly isn't seven? Finally things started to happen. At 7.06pm a group of school children came out holding huge flags. There seemed to be no logical reason for the choice of flags (we later found out that they represented the nations with players in the MLS although we still couldn't work out the Welsh representative). They went something like this - USA (obvious), Brazil, Uruguay, Wales, England, Holland and so on, snaking around the end of the pitch and ending with what looked distinctly like the flag of the Island of Åland, the Finnish Autonomous province and our friends from the Island Games back in Chapter 4). The Red Bulls fans to our left were creating quite a noise. I was surprised at the atmosphere. A huge banner was unfurled, 'We are the DC haters', along with some flare action. Well, as close to flares as you can get. Coloured dry-ice in buckets was apparently a safer option (genuinely) although coming from a country where in most States you can legally wander around with a firearm, I do find the concept of public safety baffling sometimes. It was now 7:09pm and still little sign of kick off.

DC United had brought a decent amount of fans themselves. All the myths about no fans, no atmosphere and no decent beer at US soccer weren't true (well, the first two anyway). The noise built to a crescendo when the referee led the teams out and, to Danny Last's delight some 3,500 miles away, picked the ball up off a plinth at the end of the tunnel. 7:11pm. Of course we all stood for a rousing rendition of the national anthem, perfectly observed as always, and then it was game time finally at 7:13pm. The Red Bulls fans built up to a climax, and continuing the sexual metaphor, then embarrassingly shot their bolt in a matter of seconds. Twenty nine seconds on the clock (7.14pm) and DC United had scored. the excellent Chris Pontius rose above the static Red Bulls defence to head home the first cross into the penalty box of the evening.

One of my main annoyances with watching American sports is the constant crowd movement up and down the aisles to go and get food. The average sitting time per fan (hardcore supporters aside) must have been less than 20 minutes. Granted there's a lot on offer, but do these people actually try to watch any of the game? After telling one fan to sit down and shut up, I got a small round of applause from some other fans around who were also here to enjoy a cracking start to the game. The Red Bulls started to come back into the contest and it didn't take them long to realise that DC United's keeper, Bill Hamid, was basically crap. He simply couldn't hold on to the ball and there wasn't any surprise that the Red Bulls finished the evening with 20 shots on goal.

The inevitable equaliser came in the 20th minute when Brandon Barklage hammered the ball home after a corner wasn't cleared and Hamid flapped in the air.

The Red Bulls continued to dominate the possession and it was no surprise when Barklage scored his second in injury time at the end of the half with a shot across Hamid which he tried to catch/punch, and failed miserably. Half time, 2-1 Red Bulls. In the land of showmanship and world-class entertainment I was expecting a great half time show, perhaps something from the Boss himself as Springsteen only lives around the corner. Alas it was not to be as instead we watched a 13-a-side kids game where 24 players swarmed around the ball whilst two keepers looked on bored.

The second half saw the Red Bulls continue to dominate and ten minutes in Jan Gunnar Soli (who once holidayed in Åland and Wales apparently - flag mystery solved) scored a third. Game over and the Red Bulls were going to the top of the Conference table. DC United somehow found some energy and looked dangerous, perhaps because of the introduction of Henry who looked bored and completely uninterested every time the ball came anywhere near him. After Pontius scored his second to make the score 3-2 the Red Bulls tactic seemed to be to lump the ball up field to Henry and see what he could do. Henry of Arsenal circa 2004 would have made mincemeat of the DC United defence but this is Henry 2012, and he no longer had the pace or interest to take on DC United single-handedly.

The referee's final whistle marked a great win for the Red Bulls but it wasn't quite enough to take them top of the table. We headed back to Harrison station for our return into the metropolis. My experience of the MLS this time had been a positive one. Decent game, decent view, decent atmosphere, decent ticket prices. Despite the franchising of the game/club, the mix of families and hardcore fans was good to see and one that will only reap benefits in the years to come.

As jet lag kicked in at 3am I sat in the window of my hotel room, high up in the gods, and looking back towards New Jersey. I thought about my afternoon and all I had enjoyed and then jotted down five things I learnt about my visit to the Red Bulls and the MLS in general:

1. When clubs say a game is a sell out, it is actually only going to be 80% full at best. Clubs may have technically sold the seats but many will be using ticket promotions, multi-game tickets and the

ticket exchanges such as Stub Hub were they are readily resold.

2. 'Scalping' or plain-old ticket-touting, whilst illegal in the US, is ignored by the police. On the walk to the Red Bull Arena scalpers line the route freely selling tickets. One old lady (an unusual demographic) used the flattery approach to get our attention - "Hello pretty," she said, although it appeared she was talking to Katie and not me.

3. MLS clubs should not be building their business model around aging professionals who are only interested in one last pay-cheque. The vast distribution of wages between the teams means that these 'designated' players equate to three or four (minimum) wages of their team mates, yet often their efforts are only a quarter of some of the lower paid players.

4. The MLS fans need to watch a few more European games, rather than Green Street, Football Factory or ID to get an idea about really building an atmosphere in a ground. These films are just that, films, or to put it another way, works of fiction.

5. Remember to stock up on beer before the start of half time as they stop selling alcohol after the break to prevent the fans go-ing 'too wild', wild being defined in a US sports sense as someone who says the word 'awesome' or 'twat' too many times for the officials liking

Three months after my first trip west from New York to the barren lands of Harrison, I sat on a virtually empty PATH train retracing my steps. Once again Luge Pravda and Katie were with me. Back in June it had been a boiling hot afternoon. Now the nights were drawing in and the Yankees were at home, meaning the locals weren't so seduced by a night at the Red Bull Arena. Whilst those sitting at home or in the Yankees Stadium in The Bronx would be cheering on people called A-Rod and Jeter, we were going to see the magic conjured up by genuine Wizards. Or, the team that at least used to be called the Wizards.

It appeared that a PR agency decided that 'The Wiz' wasn't an MLS-type name anymore, so they were rebranded as 'Sporting Kansas City', or SKC for short. Another franchise struggling to find an identity perhaps?

Soccer is in a confused state in the US. At the grass-roots level it is the most popular sport played by youngsters at school, especially girls. To back that up the interest among the younger generation in the Premier League or La Liga has never been bigger. With every visit I make to New York I see more and more bars now proudly displaying signs saying they show live Premier League games. And why wouldn't they? A 3pm Saturday kick off in England means people in the bars at 10am, more often than not combining that cheeky first pint of the weekend with a full English breakfast. For visitors from England it means that they can still enjoy their fix from back home and be up the top of the Empire State just after midday - everyone's a winner.

Earlier that very year I had watched West Ham v Millwall on television at 7.45am in the Football Factory, quite literally in King Kong's shadow. The owners had obviously taken a leaf out of Currys' book, with TVs on every spare inch of wall space meaning nobody had a restricted view. Add in a couple of waitresses dressed in football kit (Newcastle United in this case to keep the neutrality) who handed you another beer as soon as you had an empty one and you have a perfect recipe for happy soccer fans.

New York isn't the only city in North America that lacks a soccer identity in terms of its local team, but it is the best example to analyse. The MLS has come a long way in the last few years, becoming more competitive and being able to defocus from just the exploits of one player in Los Angeles and on to the league as a whole. It may surprise some observers from outside North America that other teams actually exist and the Galaxy is not the biggest team in the league. In early September the derby between the Portland Timbers and the Seattle Sounders drew a sellout crowd. I say 'derby' in inverted commas as it is just about the biggest rivalry in US soccer although the two clubs are actually separated by 175 miles. A packed house, full of atmosphere that you rarely see in other US sports witnessed a one-all draw. Few would know that there are now three teams from Canada, one of whom, Toronto FC, play in front of sellout crowds every week.

So soccer is slowly becoming the sport of choice for many Americans on a national level. Now recognised as a global game it doesn't take all day to play or watch as opposed to baseball and American Football. Also, the US national teams are getting better year on year - the US women's team took Gold in the Olympics; the US men's team continues to be a fancied dark horse at every tournament they enter. Sooner rather than later they will bring home a major trophy and then soccer will have truly arrived.

But in New York there is still an issue. Without a team to call their own, New Yorkers are missing a slice of the football-shaped apple pie. Ask any resident of the city who their team is and you will hear the Giants, Jets, Yankees or Knicks depending on which is their favoured sport. The Yankees are one of, if not the, biggest sporting brand in the world. Forbes magazine recently valued the brand at $1.78 billion. Their annual revenues are around $440million. It does help that they play around seventy-five home games a season with an average attendance of forty-thousand and once inside the stadium fans spend around $53 dollars each on average (bear in mind a beer at Yankee Stadium is $12). The Giants on the other hand do not go down the 'pile them high, sell them cheap' admission model. NFL teams only play eight regular season games at home and can therefore charge an average ticket price well over $150, and consequently that average fan spend once inside the stadium is well north of the $53 mark.

Back to the Red Bulls. The team, backed with the money and marketing knowhow of the Austrian beverage giants, have done a good job in trying to keep the interest high both in New York as well as in New Jersey. But there is so much untapped potential. Nearby Newark (the stadium is almost at the edge of Newark Airport's runway) has a population of near 280,000 in addition to the millions who live across the Hudson. New York City could be about to start falling in love with Soccer again when a team arrives they feel they can truly call their own, but still huge obstacles remain. Next season the New York Cosmos will join the North American Soccer League (NASL), the second tier of US Soccer. Second tier would suggest there was some chance to move up to the first tier based on merit, alas, such a concept still doesn't exist in US sports where the closed-shop franchise model is king. The Cosmos' only short-term hope of bringing top-level football back to the city was to buy a MLS franchise and move it to New York. Alas, Manchester City beat them to it and founded New York City who will join the MLS in 2015.

Still pondering the missed opportunities we had boarded a packed train at the World Trade Center in New York but full of commuters on their way home, not football fans, who alighted long before the train pulled into Harrison. As we walked from the station we questioned whether the game was actually taking place at all. The parking lots were empty, the scalpers were desperate to off-load their tickets and the stewards looked bored. With just 30 minutes to kick off the place looked almost deserted. It couldn't have been more different from our last visit when DC United were the visitors.

With just 10 minutes to go to kick-off there was not a single seat taken in our whole section. In fact, there only seemed to be a thousand or so in the ground. Perhaps there was going to be a last-minute rush? No, although we were joined by a group behind us who seemed to have mixed up the Red Bulls and Yankees. The teams emerged and the sparsely populated home end unfurled a banner aimed at the 17 Kansas fans in the section next to us. "You're not Kansas anymore. SKC - No Heart, No Brain, No Courage. No Wizard can save you now". A group of home fans berate their opposition in an empty stadium. A strange feeling to say the least.

Three months ago I was very critical of Thierry Henry, suggesting that the Frenchman's lethargy in running around the pitch was simply symptomatic of a final move in his career purely for the money. Anyone who saw this game couldn't disagree with that statement this time. Henry was plain awful. He hardly broke into a sprint at any stage, stood hands on hips most of the time whilst the game went on around him. Yet his striking partner, ex-Everton and Australian international striker Tim Cahill, put in a decent shift, coming close to a goal with one of his trademark headers from distance.

By the time his header hit the bar in the first period the Red Bulls were two-nil down to goals from Kansas's Charles Sapong and Kei Kamara, both from set-pieces where New York simply didn't pick up their men. Harsh perhaps on the home side, but with virtually every attack ending with a wasted ball to Henry, it was hardly a surprise. The group behind us, who were obviously used to a different type of ball game started getting involved in the game, including such classic moments as:

"Let's go Red Bulls!" as Kansas scored their first, go where exactly?

"Cahill, you ass, why did you head that ball?" in response to a header from the edge of the box that scraped the bar.

"Why haven't they changed ends after they scored?" - no explanation required.

"Let's take Cahill off now and bring him back on later in the game," which if possible would also ignore Henry's complete non-performace.

"So if Kansas wins 2-0 do they get 2 points and Red Bulls 0?" *sigh*

I could understand if this was their first ever trip to a game but one of them mentioned this was the fifth time he had been this very season.

It was hard to take any positives out of the game as an adopted Noo Yorkah. The fantastic sunset was probably my highlight. The Red Bulls were poor, the attendance very disappointing (on the way back in conversation with a fan he seemed to blame it on the fact the Yankees were also at home) and although the official number was 10,286, that felt far-fetched to say the least. On top of all that a beer was an astronomical $12 - nearly 60% of the match ticket. Create the environment and they will come, keep putting up prices and they'll soon leave when something else becomes available.

It was a frustrating evening. No matter how much I wanted the Red Bulls to deliver for me they simply couldn't either on or off the pitch. At the end of the day and despite my first very positive experience, the sense this time was that the New York Red Bulls are a pretty soulless business venture. If the owners decide one day that it is not viable they will simply sell it, or relocate it to somewhere where it will be. With the spectre of the Cosmos looming over the horizon with a much fabled and exaggerated history plus an established global image already there, perhaps now it is the time for the Red Bull marketing people to come up with a Plan B.

New York is definitely and undeniably a sport crazy city. You just need to catch it on a good day. Saying that, the MLS is starting to gain some street cred both within the US and in Europe. It will be interesting to see if that level of interest can be sustained in the post-Beckham era. Still, if you believe the press, they have the arrival of Frank Lampard to look forward to one day...

Chapter Sixteen

Good Old Uncle Velbert
Germany - the original football tourism hotspot

17th August 2012
SSVg Velbert 0 SC Verl 3
The Sunflower Stadium

18th August 2012
Alemannia Aachen 0 Monchengladbach 2
New Tivoli

20th August 2012
FC Hannef 05 0 1860 Munich 6
Stadpark

> *"...the notice also said no naked flames, no guns and*
> *certainly no nude people on the pitch..."*

English non-league football is the best in the world. The smell of horse liniment wafting into the bar, the home-made flapjacks, the fact players are missing from games because their wife needs them to put up a shelf and the ludicrously named stadiums. I long for a day when I get to hear Gary Lineker or one of his pals introducing the North West derby from "the Giant Axe, home of Lancaster City". We also have the 'Dripping Pan' hosting the East Sussex derby in Lewes and Newport County now play at 'Rodney Parade', possibly the only football ground in the world whose name could also double as a middling porn-star's, maybe even top-line if shortened to 'Rod'. Add in a liberal sprinkling of local beers that can be drunk whilst watching the fun on the pitch, the occasional sunshine and cheap admission, and all in you have the perfect formula. Of course, ninety-minutes of football often spoils a great day out but in the value for money stakes it's a winner, hands down.

But what is the situation overseas? We've taken in games at this level in Denmark, Sweden, Italy and even Czech Republic in our adventures over the past two years, but never the real home of football tourism, Germany. We all secretly admire how the Germans do football. Cheap ticket prices, beer, fantastic fan culture, beer, sausages, beer and a decent transport infrastructure that has you moving from point A to C via Q in the bat of an eyelid all whilst in luxury that would make British Rail blush. Oh, and the beer, did I mention that? So when an idea was floated for a weekend of football in Germany prior to the start of the Bundesliga, I'd signed up before the ink was dry on the contract.

To organise such a trip you need to call on German non-league football's equivalent of the A-Team; Danny Last, Kenny Legg and Michael Stoffl. In true A-Team style, Danny is 'Bad Attitude Baracus' due to his loathing of flying and his love of a glass of milk before bedtime, Kenny is 'Face', a man who can get a waitresses attention in the blink of an eye, and Stoffers is Stoffers. Me? I drive the van.

Kenny is famed the length and breadth of South Dorset for his award-nominated blog 'Adventures in Tin Pot', but had recently relocated to Germany. We are bound by the official secrets act as to the exact nature of his job but we understand he came within an inch of being in *that* scene from the Olympic Opening Ceremony when Daniel Craig was umming and ahhing over his fear of corgis. A new habitat hadn't stopped Kenny's eye for a non-league ground or some club-endorsed slippers, and so he had cunningly rebranded his website in true Marathon/Snickers style to 'Das Adventures in TinPot'.

"Come on over and let me show you a good time."

That line could have been whispered from the mouth of Hayden Panettiere at the Playboy Mansion (have I mentioned I've been there before?) and still it wouldn't have seemed as attractive as a weekend of football, beer, football, beer, sausage and more beer in Düsseldorf as suggested by Herr Legg. Before you could say bratwurst, Danny and I were booked on a train (well, three trains but you know what he's like about "gettin' on no damn plane fool") for a weekend at Tinpot towers.

Remember a few months ago when we sauntered out to Rome to stay at Chez Lloyd's for the Eternal Derby? Three-storey villa in the hills overlooking Rome? Supermodels as neighbours and a fridge full of salami and Peroni? Our hopes were high of a similar class of accommodation in Germany. After all, Kenny was bowing in front of the Queen every day so entertaining her subjects on foreign soil would be of the utmost importance and no expense would be spared.

Our plan, after arriving on the Rhine was simple, yet cunningly sophisticated. Three games, three new grounds, three days (well, actually four for Danny who was staying on to find some Rot-Weiss Essen slippers). A few beers perhaps, maybe a sausage or two and basically some cheap laughs at men who wear denim jackets with lots of badges sewn on them and still think David Hasselhoff is a fashion icon.

The Current Mrs. Fuller was so keen for Danny and me to go that she personally drove us to Ebbsfleet International. A two-hour journey of unbridled joy playing Stick Cricket on the iPad, a smooth five minute walk in Brussels to our ICE train and before you knew it we were gliding into Düsseldorf Hauptbahnhof. One final change onto the S-Bahn and we were at Kenny's door. A quick sweep for listening devices via a tour of the west wing of the property and before Stoffers could say "Sechzig", we were in one of Kenny's locals supping the first of many Alt-beers of the weekend. Those back home would have just been tucking into their Rich Tea for elevensies.

A couple of beers in the sunshine, including the world's shortest pub crawl that involved walking three yards between bars, felt like a good way to spend a Friday afternoon before Stoffers rose to his feet.

"I have an announcement to make. It is time to depart!"

And with those words he started walking towards the bus stop. Not having a clue where we were heading we drank up and followed. We had let Stoffers organise our Friday night game and he'd promised us a treat. All day he'd been using words and sentences like "lovely jubbly", "kushty" and "don't be a plonker" for no apparent reason. As we were served our lunch he told our waitress that "...this time next year we'd be millionaires". German humour, we thought, best in the world?

As we boarded a bus he finally revealed where we were heading through the medium of song. "Go West, where the air is clean!" he shouted out, scaring the driver who nearly swerved into a traffic bollard. We calmed him down and discovered that we were heading for a small village called Velbert. It appeared that Stoffers had been trying to "Only Fool and Horses" us all day with a vague link between the name if the village and the character Uncle Albert. "Why didn't you just say 'During the war' then?" asked Kenny, although Danny and I were dreading the obvious follow-up.

"Don't mention the war!" Shouted Stoffers, again causing the bus driver to nearly hit a lamp post. We held our breath, "I mentioned it once but I think I got away with it" came to mind.

As I said, German humour, best in the world (?).

Velbert is such a special place that it is one of the few places in Germany that doesn't have a railway station. They like to keep themselves untouched by technology here, and only installed their first post box in April. Bus number one took us to the centre of Hottsville. It was like a scene from an updated Valley of the Dolls with young women everywhere walking around in the tiniest shorts, cropped tops and leaving nothing to our collective (and far too easily led) imaginations.

"No time for indulgence," boomed Stoffers as he marched us across the road, picking up our tongues, removing our cameras and wiping his glasses clean. "These are not real German women. They are merely here to trap you into staying, once you are in their web there is no escape". Tempting as it looked, his words of warning reminded me of a bad night out I once had in Worksop that almost led to me getting married dressed as Michael Caine to a girl who claimed to be the cousin of John Noakes. Not a night you forget in a hurry or ever want to repeat. Bus two soon arrived and took us deeper into the forest where we had to wait for bus number three. Velbert had better be worth all this mystery and public transport stuff.

What could I tell you about the place? I'm sure if I mention that it is twinned with Corby you can fill in the blanks yourself, so let's concentrate on the football instead. We were heading for the Stadion Sonnenblume, which all you students of German will know means 'sunflower'. The ground is located in a sleepy hollow, surrounded by trees. The distinct and noticeable lack of floodlights had Danny in a sulk straight away but the promise of a dog or two, a beer and a large portion of German non-league clothing had him smiling again within minutes. He mistakenly thought that based on the name of the stadium there would be giant Sunflowers if no floodlights. After explaining that was mental once again disappointment took hold.

I am sure you don't really want a detailed report on this fourth-tier German game, right? Good because I can't really remember much of the details. There were three goals all scored by the opposition, one of which was so far offside that Ray Tinkler even saw it (kids - ask your Dad or Uncle YouTube), a bizarre sending off and of course some dogs despite a clear warning outside the ground that canines were banned. Not one but two dogs had flaunted the rules and regulations that clearly said 'Nich Hunde!'. The notice also said no naked flames, no guns and certainly no nude people on the pitch ("Keine nackten Leute auf dem Platz"). Good advice I think you'll agree.

First things first, a drink and some food. Hmm, what to choose? I know, how about a beer and a sausage. Velbert use the world famous bingo card system to purchase food and drink. You buy a card and then when you want something one of the ladies shouts out what she has and you cross it off your card. Or something confusing like that. Quite why you couldn't just pay them in Euros is lost on me, possibly that famous German sense of humour again no doubt.

The music was blaring out from a little hut set in the hill-side above the terrace. It looked like a beach bar shack, but was actually the press stand. The crowd milled around in the sun-shine as the players went through their moves on the pitch. The visitors were clearly the better side and so it was no surprise when they took the lead from a well-worked training ground move. The main talking point came in the second half when one of the Velbert players was sent off for a tirade of abuse aimed at the referee. Instead of simply walking back to the changing rooms around the pitch and down the tunnel, he decided to jump in the stand, walk up to the path that went around the top of the arena then sit on a grass bank watching the rest of the game like a child being made to sit on the naughty step. During the second half Stoffers announced he had found a much better route home that only involved two buses. "Do we still have to stop in Hottsville?" I asked, already formulating a plan for the evening. "No, this is not possible."

After a night of drinking in the party capital of the North West Rhine region we returned to Chez Legg and retired to our own luxury suites. Before long the breakfast waft of freshly brewed coffee and pastries filled our nostrils waking us up. And there were those who thought we'd all be kipping on the floor of a one-room bedsit with someone's feet inches from your nose and the smell of guff heavy in the air. Where's the romance in that? Saturday was a day for sunglasses. Not that it was a late (late, late) night in the pubs, bars and clubs of downtown Düsseldorf, or the fact that temperatures were going to hit the big 4-0 later on. The main reason was that we were heading westwards to the historic town of Aachen, where the New Tivoli was our venue. The home of Alemannia Aachen is one of the finest new-style stadiums in Germany (and there are quite a few to choose from) but its most notable feature is its yellow seats. Really bright yellow seats, nearly 25,000 of them in fact.

Our journey had the word problem written all over it. A train-ride from Düsseldorf to Aachen skirting close to the Dutch border doesn't sound difficult but add in the fact that our journey would take us via Mönchengladbach, and you have a recipe for carnage. Thousands of Borussia Mönchengladbach fans would be hopping on our train full of weekend cheer and no doubt a beer or three to make the half-hour journey to Aachen for their first game of the new season, a season where optimism hasn't been as high for well over a decade.

Differing fortunes is a simple way to describe the current situation of the two clubs. After a spell in the Bundesliga for a few seasons, Aachen celebrated the opening of their new stadium by getting themselves relegated not just once, but twice, to the Bundesliga Three. They aren't the only big team now competing at this level. They will renew acquaintances this year with the likes of Hansa Rostock and Karlsruher SC in a situation similar to the nPower League One in 2011/12 when the likes of Sheffield United and Wednesday, Charlton Athletic and Stevenage all locked horns.

Borussia Mönchengladbach, once a regular in the latter stages of European competition, have gone through the 'punching below their weight' barrier for a number of years. In a similar situation to Aachen, their recent brushes with relegation coincided with a move to their impressive 50,000 plus capacity Borussia Park stadium. The fans, in my view, are some of the most passionate and noisiest in Europe, and for the first time in years were entering the season with a real sense of optimism. Last season they started as one of the favourites for relegation but ended up in the Champions League places after a top four finish for the first time in over thirty years. Whilst Aachen would be welcoming Rot-Weiß Erfurt at the New Tivoli for their next game in midweek, Borussia would be entertaining Dynamo Kiev in the Champions League qualifiers.

In England an early round cup game like this would be viewed with some contempt not only by the teams but the fans as well. Clubs can discount prices back to pre-Sky TV levels (kids - ask your Dad about when the First Division used to mean the top level of English football) but nobody wants to see two sets of reserve teams play and then the losing manager making an excuse about "concentrating on the league anyway". Here in Germany the cup is taken seriously by all concerned. Despite their Champions League game in just 72 hours Borussia went into the game fielding a full strength team. The draw for the cup is seeded in a way so that the teams from the lower league play at home, with ties being settled on the day via extra time and penalties if required. So one of the most anticipated matches of the round would see a sellout crowd in Aachen watch a game for more than just local pride.

The first forty-five minutes of our journey passed in relative calm. We were, if truth be told, a little fragile from the excesses of the night before, but a liberal dose of an English breakfast done German style with a salad no less, had perked up our outlook on life. Then the train pulled into Mönchengladbach. "What's it looking like out there?" Danny asked me as I peered out of the window. "All quiet on the western front at the moment." A few German riot police stood on the platform and it looked like only a few of the Borussia fans would be joining us.

And then, like the sun rising slowly above the ocean, came the unmistakable noise of a crowd building. Football fan noise. Ultras noise. Then they were upon us. Hundreds of them invaded the train, not in a bad, hooligan way, but in a bad for a hangover way. The riot police also climbed on board the fun bus for the journey just to make sure nobody got too rowdy but these were passionate football fans, not violent thugs.

Forty-five minutes later we arrived at Aachen West and everyone headed off the train. Well, not quite. It appears that all the Borussia fans were alighting here. Warning bells sounded in our collective heads but we just put that down to the headache tablets wearing off from our morning of suffering. We were funneled down the platform, through a tunnel and onto buses laid on for the away fans. We were cast as Ultras, but with pasty tans and a more conventional dress sense.

The buses took us straight to the New Tivoli, despite kick off still being a good few hours away, and pulled up into a locked car park. We were in the first batch of away fans to arrive and it looked like the open-air car park with no shade or 'facilities' would be our home for the next couple of hours. Fortunately Stoffers was on hand to negotiate safe passage out of our prison, pointing out our dress sense and accents which got a hearty chuckle from the riot police. We were now free to roam the New Tivoli.

Inside the ground after the customary entry search from the thorough female security guard (three times for good measure) we headed for the club shop, and what a club shop it was. Some clubs put their badges on anything and everything, priding themselves on levels of tat never seen since Ronco went out of business. But not Aachen, oh no. Club crested egg timers for just 50 cents, dog scarves and a t-shirt for girls saying "Sorry darling, these babies are reserved for Alemannia Aachen" across the chest. Classy. Christmas shopping complete in less than five minutes. Now that deserves a drink or two (or three or four...) to celebrate - to the bar Stoffers!

A brand new bar no less, filled with history (match poster from a game versus Swansea Town anyone?) and waitresses who only needed a nod and a wink to deliver another round of Bitburger. Our attentions were distracted by the weird and wonderful guests who were filling up the place. Old man with Aachen scarf wrapped around his waist? Check. Tall woman with short skirt and Alemannia Aachen tattooed up her inner thighs? Check. Very drunk real life Barney Gumble from the Simpson's bouncing around the room? Check. George Michael? Check..... whoa, back up a little there? George Michael? Absolutely. Of course it was him. Why wouldn't it be him? Even middle-aged

Anglo-Greek music stars that bored the world at the Olympics Closing Ceremony need to let off steam sometimes and have a nibble on a sausage or two at football.

Possibly.

Pre-match warm up complete, we made our way into the stadium for what had been billed by Kenny Legg as a potential "bananenschale" (banana skin). German football clubs are characterised by their ultras groups, clubs do not just have one, but many. The different factions normally have scary names like 'the Death riders' or the 'Sud Curve Crazies'. Here at Aachen they have 'the Karls Bande', 'Aachen Ultras' and 'Aachen Fanatics' who to a man broke into You'll Never Walk Alone, stirring at Anfield, spine tingling in the New Tivoli, to greet the two teams onto the lush pitch. Time for the magic of the cup. The only thing missing was a tinfoil-wrapped cardboard version of the trophy being held up in the crowd somewhere.

Borussia were on a hiding to nothing. Lose and the press would be all over them, especially with their Champions League game coming up against Dynamo Kiev; win and everyone would simply put it down to the higher ranked team doing their job. So they took the easy route and won in a very professional manner. They took their time to break down a spirited Alemannia side in front of an impressive 31,000 fans but in truth, they were never in any real danger.

Despite some early neat play by the Aachen midfield it was the visitors who held the upper hand and could count themselves unlucky not to go in at half time at least one goal to the good. In fact it took until the 70th minute when they finally took the lead. Granit Xhaka found the space and the killer pass, Juan Arango did the rest. Back of the net as Alan Partridge was prone to saying. Aachen threw men forward looking for an equaliser to take the game into extra time but as their final corner was cleared, Borussia broke in efficient and deadly style, Harvard Nordtveit eventually finishing off the counter-attack to put the result beyond any semblence of doubt.

Keen to avoid being kettled back onto buses and trains at the end of the game we headed back to the bar. Alas, as George Michael had headed back to Hampstead Heath, we were left with a variety of German football fans in all shapes, sizes and volumes to keep us amused. We remained until last orders (we wanted to show those Germans a thing or two about drinking) before heading back to Chez Legg, via a number of Düsseldorf's finest bars of course. In the words of the Beastie Boys, 'No Sleep 'Til Bonn', and day three of our German adventure and more cup action lay ahead.

It doesn't matter what the country is, the cup is full of stories of wonder, awe and inspiration. David beating Goliath, George slaying The Dragon and *those* goals by Ronnie Radford, Ricki Villa and Trevor Brooking. In France there was the story of plucky little Calais taking La Ligue champions Nantes to extra time in the 2000 Coupe de France; in England we had fourth-tier Chesterfield coming within a poor David Elleray decision of a Wembley date with Chelsea and of course in Spain back in 1980, Real Madrid beat their second team Castilla in the Copa del Rey to name but a few cup shocks that make the geese bump.

This season in Germany the hopes of a giant killing in the DFB Pokal rested with the opponents of the two sides from Munich. In the red corner, German super-beings Bayern München were due to take on newly promoted Bundesliga 2 side Regensburg, whilst the 'people's club' 1860 were drawn to play against FC Hannef 05, a tiny club from a few miles outside the former West German capital of Bonn, the town that gave (and continues to give) us Haribo. Named after the founder HAns RIegel and the town BOnn, the gummy sweets are a worldwide sensation. Today they produce a mere 80 million sweets per day in their 13 worldwide factories, enough to keep dentists the world over in Audis and holidays to the South of France for years to come. That reason alone was sure to bring the visiting fans to town, let alone the fact that gummy bears can be used as currency in the shops here. With hordes of Bavarians preparing to descend on the small village it was a wise decision to move the game down the road to SC Bonner's 10,000 capacity stadium. It was here back in May that Hannef won the Middle Rhine Cup and thus gained a pass into the DFB Pokal. This would be the biggest game in the club's history, and we were here to witness it.

1860s history is a bit more glamorous than Hannef. Winners of the Bundesliga in 1966, they have been out of the top division since 2004 and despite playing at the 69,000 seater Allianz Arena, things are not as good as they could be. The club and its fans crave a move back to their former ground in Grünwalder-strasse, ending their unhappy marriage of convenience with the red half of the city. They have won the Pokal before, the last time being in 1964 when they then went on to reach the final of the

European Cup Winners Cup (kids - ask your Dad) where they lost to West Ham United at Wembley Stadium.

It was almost like Groundhog Day for us as we started the morning, bleary eyed, staring at our Englischer breakfast with salad. Unfortunately Kenny's single room hadn't magically expanded overnight and the sight and smell of Stoffers feet once again acted as my alarm clock (still better than Huddo's alarm cock). We had to get an early train to Köln where we saw some of the most bizarre sights on a Sunday morning as the city's exhibition centre was hosting the Gamesco conference. The train was full of people dressed as elves, sprites and various members of video games, although there was a distinct lack of Jet Set Willy's (kids - ask your Dad again if he's not sick of the questions by now).

We arrived in Bonn and immediately hopped into one of the supporter's buses to avoid being mistaken for travelling fans and route-marched to the ground. Whilst the centre was sleepy the vicinity around the Sportpark was rocking. The mercury was due to hit 40 again today and we had all taken precautions against the effects of the sun by sporting our sunburn from yesterday's outing. After the customary pat down, twice this time by the young security girl, we walked into the huge bowl that is the Bonn Sportpark. Home to SC Bonner with a capacity of 10,164 it can be summed up in one word.

German.

Back in the 1970s most football grounds in Germany, Austria, Poland and the Soviet bloc looked like this. Some of the great old grounds were characterised by towering floodlights, athletic tracks with one covered main stand and huge banks of terracing. Gelsenkirchen had the ParkStadion before they built the Veltins Arena next door; Munich's OlympicStadion had a fancy glass roof but was essentially in the same design, and redeveloped stadiums in Hamburg, Hannover and Cologne are all constructed on the foundations of this same model.

The most stunning aspect in Bonn had to be the floodlights that not only extended upwards by about 70 metres, but also tilted at an angle of around 30 degrees into the stadium. Quite bizarre. So bizarre that a beer or two was needed to get over the shock. Fortunately the Kölsch van had arrived and we were soon two-handed toasting, drinking to the good health of German Footballing Weekends with our newfound best friends from Munich.

We took our place on the terrace in the covered main stand with the rest of the 1860 hardcore fans. This was a journey and a half from Bavaria but that hadn't stopped the six hundred or so who were now belting out the classic songs to the tunes of Shakin' Stevens, Pet Shop Boys and Slade. Everyone was welcome as long as you had a beer in both hands - old blokes with mullets and leather waistcoats (and nothing on underneath - a great look for the ladies in the crowd), men wearing badge-laden denim jackets and girls with their boobs pieced. Everyone.

Let me just rewind on the last point. Germany loves a piercing. I've never seen so many pierced people in my life as I had in in the past few days. All the usual suspects were covered in the 1860 crowd, ears, nose, eyebrows and belly buttons, but one girl who had stripped down to her bikini for the game, had her boob pierced. Twice. We aren't talking nipple-piercing here, we are talking about her actual boob. Twice. Thank heavens she didn't appear to have implants otherwise they would be leaking all over the shop. In fact it seemed like a fashion parade for the girls to expose as much naked pierced flesh as possible. Not that I was complaining of course. In fact we raised a glass in honour of the latest fashion craze sweeping the nation just as the two teams entered the arena.

In the end it was literally a walk in the Sportpark for 1860. Just like Borussia yesterday, they were professional in their execution of a team playing five levels below. The first goal didn't come until the 30th minute, by which time the home side should have taken the lead when a one-on-one ended up with the home striker smashing the ball against the bar. Two goals in as many minutes in the first half broke Hannef's dreams of a giant killing, whilst three more in a short period in the second half extinguished any brief hope of a comeback.

The 1860 fans had prepared for the sunshine by all donning beanie hats and throwing around blue balloons to welcome the teams onto the pitch. From the moment the sides appeared the songs began. We stood up, sat down, jumped around, clapped, cheered and kept silent all because a man at the front told us to. It was bloody great. I'm no wallflower when it comes to football but even this was a step above from anything we have ever seen in England. The riot police stood in the sunshine, keeping an eye on events but the whole section was essentially self-governed without any hint of trouble.

Half time saw the only real fan action when a water fight

broke out on the concourse, started by a riot policeman squirting a water bottle at an 1860 fan who then took a drenching in good spirit back. A few fans, including one who would have needed an E-cup bra if there was a market for them (we're in Germany - of course there is a market for them) simply sat drinking beer in the sunshine, ignoring the events on the pitch.

Full time saw a comfortable 6-0 win for 1860 thanks to goals from Guillermo Vallori, Benjamin Lauth, Ismael Blanco, Kai Bülow, Daniel Bierofka and Moritz Stoppelkamp. The home players milled around the main stand, talking to family and friends about the biggest game of their careers. I had 'acquired' a press pass and so it would have been rude not to take the opportunity to venture onto the pitch and have our picture taken. Nobody gave us a second glance as we acted like kids on Christmas Day. I got some strange looks with my pass on and it appeared that everyone else in 'my company' was working hard taking away all of the TV equipment, whilst I was larking around with a beer so we decided to head off before we were rumbled.

Unfortunately, after a couple of beers in the centre of Bonn it was time for my departure from German shores. The rest of the A-team had another full day of mirth and mayhem with a visit to Rot-Weiss Essen but for me it was Easyjet, SouthEastern trains and a day at the grindstone in London.

There is no such thing as a bad weekend in Germany. Wall-to-wall football, a love of a beer and a national dress that involves girls squeezing into dresses two sizes too small is a winner (we will hold judgement on grown men wearing leather shorts though). Kenny Legg was our new hero. Danke Germany, danke Kenny. We will see you again very soon.

Chapter Seventeen

How Many Balloons Go By?

Reasons to love (German) football, part II

19th October 2012
VfL Bochum 0 Hertha Berlin 2
The RewirePower Stadion

20th October 2012
Fortuna Düsseldorf 0 Bayern Munich 5
The Esprit Arena

21st October 2012
SC Paderborn 1 St Pauli 1
Benteler Arena

"...a good sing-song, a sausage or two and lashings of beer
are nearly as important as what happens on the pitch..."

> Ninety nine Decision Street,
> Ninety nine ministers meet,
> To worry, worry, super scurry,
> Call the troops out in a hurry,
> This is what we've been waiting for,
> This is it boys, this is war.

If there has ever been a finer verse of German music written then I'm a Dutchman. Nena's seminal '99 Red Balloons' was a lesson in life, love, war and peace. When you're 14 any woman wearing a short leather skirt, knee-high boots and fishnet tights on Top of the Pops looked like a goddess, even if she was singing a load of tosh and sounded like a strangled cat. Even my Dad remarked upon it back in the glorious summer of 1984.

"Remarkable set of lungs on her, young Stuart"

"She's German, Dad"

"Really? I met a German girl once. I was in Düsseldorf back in 1952. Hair everywhere. Piece of advice for you son, when you start courting be sure the girl knows how to use a razor."

And with that life lesson my Dad sent me out into the world.

Fast forward nearly thirty years and I was back in Dussers as Mr. Last is fond of calling it. Just eight weeks after I'd left the fine city of Düsseldorf I was back here again with Danny, this time with Big Deaks filling the ample shoes of Stoffers. This was fast turning into our new European HQ for continental operations, replacing Copenhagen (code named Denners) which now no longer had the same tax breaks, commitment to green issues and above all cheap beer. From Düsseldorf, German footballing missions could easily be marshalled, with the borders of Holland and Belgium within striking distance if we got bored, which quite frankly would never happen. We also had our man in the field Kenny Legg there, and it was at his request that we dropped tools and headed to the land of Beat Uhre. After August's visit poor Kenny had run out of PG Tips, Marmite and copies of 'Caravanning Monthly' written in English so he sent out a distress call.

"Low on essentials, any chance of an air drop at some point? P.S got tickets for Fortuna Düsseldorf v Bayern München and Paderborn v St Pauli if you fancy hanging around for a day or two...or three."

He had us at 'Low on essentials'.

Gatwick may well have gone through a multi-million pound

facelift but queuing to get a beer at Wetherspoons so early in the morning turns my stomach. But then again we were on holiday, albeit for 72 hours only, so make mine a pint of JW Lees Chocoholic please. Big Deaksy was thrilled to have made the starting lineup for the trip, joining Danny and I for the very short hop over the Channel, down the A1 and then throwing a right over Strasbourg to land at the heart of NordRhein Westfalen before most people back in Blighty had turned off their alarms.

Our early flight meant an early arrival in Düsseldorf. It would be tempting and very easy to have simply parked our bums in the nearest Brauhaus, sinking litres of Alt-beer whilst waiting for Kenny to finish work. Unfortunately, the work of the British Government isn't a 9 to 5pm role here in Germany. Oh no, on a Friday they finish at 4pm. Still, we didn't want to be gibbering wrecks by the time he changed out of his Dirndl, well, no more than normal anyway. A plan emerged thanks to the combined brains of Fuller and Last.

"What about a tour around Borussia Dortmund's ground? Biggest stand in Europe, most passionate fans, best football tack in Europe?" said Danny.

"What about a tour around the DAB brewery? Thirty-minutes of chat followed by two free litres of Dortmund's Awesome Beer?" I retorted.

"Can we do both?"

That's why we bring Big Deaks – he's a goldmine of common sense and fine thinking.

Of course we could. Add in an evening visit to VfL Bochum versus Hertha Berlin and you have one of the best days ever. Thanks to those good folk at NH Hotels we were able to have our rooms from 9am (gratuitous corporate plug - tick) and we changed into our German finest before heading for Dortmund with our free rail travel. It was at this moment I thought I would begin crafting a small list about what's great about travelling to German football.

Great things about German football #1:
Most clubs give free travel on match days in the region if you have a ticket to the game.

So our €15 ticket for Bochum allowed us to travel across to Dortmund and back before we'd even had a sniff of a game. Unfortunately time was slightly against us and just the one tour was possible so we chose the Signal Iduna Park over the DAB brewery. Marks out of ten? Just a six from the English jury - far too much talking in a foreign language and not enough letting us on the pitch for a kick about. You cannot fail to be impressed by the sheer size and yellowness of the ground and with the derby versus Schalke just twenty-four hours away, the grass was having a final laser-guided cut. Who said footballers were pampered these days? The final part of the tour saw us in the police cells underneath the Nord Tribune. "Hopefully these will not be full up after tomorrow's game versus Schalke," joked Wilhelm our guide. Two cells? Of course they were full after over 150 were arrested before, during and after the game.

The NordRhein area of Germany is essentially one big footballing corridor. From as far south as Köln right the way to Dortmund, the railway passes through towns that all seem to blend into one huge conurbation, differentiated by their footballing identity. Leverkusen, Duisburg, Düsseldorf, Essen, Bochum and Dortmund certainly makes a more interesting sounding train ride than my daily one of Mottingham, Lee, Hither Green, Lewisham and New Cross. Football is normally only a short hop away and after leaving Dortmund we soon arrived in Bochum, the cultural capital of the region (not my words I hasten to add) famed for its museums like the Farmhouse Museum, the Mining Museum and the Museum of Medical Tools. Scintillating. Our time for such culture was limited to just a quick look at the map before our next train steamed into Bochum railway station.

Kenny and his mate Stelios were waiting for us at the station, a pint of local Hërvel in each hand. We headed up to the ReWirPower stadium and joined the throng of home fans in the huge beer garden next to the ground. Plenty of characters here all dressed in their Bochum finest enjoying the October sunshine. I still find it strange that games are played in Germany at 6pm during the week when we Brits would be just logging off our computers, but football and beer are more important than risk analysis reports. It's all about a work/life balance and understanding the priorities in life so a Bochum fan was explaining to me. "Football, beer and hardcore pornography are a staple of life here. Oh, and Christmas Markets - but they are just a front for wife-swapping and dogging. You know the word 'Hunding'?"

There was literally no way to answer that without lowering your opinion of me still further, so I stood in stunned silence. Before my new friend could ask to come visit in England and sample our own 'Christmas markets', we headed into the ground. Two beers in hand we climbed to the back of the terrace for the visit of the league leaders Hertha. Beer and standing on a terrace – the sort of thing that gives football authorities a heart attack in England. Of course there were no issues, no trouble, no need to even have the police anywhere near. Allowing fans to drink in the ground also stops the English problem of the crush five minutes before kick-off outside and in the walkways. That gave me pause to go back to the list.

Great things about German football #2:
Football, terracing and alcohol can and do mix, even in huge numbers.

VfL Bochum are one of a number of German clubs that yo-yo between the two top divisions. With a relatively modest sized stadium, crowds tend to be...well, relatively modest. The stadium was the one of the first redeveloped in Germany in the 1970s. They are one of the oldest sports clubs in Europe having been formed back in 1848, although the football club didn't come into fruition until 1911. Their best seasons came in 1997 and 2004 when they finished in 5th place in the Bundesliga. Whilst the RewirPower Stadion is showing some signs of age, it is a classic old-style German ground with covered terracing at both ends where the respective hardcore fans gather and create the atmosphere. Another cracking little place to watch football.

Men v Boys is a fair summary of the games we saw over the weekend, starting with Hertha's dominance over Bochum. Berlin had gambled on an immediate return to the Bundesliga after their play-off defeat to Fortuna Düsseldorf in May of 2012. No longer is their team one dominated by Germans, eight different nationalities started the game under Dutch coach Jos Luhukay. Two well-worked second-half goals from Peer Kluge and Marcel N'Djeng didn't really do the scoreline justice although they could've had an injury time third when they missed a retaken penalty (having scored the first time around).

This was what watching football was all about for me. A beer in each hand, swaying to a German version of 'Three Lions' (specifically the chorus) whilst an enjoyable game unfolded in front of us. German football fans are passionate about their team's performance but a good sing-song, a sausage or two and lashings of beer are nearly as important as what happens on the pitch. Here we were playing our part. At some point the referee brought proceedings to an end and we all linked arms and Poznaned to the exits in the chilly night air.

We heartily slapped our new best friends on the back, promising to keep in touch, although leaving the invitation to visit the Christmas markets hanging in the air. The night was over for Bochum but for us it was just beginning. A brief pit stop on the way back to the station to look at some lovely Bochum net curtains in a supporters bar and then we were on our way to the bright lights and big city on the Rhine. Düsseldorf provided another exceptional evening's entertainment ending in a visit to Herr Legg's local, immediately dubbed the 'Legg Arms' as we had no idea of the literal translation of its real name. One final rendition of 'Every Rose Has Its Thorn' and a small discussion about The Scorpions' limited back catalogue and it was time for bed. Tomorrow promised to be a day that would live in the memory for years to come.

Saturday dawned and the main event was upon us. Seven games into the Bundesliga season and Bayern Munich were yet to drop a point. In fact they had won every game they have played in the season so far bar one (the coupon-busting surprise defeat to BATE Borisov in the Champions League) and had rarely being tested along the way. As the thousands of Bayern fans descended into Düsseldorf for the 3.30pm kick off against Fortuna, few thought there would be anything different about today's game. The local press and the Fortuna fans talked about the remarkable game in 1978 when Düsseldorf beat Bayern 7-1 but it in reality they would be more than happy with a point.

Düsseldorf old town on a Saturday morning is a great place to be. Women do their shopping whilst the men go to the many bars at the Rhine end of the pedestrian streets and drink copious amounts of Alt-beer. Then the women return, shopping bags in hand and join in the fun. Add in a few dogs in football colours and of course, on this day, the Bavarian regional formal dress of lederhosen left, right and centre, and you have quite an eclectic scene, all united by two factors - beer and football.

List time again.

Great things about German football #3:
Football is a day-long event for the whole family.

It may come as a surprise to know that the Germans have very strict trading laws when it comes to the hours that shops can open. Very few shops are allowed to open on a Sunday, and on a Saturday most tend to close by 4pm. This is all part of a drive to encourage a family lifestyle and so it is no surprise to see so many families dressed up for a visit to the football. Add in deliberately cheap as chips season-ticket pricing in modern, safe stadiums and you have a perfect cocktail that we are so far away from ever understanding in Britain. Clubs simply do not realise that whilst having a 'Kids for a Quid' game v Wigan Athletic or Southampton seems a noble gesture, charging £30 plus for the same seat versus Chelsea or Manchester United is not a long-term route to success. That brings me to another point.

Great things about German Football #4:
There is no such thing as a shitty stadium anywhere near the top flight.

Fortuna Düsseldorf's home is impressive Esprit Arena, built on the edge of the city and probably the best stadium in Germany that wasn't used for the 2006 FIFA World Cup. The city invested massively to rebuild the crumbling Rheinstadion back in 2004 in the hope that some of the World Cup games would be hosted here. After all, they had big tournament previous having hosted games in the 1988 European Championships and previous to that in the 1974 World Cup. But with three other grounds in NordRhein Westphalia already a shoo-in (Schalke's Veltins Arena, Dortmund and Köln's new stadium), Düsseldorf lost out, winning the right to host the 2011 Eurovision contest as consolation, the one when Blue came out of retirement - remember?

They don't do things by halves here in Germany so in order to prepare for the world's greatest music competition, Fortuna were required to vacate the stadium for three games. They could have moved in with FC Köln or Bayer Leverkusen down the road, but instead decided to build a temporary stadium in the city-centre with a reduced capacity of 20,000. The structure was completed in just 60 days and was superb. While I'm in this wave of German football euphoria, time for another reason.

Great things about German football #5:
Tickets can always be bought legally and without any issues online via market place websites.

This was the first season back in the Bundesliga after a fifteen-year hiatus for Fortuna. So far they had started okay, picking up ten points from their opening seven games. Their fans are some of the most passionate in Germany and there was never any doubt all 54,000 seats would be sold for this game. Tickets would be hard to come by but in Germany buying one on the black market is not illegal. German eBay (ebay.de) for us in the know was our best friend and for less than a price of an Emirates burger, we had procured three tickets for the game.

The use of market place sites to buy and sell tickets was made illegal in Great Britain by the introduction of the Criminal Justice and Public Order Act of 1994. This was specifically passed to stop ticket touting during the European Championships that were held in England in 1996. That was basically pre-Internet and as we all know, the world has evolved significantly since. The act applies to tickets for any football match played in this country or featuring a British team. By denying the buying and selling of tickets on the biggest market place in the world the authorities are actually making the issue of touting worse. Online sales, through regulated sites such as Seatwave and Stub-Hub in the US ensure that the tickets are genuine and the amount they can be sold is regulated. People trying to sell their seats for inflated prices simply won't find a buyer. I know, I know, you're right, it is just common sense but it's easier to assume everyone in Britain's a criminal obviously.

double sigh

Shut up Stuart and move on.

After our pre-match warm up of some excellent Warsteiner Pils on the concourse, we headed up to the seats just in time to see the F95 hardcore fans at the far end unfurl a huge banner celebrating that victory back in 1978. Right on the referee's whistle the banner split in half and as soon as it appeared it was gone, replaced by mass flag waving - a pretty awesome sight in anyone's book. So I guess that means it's list time again...

Great things about German football #6:
Fans tifosi displays are amazing and put our support in the shade.

So distracting was the display in the first few minutes that anything could have happened on the pitch and we wouldn't have known. Bayern lined up with a 4-4-1-1 with Kroos in the false 9 position (back in the day he would have been called a link man but let's go with the modern flow) behind the league's top scorer Mario Mandzukic. Franck Ribéry and Thomas Müller gave the team width, whilst there was no place in the starting XI for new and massively expensive signing Javi Martínez.

From the first moments of the game it was obvious that Bayern had come to win, and win comfortably. They held onto the ball for minutes on end and Fortuna were chasing shadows. It came as a surprise that it took so long for them to take the lead, in fact we were on our second beer by the time that Mandzukic converted a chance made by the impressive and busy Ribéry. The second came just before half-time and goes down as a very soft goal. A corner was played in and Bayern midfielder Luiz Gustavo poked the ball at the Fortuna keeper. The ball rebounded back to him off his knee and he had the simplest of jobs to guide the ball into an empty net from a few yards out.

The second half started in much the same with Bayern threatening from the first whistle. Such was the excitement that more beer was required. Ribéry was again the creator when he set up Müller in the 55th minute to put the game beyond doubt. The Fortuna fans, however, never gave up trying to get behind their team and will them forward.

Great things about German football #7:
Fans support the team for 90 minutes irrespective of the score.

We missed the fourth goal, scored by Müller incidentally, when Danny walked in front of Deaks and me. The fifth arrived within 30 seconds of Danny finally moving his arse and was a cracker, scored by substitute Rafinha supplied again from the magic boot of the brilliant Ribéry.

The final stats didn't lie. Fortuna only mustered two shots in the whole game, only one of which was on target, whilst Bayern peppered the goal with 25 efforts. They had 69% possession during the 90 minutes and should have won by a bigger score. Fortuna knew this game would probably be a bridge too far and so on the final whistle immediately refocused their efforts for the visit of Wolfsburg next weekend.

We headed out and filled the evening in the usual way. After a heavy night in the best bars in the city, the last thing we really needed was a 7am alarm call the following morning but we're all martyrs for the cause and so, headache or not football would wait for no man. Düsseldorf Central Station at 8am on a Sunday morning was a buzzing pot-pourri of all walks of life. People with multiple facial piercings, tattoos, ripped clothes and various political slogans walked by the hung-over group of Englishmen gazing into the distance. Despite the early hour drinking beer seemed to be the main alternative to a Sunday sermon for all around.

Then it hit us. These were all St Pauli fans who were heading east, like us, to Paderborn. If one club is known for sticking their fingers up at authority then it's St Pauli. They like to do things their own way, offering up a different brand of football club and encouraging the alternative rather than the norm. Located just a stones throw from the famous Reeperbahn in Hamburg, itself the home to age-old sin, the club has endured a tormented period of trying to resist the uniform commercialisation of a football business model, yet still yearning for on-field success. Currently plying their trade in the second tier of German football, they had one of the most passionate away followings in the world. People followed them because of what they stood for rather than where they were based.

We certainly felt a bit out of place on the long train ride east, without any metal or ink on our bodies, and currently drinking just water. On arriving at Paderborn it wasn't difficult for us to pass through the riot police cordon on pure looks alone. Whilst the away fans were herded into a holding area at the station we had time to see the historic remains of St Liborius to tick the box marked 'Paderborn – culture', before we were heading to the Benteler Arena.

Paderborn is home to over 10,000 British troops and their families, and many regularly attend the 2.Bundesliga side's home games in the functional, if not spectacular stadium that opened in 2008. The club seems to have found its level in the second tier of German football whilst today's visitors, St Pauli, had ambitions of a return to the top-level. With such a big travelling support a sell out here was never going to be in doubt.

It was hard to think about the fact that back in the UK rain and chilly temperatures had marked the start of autumn, yet only a few hundred miles away we had 29 degrees of beautiful sunshine. Fans bathed in the heat, shedding their clothes accordingly (alas only the male St Pauli fans) with a beer and a sausage strategically placed to hide their modesty whilst the countdown to kick off continued.

It is fair to say that this wasn't a classic. The most impressive display was undoubtedly from the fans at either end, although St Pauli must get all three points game for:

a) Safely fitting twice as many people in a section as seats.

b) Enduring the sun in their eyes for the whole game.

And finally...

c) For singing a version of Just Can't Get Enough for a solid 15 minutes at half-time.

Neither team really pressed forward although St Pauli had two good first half chances, one of which hit the post. Both Danny and Deaks had bets on a three away win accumulator from our weekend's games and they could smell their money when Daniel Ginczek put St Pauli in the lead with a header in the 48th minute.

Alas the lead, and the boys winning position, lasted just 25 minutes before Deniz Naki scored an outstanding effort from the edge of the box to draw the home side level. The away fans hardly skipped a beat as the ball hit the back of the net. If points were awarded for fanatical and coordinated support, they would be up there with the league leaders at the top level in any country.

We still had time for a quick beer or three in the centre of sunny Paders as it had become affectionately known to us, choosing alcohol over a train ride back with the beautiful people. Another three days of fun was coming to an end. Our annual Oktoberfest of football had been a roaring success but now it was time to return home or in my case, down to Munich for work. Germany does football as football should be done. We'd paid a grand total of €83 for our three games (approximately £72) and that included buying tickets on eBay. If you want to ease your way into football tourism Germany is the place to start.

And revisit.

Again and again and again and again.

I could go on but the point has been made. I'll finish as I started, with the words of one of music's finest talents, Nena:

This is it boys, this is war,

The President is on the line,

As Ninety-Nine balloons, three matches, several sausages, some very heavily pierced people carrying brilliant banners and God only knows how many beers,

Go by.

At least that's what I think she sings...

Chapter Eighteen

Push the Bloody Button!
99 problems but a switch ain't one

16th October 2012
Poland (P) England (P)
Kazimierz Górski National Stadium

14th November 2012
Sweden 4 England 2
Friends Arena

"...no football could be played but then I remembered the
miraculous fold-away roof the stadium had..."

Wednesday 20th February 2009 - that's a date I'll never forget.

Toothache can strike at any time but when it starts suddenly whilst on a high-speed train cutting through the barren lands of Castilla La Mancha in Spain you really are stuffed. No access to a dentist there, no pharmacies selling painkillers and none of those old fashion door handles where you can loop a shoelace around to yank the offending tooth out with. Never had I wished for a return to an old a British Rail football special more.

As was the case with nearly all of the premium train lines in Europe, the staff were top notch. Sitting in first class with Dagenham Dan we had our own stewardess, Isabel, and she was there to serve us "personally" she told us. Her English was good, slipping in the words 'serendipity' and 'tranquility' into a sentence about what highlights we would see on the two-hour journey. However, she proved useless as to a means of providing pain relief for my molar. The one ray of light came when she had to reach up to one of the overhead lockers and her relatively tight fitting attire rode up momentarily distracting me. As a gentleman as well as a scholar I was far too polite to ask her to hold that position just for my comfort.

The train was heading from Madrid to Andalusia, Seville to be more precise, where we would be watching England take on European Champions and World Cup favourites Spain. It would be the last time I would travel to watch England abroad. I had grown weary of the endless suspicion, the security checks, and the hassle that travelling abroad following the Three Lions involves. I'd also got fed up of the way our own FA had been running the game at all levels for years and the contempt they had shown for the fans. There had been far too many instances of our own football authorities simply seeing the travelling fans as unnecessary hassle. An incident in Zagreb a few years previous summed it up when we fans, after coming under a savage attack from the Croatian police for daring to enter the Maksimir Stadium to watch the game, were then held for nearly two hours in a remote car park at Zagreb airport just so the team themselves could pass through the airport without any issues. The toothache I suffered on the way to Seville was agony. Whilst I can never blame John Terry personally for my current condition, it was a sign that I should knock the travelling away for England games on the head. Away trips couldn't get any worse than Seville, could they?

There had been some good times. Representing (and managing) my country in Macedonia as the England Fans Veterans XI lost 5-1 to a team LIVE on Balkan TV who would later that same season qualify for the then UEFA Cup. Of course Germany 2006 was probably the pinnacle for most fans. It couldn't get any better than cheap excellent train travel, first class stadiums and some perfect weather.

And it didn't.

Zagreb in October 2006 was a nightmare - poorly organised, terribly treated and an awful performance. Paying the best part of £500 to go on a heavily delayed day trip to Tel Aviv to watch one of the dullest games of football ever didn't help my mood either. For every Minsk there was a Barcelona, Berlin or Moscow. Slowly the other fans I used to travel with started giving it up. Rob the Red, Paul Knight and even Dagenham Dan. Trust me, you don't know him but believe me when I say that when he gives up something football-related, you know it's time to seriously re-assess the future.

I saw the England game last year in Copenhagen but that doesn't really count as I was in the press section and I was living a 15-minute walk away from Parken at the time. Oh no, come England membership renewal time in July 2012, I kept the cheque book firmly in the drawer. Admittedly I glanced an eye over to that same drawer when the fixtures for the qualifiers for Brazil 2014 were drawn, but I didn't really see anything that particularly excited me. Happy with myself I sat back smugly as the campaign kicked off, knowing I had made the right decision.

But then it started.

A little voice in the cheque-book drawer talking to me every time I sat at my desk, whispering bank-balance poison in my ear at every oppurtunity.

"Mmmmm...new stadium in Warsaw Stu, shiny and new."

Go away.

"And you know you love football in Poland Stu."

Stop it.

"Stockholm Stu, another new stadium, another shiny and new stadium."

La, la, la, I'm not listening.

"It's called the Friends Arena. Just a goal kick away from the office - you have to go there to do some training anyway."

I do have to go there for training. I'm listening.

But I'm definitely not going.

"And Airmiles Stu, you have thousands of them, hundreds of thousands, just waiting to get used on venues like, well Warsaw and Stockholm for a start."

Oh God, be strong Stuart, be strong.

And then the emails began

"It's still not too late to be cheering on Roy's Boys in the new National Stadium in Warsaw!"

I swear that the email had hidden HTML subliminal advertising because before I knew I had paid my £70 renewal fee, booked my flights to Warsaw and dug out my Zlotys. I literally had no idea what had just happened but it appeared my will power was weaker than a weak thing on a weak day. Time to broach the subject with Current Mrs. Fuller, one that would require extra special petrol station flowers for sure.

She of course asked the one question that I couldn't really answer. "Why?" I couldn't really say because of the Airmiles as she had given me a list of places she wanted to go that amazingly always seemed to be unavailable when I checked with British Airways. I couldn't even say it was because of new cultures, new cities and new experiences - I went to Warsaw twice in 2011 and travel to Stockholm for work at least every other month. I had to 'fess up that I was simply going for the new stadiums. Is that shallow? Who cares, it had shut the voice in the cheque-book drawer up and that was what's important. She agreed because she is the best woman in the world, and I was going.

I am a weak, weak man.

Poland has gone through a massive regeneration in the past few years. On my first visit in 2006 it was very grey, people looked miserable and the football stadiums were grim - none more so than the two in Krakow where I managed a sneaky look via a magic door. Fast forward to my trip with Mr. Last last December. We stayed in a 5-star hotel in Warsaw for less than £50, drank (a little too much perhaps) beer in some fantastic bars for less than £1 a bottle and the locals ladies even went out of their way to show us they didn't have any tan lines in one bar. We flew in Poznan to have a look at their impressive new stadium, wandered the club's shop (socks for me, Christmas bunting for Danny) then travelled first class across country to the capital for less than the cost of your Old Trafford hot-dog, sharing a carriage with the Italian Ambassador to Poland no less who was equally impressed with how the ugly duckling of Polksa had grown up into the beautiful white swan of Poland. The country had caught Euro-footballing-fever.

England were hardly strangers to Poland in footballing terms.

From Jan 'the clown' Tomaszewski's one man show at Wembley in 1973 to Gary Lineker's first half hat-trick in the blistering heat of Mexico in 1986, it seems that rarely a qualifying tournament goes by without us being drawn together. Poland is possibly the one country that England has a reasonably good record against.

After co-hosting such an excellent European Championships there was an air of confidence wafting across Warsaw as I landed at Chopin airport. My taxi driver tried to explain how Polish coach Waldemar Fornalik would line his side up against the Three Lions, concentrating more on the overlapping runs of Grzegorz Wojtkowiak than the pedestrians crossing the road into the city centre. Two-nil Poland was his parting shot to me but a few days previous, England had comfortably beaten the mighty San Marino 5-0 at Wembley. Surely we were now the best team in the world again?

I didn't see the San Marino game, I didn't even see a report or the goals on TV. It was CMF's birthday and so after a very pleasant night out at the theatre in the West End we headed off to Bruges for a weekend of silky chocolate, double-cooked chips and triple brewed beer - a million miles away to the fare on offer at our national stadium. As my daughter would say, the weekend was "well-reem".

All of my comments so far may lead you to think I'm anti-England. Nothing could be further from the truth. When it comes to football I want my nation to win every game. I just wish I didn't have to feign interest in certain aspects of following them. I'm not and never will be 'England 'til I die'. I've never been in an Irish Bar whilst abroad watching them, never sung 'No Surrender' or jumped in a fountain. I want to travel abroad to see a national side that inspires the watching fans, plays good football and makes people proud to say I'm an England fan. In terms of inspiration, the thought of Ashley Cole being lauded for reaching 100 caps leaves a bad taste in my mouth. Here's someone who sums up what a modern footballer shouldn't be in one small, spiteful package. Thankfully, the other toxic twin (England's Brave John Terry) retired from international football just before the FA banned him. Even then they showed no consistency after the Suarez case last year. These are the things that grate, but in purely footballing terms, I'm very much an England fan, and always will be.

This game would certainly be a test more for the Poles than England. After two years of friendlies in the build up to Euro2012 the White Eagles came into the tournament in some confusion as to how good they really were. Three games later the national team confirmed what many thought - that by the third week of the tournament they'd all be watching the games on TV. Drawn in a qualifying group for Brazil 2014 along with Euro co-hosts Ukraine, Moldova, San Marino, Montenegro and England, on paper they would fancy a shot at being group runners-up and ultimately a play-off spot. So far whilst England could boast 7 points from their opening three games, Poland sat in 3rd and could technically top the group with a four-goal win over us.

But that wasn't going to happen. The powers above (in more sense than one) had a different plan for the evening. Apart from the McClaren years, England's qualifying form for major championships has been nothing short of outstanding. Rarely are they troubled on their travels whilst away from Wembley; they may not always entertain, but they constantly deliver. So what could possibly go wrong in Warsaw?

Well how about the plans (and finances) of thousands of fans being adversely affected by one single person? I refrain from swearing in normal circumstances for the sake of offending my younger audience but on this occasion I will make an exception. What fucking fucker decided not to fucking push a little fucking button that would close the fucking roof of this fucking brand new fucking stadium when the fucking weather forecast was for fucking rain ALL fucking day?

One fucking button.

One fucking second of activity and those thousands of fans would've been happy.

The day before, both teams were consulted as to whether to close the roof. Not armed with a weather forecast that said it would be raining in biblical proportions all day, they said no. But surely someone had some sense and the power to reverse this decision when it started pissing down something terrible on Tuesday morning.

At 6pm as I trudged through the streets of Warsaw looking for my hotel I started questioning whether the game would go ahead. I wasn't just wet, I was soaked to the very core. Every item of clothing I was wearing looked and felt like it had been dunked in a swimming pool - surely no football could be played in these conditions? But then I remembered the miraculous fold-away roof the stadium had. A year ago I had come to Warsaw to have a butchers at how the stadium was progressing. I spoke to a local football expert who extolled the virtues of the "ingenious" roof. I remembered a similarly designed canopy-style cover installed at the Commerzbank Arena in Frankfurt. When the stadium hosted the final of the 2005 Confederations Cup between Brazil and Argentina in a torrential storm, the roof was closed. Unfortunately all of the water pooled in one corner of the closed canopy causing it to rip and dump thousands of litres of water onto the photographers below. Lessons learned, according to my friend, after all, the Polish FA wouldn't want the embarrassment of a postponement on their hands.

Hotel found I stood under a hair dryer for 20 minutes and put various undergarments in the microwave. I turned on the TV and saw the crowd filling up the seats. A TV presenter holding an umbrella at pitch level turned to the sky. To coin text speak rather than be forced to swear again - WTF? The roof was open. Rain was pouring through the opening onto the pitch. A feeble attempt to get a ball to roll demonstrated that the pitch was unplayable, yet the teams were being displayed on the screen. Perhaps they knew something I didn't so I headed onto the tram and made the short journey to the stadium. Fans huddled under umbrellas as they made their way into the ground. At 8pm my ticket disintegrated as I handed it over to a steward to check on the outer perimeter. "No problem - game will be off," said the steward on the gate. The Polish police were standing by happy that no hooligan from either side would really want to be trading blows in the rain.

The England fans were all congregated in a small, but dry concourse area tucking into the delights of Polish football food. I grabbed a drink and headed up to my seat and looked down at the pools of water on the pitch. There were no ground staff making an effort to drain the pitch, nor were there any players warming up despite there now only being 20 minutes until kick off. It didn't take a genius to realise there would be no football played tonight yet the fans from both sides were kept in the dark as to what was going on. Text messages from back home gave us more information but for us in the stadium it was torture. For the next hour we saw highlights of Euro2012 SIX times, accompanied by the whole back catalogue of Coldplay. Wasn't the rain punishment enough? Ironically, the roof couldn't now be closed as it was raining too hard and it would cause the canopy to collapse when it started to pool.

The 9pm kick-off time came and went and there was no sign

of any players or officials. Bizarrely, still no efforts were being made to clear water from the pitch, yet the rain continued to hammer down. At 9.15pm the referee and his assistant made an appearance to a chorus of whistles from the frustrated crowd. Their attempts to make the ball roll on the pitch were observed by a thoroughly soaked Roy Hodgson. Pitch unplayable, game off surely? Oh no. Another bizarre decision on a day to forget for the Polish FA saw us being told that a further pitch inspection would be carried out in half an hour. How on earth they thought the situation would improve in that time with the rain falling just as hard and no effort being made to clear the surface of the lakes of water I'll never know.

Hmmm...what to do to amuse the crowd? I know thought the stadium announcer, I will put some more Coldplay on, yay – that'll cheer them all up. In the darkest hour came a ray of light. A pitch invader from the Polish section managed to hurdle the perimeter fence, escape the feeble attempts of the stewards and ran the length of the pitch before performing a perfect sliding dive in the penalty area. 'Bring on the Belgians' as they would have said in 'It's A Knockout' (yet again ask your dad kids, he must be sick of all these questions by now).

At 9.45 came another pitch inspection. This one lasted all of 10 seconds. Ball thrown in the air, lands firmly in a puddle and doesn't move. Referee picks it up and walks back down the tunnel, shaking his head. Yet still an official announcement wasn't forthcoming for over 30 minutes, by which time we had all had texts from back home saying the game was off and would be replayed at 5pm on Wednesday. Very handy for the 75% of us who by that time would be back in the UK. I should add by this point my line of communication had collapsed; iPhones and water do not mix very well and the rain had now soaked into every nook and cranny causing my pride and joy to short-circuit. This trip was already up there with the toothache in Spain.

I had no idea how they would re-ticket the game. Few fans had anything left apart from a mush of, well, mushiness. The frantic race for most fans to rebook flights and hotels was already underway as I made my way out of the stadium and on to a waiting train. Thanks to one person's incompetence the additional cost would have to be borne by the fans who wanted to watch the game. Ridiculous.

So possibly the worst ever away trip came to an end with a flight back to the UK with our favourites Ryanair. I'd personally like to use this book to thank that one individual who decided to not press that button which closes the roof. Thanks to that idiot I wasted one-and-a-half days annual leave, about £150 and now needed to replace my iPhone. If there is any justice in the world they will be fired, or made to personally apologise to all those fans that had to miss the re-arranged game because they couldn't change their travel plans. Perhaps just an offer to do some light chores instead? But they won't will they? After all they are part of the football family and will probably find themselves promoted to work at UEFA or FIFA head-quarters in ticketing and logistics for the next tournament.

Over a nice cup of tea back at home, CMF had that smirk on her face, the one that women have when they know they're right. She didn't have to ask the question "was it worth it?" as it was written all over her face. I would take toothache over being soaked to the skin, attending a game that would not take place and then ruining my iPhone.

And I still blame John Terry and Ashley Cole.

Did I learn my lesson and vow never to travel again (again)? Of course not. Less than forty-eight hours later I was uttering those immortal words that get me in so much trouble time and time again, "I'm in", when I received an email asking whether I wanted a hotel room in Stockholm.

Like I said, I am a weak, weak man.

After the farce in Warsaw I needed a bit of re-assurance that lightning wouldn't strike twice in Stockholm but I had no worries about the weather affecting the game. Two weeks previous to my arrival in the capital of Sweden the lights dimmed and a lone voice welcomed over 45,000 people to the opening of Europe's second largest indoor arena (Schalke's Veltins Arena is classed as the biggest should you want to know). The 2.8 billion Swedish Kroner Friends Arena had finally arrived, after years of talking, debating and finally construction in Solna, just north of the city centre in Stockholm. The opening event featured the best of Swedish music including appearances by Björn and Benny themselves (obviously coming out as ABBA must be short of a few quid) as well as 1990s favourites Roxette. Alas, other classic Swedish music acts such as Ace of Base, The Cardigans and Europe were missing from the line up on that opening night.

But the Arena wasn't built just for Swedish House Mafia concerts. It will primarily be a football stadium, the home of AIK and the national team. It was only fitting that the opening game to be played here should be against a team who has a passionate away following, who could generate some real noise and atmosphere. Unfortunately, Denmark had a previous engagement with Turkey so England agreed to step in. The good news was that I was already due to be in the city for work purposes when the game was scheduled; the bad news was that it was likely the exclusion on the England band from previous away matches in Poland and the Ukraine would be lifted for this game.

I've enjoyed a good relationship with football in Stockholm over the past few years, coincidentally tying in work trips when there were games in the city. As well as trips to Hammarby and IF Brommapojkarna, I'd been a frequent guest at the Råsunda, the home for at least another week of AIK, primarily to watch Kenny Pavey, the finest Englishman never to play for the national team (remember him from chapter two?). The face of football in the city was about to change dramatically. Not only were AIK about to get one of the most modern new stadiums in Europe to call home, city rivals Djurgården and IF Hammarby were about to move into the new Tele2 Arena in the south of the city for the start of the 2013 season.

I have spent enough nights in the city to know where to go to drink proper beer, rather than the watered-down, Government-friendly bars that most of the England fans would camp out in during the run-up to the game, spending a fortune on a beer that has less alcoholic content than a can of Shandy Bass. So it was a no-brainer that once I had set up my work schedule for the day I would be heading north to the new promised lands in Solna.

After the debacle of Poland many people questioned why I was here at all. I'd replaced my iPhone at a cost of "just" £200 and whilst the FA promised a refund of our ticket money, a month down the line I was still waiting. As with most organisations they are very quick at taking money off you, but very slow at refunding it.

Still I needed to console myself. Having enjoyed a spot of list-making in Germany I was at it again. I re-assured myself as to why I was travelling to Stockholm as my plane flew over the North Sea.

1: It was a historic night for Swedish football. The opening of the biggest stadium in the Nordics, one of the most modern in the world and one where the roof actually worked and would definitely be closed.

2: I need to visit our sales office in Stockholm every few months and hadn't been since May and they missed me. Probably.

3: I had a room booked at the Jumbo Inn, literally a hotel in a jumbo jet.

Point three was probably as exciting as the visit to the new stadium. I love aeroplanes. I have no choice but to in the job I currently do. On average I fly over 100 times per annum so being able to actually stay in a jumbo jet for the night was high on my list of to-dos especially as the house maids were dressed as air stewardesses (I was hoping Virgin/Singapore rather than the surly Ryanair variety).

As usual prior to any friendly international there had been a significant number of withdrawals from the squad the weekend before. Five players pulled out on Sunday, and three potential replacements had produced a note from their mum on Monday morning meaning the 21-player squad includes new faces such as Wilfried Zaha, Fraser Forster and Carl Jenkinson, the latter having previously represented Finland at under-19 level. Just a few months before, these three would have been hoping for a spot in their respective team's Capital One League Cup side, yet here they were travelling first class to Scandinavia in their lovely new England tracksuits.

I wandered around the city like a local primarily because I thought I was one. I know enough Swedish to get by and be understood and could thus join in the banter in the office about the game. Of course the Swedes would win; of course Zlatan would score and of course it would be the best stadium ever. Over dinner and a few proper beers in a local restaurant my work colleagues replayed the game at Euro'92 to me, demonstrating Brolin's winner using the (fat) salt and pepper pots. I bade my colleagues farewell and headed onto the T-Bana for Solna Centrum. The guide the FA had put together for the fans was useless, full of dead links, although fortunately the always excellent Free Lions, put together by the Football Supporters Federation, had full details of the routes to the new stadium. I exited from the metro station right in front of the Råsunda, which would be hosting its final game in a weeks time when Napoli were visiting in the Europa League. Now there are two sets of fans that would willingly start the demolition process on the historic ground free of charge...

The route from the station was well sign-posted, albeit dark and wet as we went up hills and down dales. Eventually the sky turned blue and yellow as the new stadium lit up the night. It certainly looked impressive, with an outer shell pulsating blue and yellow as Swedish rock music blared out. Having had to carry around my laptop bag all day I was expecting some issue when I entered the stadium. Instead I had a not-too unpleasant rub down from one of the Corrs, who had found a new job since stopping touring clearly, and she asked if I had anything "interesting" in my bag. What do I do? Show her my collector's edition of 'Private 73 - Swedish Saucepots' featuring and I quote, "Amazonian haired women" (and we are not talking about hair on top here), or my iPhone mobile charger shaped like Spider-Man? I kept my mouth shut as she moved her hands from my body onto the bag, giving it a seductive squeeze and a wink as if to say my secret was safe with her.

"From Miami to Ibiza," sang the Swedish House Mafia as I entered the stadium, quite apt as the temperature had risen by a good ten degrees. Perhaps it was the collective heat generated by the England fans that also had a thorough security check, or maybe just all part of the modern design of the stadium which ensured that a temperature of 20 degrees was kept constant as scientifically that was the optimum temperature for the players to perform at apparently.

First impressions were very good. Wide concourses, plenty of food outlets, soft drinks which you could top up as much as you wanted a la Pizza Hut, a special Arena sausage (made from 80% "great meat" although it was the remaining 20% that worried me) and very surprisingly, beer. Some England fans hadn't realised that the cheaper variety was the alcohol-free kind, a fact that became more amusing as the evening wore on and they got 'drunker and drunker' on the placebo.

The stadium had excellent sight lines, seats with masses of legroom and four huge screens that hung from the ceiling. With the roof closed it had an almost surreal feel about it. At one point durng the warm-up, Hodgson looked up to the roof as if he was reliving the nightmare in Warsaw. Talking of Roy, the fans were treated to an interview he gave with Swedish TV prior to the game. I always find it strange when we see and hear an English-man speak a foreign language fluently. We see the reverse all the time in England but because we see so little exported talent from our shores it always makes you want to applaud them for basically bothering to learn a local language. Roy of course is still a hero down at Malmö FF where he heralded in a golden age for the club and signed some quite good players as it turned out. Such as Zlatan Ibrahimovic, but he's rubbish, right?

With this being the first game in the stadium we expected some pomp and circumstance. What we didn't expect was six bloody great big horses running around the edge of the pitch, ridden by knights holding various flags. They provided the guard of honour for the teams as they emerged and we stood up for the national anthems. The Swedish authorities decided on the two-verse approach for England, thus trying to gain the upper hand by silencing the England fans. We had already broken into applause at the end of verse one, the band had started and we were back in our seats before we realised they were singing the lesser known second verse "Our lord our God arise". Just like the missing third verse rapped by Vincent Price in Thriller, none of us knew the words so we just repeated the first one. Spare a thought though for some of the players as they'd only just learnt a) we have a national anthem that didn't feature 50 Cent or Dr Dre, b) it has words and c) they are supposed to sing it. Now they find out there's a second bit to it? I think we best leave the fact that there are two more verses to another day.

The horses dissipated without any Blue Peter elephant antics and the TV presenter on the side of the pitch tried to persuade the young mascot to take the match ball onto the pitch so we could start the game but he was having none of it. With his image being beamed to a global audience of millions and blown up to 6 metres wide on the huge screens above, he froze. Stage fright is a bugger and he had it bad. Eventually the referee persuaded him on to do the ceremonial kick off with Zlatan. Finally done he picked up the ball and ran off, only problem being that he had taken the match ball with him so a further delay ensued whilst someone went and got it back, swapping it with him for a bar of local chocolate 'Plopp'.

The game was easily summed up in three parts. Firstly, there was the section where England were crap, secondly we had the bit when when we realised we were playing a one-man team with very little substance, and then finally there was the time when Joe Hart went a bit funny. Make no mistake, Sweden deserved the win but the way that England handed it to them on a plate with some of their own IKEA special sauce and that strange something-berry jam made us realise actually we still aren't world-beaters, as if we needed any reminding.

It was certainly a new-look England team that started the game with Raheem Sterling, Leon Osman and Steven Caulker all making their debuts. For all of his boundless energy and apparent fertility, young Sterling cannot defend. Never really an issue if you are playing in front of a good full back. But he wasn't. He was playing in front of Glen Johnson. First question. Why does Johnson have the letter "G" on the back of his shirt? There are no other Johnsons in the current squad, nor has there been since Adam lost his way at Man City and ended up in the North East. Of course he could always get a recall and thus they'd save on money by already having his shirt printed but could you say the same for Wayne Rooney (the lesser skilled John is skill kicking around in Yorkshire), John Terry (brother Paul is the one player slower than England's Brave JT) and of course Stevie G himself has a cousin, Anthony, currently playing for Huddersfield Town. But back to Johnson (G)'s walkabout with just twenty minutes gone. Sweden exposed the space down the England right, the ball was played across the area and Zlatan got to it first. His initial shot was blocked by Caulker but he made no mistake from the rebound.

The roof almost came off the stadium. Prior to this you could actually hear a pin drop. It was deathly silent, something completely the opposite to the big games I'd attended in Sweden in the past. In fact the goal woke up a fair few thousand fans that had been happily snoozing in the quiet, warm indoor environment. To stop them going back to sleep a Mexican Wave was started, and of course we all joined in. We love a Mexican Wave us England fans (apparently).

At this stage the familiar thought went through my head. "Why do I bother spending time and money to watch England play?" It was simply another below average performance against another average team. Then something strange happened. We started playing the ball around like a top-ten FIFA world team. Ashley Young got the ball wide, beat his man, decided not to dive for once and sent the ball across the six-yard box where Danny Welbeck couldn't miss. One-all.

Confidence breeds confidence. Gerrard and Osman put their Stanley Park differences to one side and started bossing the midfield. Then all of a sudden England had the lead. Gerrard swung in a free-kick, the Swedish defence left it for the keeper, the keeper left it for the defence and all it needed was for Caulker to get any part of his body on the ball to score. And so the young Spurs centre-back celebrated his debut with a goal to put England 2-1 up. This wasn't in the script.

By half-time the pitch was a mess. Prior to the game I had met up with Pras, the Swedish Marketing Manager for a Championship club (not specifically for Sweden but he is Swedish and a Marketing Manager) and he had relayed his concerns about the surface that had only been laid the week before. After just forty-five minutes his fears seemed to be coming true as it looked like it had been toasted in parts, with clear parallel lines running across it from where the turf had been laid. Various divots were scattered around which the groundsmen tried to work on, but to no avail.

The first part of the second half was a typical England performance. Little threat, square passing and lots of substitutions. On came Stoke City's Ryan Shawcross to shore up the defence and nullify any threat from that pesky Zlatan. The appearance of Shawcross in an England shirt still gives middle-aged ex-players like me that one day I still might get a call-up by Roy. The Swedish captain Zlatan wasn't having the best of nights despite his goal in the first half. He'd seen little of the ball and more often than not tried to drop too deep to get it. "You're just a shit Andy Carroll" some of the England fans sang to him, obviously forgetting that West Ham loanee Carroll had been overlooked for a player who plied his trade in the Championship (Zaha) and another who could still play for another country (Jenkinson). Of course this all meant there was absolutely no irony when Ibrahimovic equalised with a little less than twenty minutes to go as the England band played the theme tune to Steptoe & Son.

Now would've been a good time to bring on one of our substitute goalkeepers. After all, isn't the point of friendlies an opportunity to blood some new players, try out new formations, such as Osman, Zaha, Shawcross and Caulker? With Gerrard now off the pitch to pinch himself as to how he had just played for his country for the hundredth time, Joe Hart was the most senior player on the pitch. Joe Hart, a man who still looks like he's yet to start shaving. What was Hodgson hoping to learn that he didn't already know about Hart? And what's the point of having two untested keepers on the bench if you will never play them in friendlies?

As the game entered the last ten minutes of the ninety, the

goalkeeping irony came back to bite England firmly on the bum. Zlatan's free kick from 25 yards was well hit but should not have beaten the wall, let alone an almost static Hart. Three-two and at last the home fans had woken up. The script was written for them to win their first game in the new stadium. What was it I had said to a work colleague over dinner? Ah yes.

"The problem with Ibrahimovic is that he can never raise his game when it matters."

You know what's coming next don't you.

What on earth was Hart doing in injury time, wandering out of his area to head a ball straight up in the air? The next few seconds seemed to pass in slow motion. You could see Hart mouth "shiiiiiiiiit!!!!" as Ibrahimovic looked up and turned away from goal. He leaped and connected with an overhead kick some thirty-yards out. The ball sailed high up into the air, the crowd all looked skywards, as too did the English defenders frantically trying to get back on the line. Of course the script had already been written for this historic night and the ball defied physics by coming almost straight down and just under the cross bar. The stadium went rightly ballistic; it was part luck, part genius. If a 'normal' player had scored the goal we would have said it was lucky but because it was Zlatan (what I call the Beckham/Cantona effect where everything you do irrespective of how lucky or shit it is has to be classed as genius) it was a stroke of pure, eye-watering, breath-taking magic.

Quite a few of the England fans applauded; we are all foot-ball fans at heart and it was a goal worthy of the highest inter-national stage. Zlatan ran to the crowd, took off his shirt and milked the applause raining down on him. Of course despite the situation, the referee had to be the fun police and book the Swede for taking off his shirt, but we all know that he has to follow the rules as they help control the fun.

The rest of the game was irrelevant. The final whistle followed a few minutes later and it didn't take too long for the fans leaving the stadium to change their position from the brilliance of the goal, to the fallibility of the England keeper. He made some poor judgment calls in the second half and as a result England lost the match. Once again you have to ask the question what he was doing on the pitch when we had two untried keepers on the bench desperate to prove themselves.

The journey out of the stadium to the station was cold and wet, although still not on the Warsaw scale. My first-class cabin on Jumbo Inn awaited me, complete with a selection of free light refreshments all served with a smile. Thursday morning dawned after a lovely night's sleep and I had already dealt with the texts from my Swedish (and French colleagues) about the "lucky goal" and "one trick pony" before breakfast. One player was the difference yes, but surely a team who are ranked sixth in the world shouldn't have been beaten like that. Hats off to the Swedes for having the balls to build such a great new stadium and let's hope it won't be so long before we come back and exact footballing revenge.

Swedish football has always been on the cusp of something good. Despite a run to the FIFA World Cup semi-final back in USA94 there hasn't been much to cheer about. Could the massive investment in the stadiums be a sign of the dawning of a new age of football in these parts? Only time would tell, but I'm happy to take on the job to report on their progress on a regular basis if it means spending more time in Stockholm. Possibly one of the best cities to visit in terms of relaxation and natural beauty (and I am not just talking about the locals here), the added bonus of three decent football teams makes it a definite stamp in the Football Tourist's passport. Just remember to remortgage your house before you arrive though...

Chapter Nineteen

Silent Night
New money? French bread

4th December 2012
Paris Saint-Germain 2 Porto 1
Parc des Princes

5th December 2012
Lille OSC 0 Valencia 1
Grande Stadion

> "... the toaster I was looking at not only burnt the club's
> name onto bread, but also played 'Allez Lille LOSC'..."

Paris, the City of Lights. Home to Pepé le Pew, dancing polar bears (well, every fridge magnet I saw for sale in the city had them on), the birthplace of pole dancing and once home of the object of Obelix's affections, Falbala. This is the most visited city in the world and one where the traffic jams stretch from La Défense in the west to Disneyland in the east. This is a land where a small hotel room no bigger than a six-yard box can set you back €550 just because you can see the top of the Eiffel Tower on a clear day by hanging off the roof-top TV antenna. Paris, home of dreams, nightmares and everything in between. In truth I'd rather be in Blackpool than Paris.

So why am I here if I don't like the place? Good question as my normal cheery outlook seems to be slightly clouded by the comments above. Let me set the record straight. I've spent more time in Paris than any other city on this planet, bar London and Copenhagen, thanks to a year-long work assignment that saw me in the city every Tuesday and Wednesday for 52 weeks. Sounds brilliant, right? Well, what if I was to tell you that our Paris office was actually in the western area known as Boulogne where our neighbours were transsexual prostitutes? The 'high-class shopping experience' promised in all the brochures in my case was a store that made your local pound shop look upmarket, even six months after it had closed. My version of the 'local fine dining' promised was a burger bar that had once closed down after a dead cat was found in the freezer on an inspection (true and horrible story).

Like I said, I'd rather be in Blackpool than the Paris I had been posted to.

With some of the most bizarre employment laws known to man in power in France, I was sent to the Cite l'amore to 'cut through the red tape', which was American speak from our head-office for 'let's take a chance we won't be sued for firing people without months of employee consultation periods'. Since the heady days of 2001 I've been a regular visitor, and perhaps Paris and I got off on the wrong foot as I've always had a mild dread of trying to do anything that involves negotiation, contracts or due process here. Don't get me wrong, I love the Parisians to death, but sometimes cannot understand the quirks of life in the city. The city is simply an enigma to me.

If ever one establishment summed up this enigma it had to be Paris Saint-Germain football club. The premier team in one of the premier cities in the world, alas, their standing has never been one of Premier League quality. For a club that are actually younger than me (that makes me feel very old) their dominance of the media would lead you to believe that they are the most successful team in the country. They aren't, that title could be said to belong to Saint-Étienne or more recently Olympique Lyonnais. Olympique Marseille would also have a thing or two to say about who was the biggest club in the country with over 60,000 packing into the Stade Velodrome come rain or shine, success or failure, and even regional sides such as Nantes, Lens and Lille would say they were more successful than PSG. But that is all about to change if you believe the hype.

In England we have seen numerous new dawns in terms of football. The creation of the Premier League in 1992, the arrival of Roman Abramovich and his millions of roubles in 2003, and then four years ago the black gold arrived. The gold-plated Rolls-Royce rolled off the Calais to Dover ferry from the Middle East and headed up the M6, with Sheikh Mansour bin Zayed Al Nahyan (known as Dave to his mates probably) in the driving seat. Manchester City went from being the perennial underachievers, playing in the third tier of English football just fifteen years ago, to out-scoring and out-spending anyone on the planet. Money does buy success whatever people may say, and the Abu Dhabi dollars delivered the Premier League in May 2012. But at what price? In November 2012 it was revealed the club spent over £10m last season on agent's fees alone and that their wage bill was over £500,000 a day. Ten million pounds is the equivalent of the operating budget for every non-league team playing at levels 3, 4, 5 and 6 of the pyramid, that equates to over two hundred and fifty grass roots teams.

Welcome to football in the 21st century.

A transfer policy that is based on bringing in the game's biggest mercenaries, coupled with buying up English talent to sit on the bench so that none of their rivals can have them may have worked last season, but this season it all seems to be falling apart especially as they cannot buy European success, where it really matters to be seen as a real giant of the game. After a poor Champions League campaign last season, they followed it up with a disastrous one this time out failing to even qualify for the Europa League consolation spot. They would be joining the likes of FC Nordsjælland, OSC Lille, Montpellier and Dinamo Zagreb in getting the wooden spoon. Not only that but they earned the honour of the worst ever record attained by an English club.

So how are Manchester City's finances relevant to Paris? Well a similar situation is playing out in the city thanks to the massive cash injection from the Qatar Investment Authority. Their arrival saw the appointment of Carlo Ancelotti as head coach and the acquisition of Zlatan Ibrahimovic and Thiago Silva, amongst other marquee players in the summer. The title race was done and dusted before a ball had been kicked apparently and Man City were the model to follow.

Unfortunately, the wheels on the wagon haven't been on long enough in the French league to be considered to now be falling off. Form in the early part of the season has been poor to say the least based on expectations and the quality and quantity of their squad. Defeats to the likes of Nice, Rennes and Saint-Étienne has seen pressure heaped on the Italian coach, just as it has been on Roberto Mancini at Man City. Without a league title since 2004 although they did finish runners up to Montpellier last season, the first time in eight years they have finished in the top two, they simply have to win the league.

But in the Champions League it has been different. Whilst Manchester City had struggled Paris Saint-Germain came into the final game of the group stages knowing they had already booked a place in the knockout phase along with Porto. The final home game against the Portuguese side would determine the group winners, and I had a window..

Coincidentally I happened to have planned a visit to Paris for work purposes on the very day the game was taking place. No seriously, genuine coincidence in this case - I mean what sort of shallow individual would use the fact that his employers would pay his travel and accommodation just to watch a football match. Honestly, some people. But of course once I had found out this massive stroke of luck I asked the question – "How can I get a ticket for the game?" and as luck would have it, my French colleague Patrick knew a man, who knew a man, who once knew a woman who knew someone who we cannot talk about.

People often ask how I manage to get tickets for all of these games wanting to know my secret. Well, the secret is there isn't a secret - it's all about who you know. I've spent years building up a network of contacts, people who can help me out just like I help them when they want tickets for West Ham or God forbid some rubbish at The Emirates or Stamford Bridge. What's more I'm on Twitter, Facebook and most of the other usual channels and if you want a ticket, I can usually put you in touch with someone who may well be able to help. Modern life may be challenging in some respects but in terms of building connections, it is undeniably magnificent in almost every way.

So when I arrived in the office in Paris there on my desk was a beautiful silver ticket for the match, looking like it had been freshly unwrapped from one of the five prized Wonka Bars. Of course when you have that little beauty winking at you in the weak Parisian sunshine, work is almost impossible. The whole office was abuzz with talk of the game. Football fever had at last arrived in the city, sure it might have taken tens upon tens of millions of Euros to turn the locals on but let's face it, money is one hell of an aphrodisiac.

With talks of reputation-management strategies and on-line contingent-liabilities wrapped up for the day I headed to the world's worst value hotel, got changed and then went for my pre-match fitness test with the legend that is Hadyn. There is nothing this man doesn't know about fine food and wine in the city and he regaled us with tales of recipes featuring stuffed duck necks and tripe. Combining his ample skills in online brand protection planning with a passion for producing his own food on his Essex farm gives him an aura when in any restaurant. Unfortunately the fare on offer in Restaurant Marco Polo had him only recommending the Kronenbourg at €8.80 a pint and some assorted nuts. He's a rugby man and so had no interest at all in the Champions League game, preferring a nice bottle of Chateauneuf than watching Zlatan Ibrahimovic, so I enjoyed his company for a while and then left him to it.

I've been a sporting spectator in the city frequently, although primarily to watch rugby. In fact my visits to the Parc des Princes read 'Rugby 6 vrs Football 1' prior to this game. There had also been a few trips to watch Stade Francais in the H Cup (it's a cardinal sin to mention the Heineken word in public in France) just across the road from the stadium. This trip to watch PSG was long overdue.

There are no easy journeys on the metro in Paris. Every line seems to snake around each other meaning to get from point A to B you often have to go via H, P and X. A relatively easy trip from Opèra to the Parc des Princes directly westward took Patrick and me up, down, left and finally right underneath the Parisian streets. The game had sold out weeks ago and outside the stadium there was a crackling atmosphere - something which can be a slight rarity at French football. The smell of strange grilled meat filled the air, the babble of the crowd was punctuated by the sound of police sirens and those bloody half-and-half Champions League scarves were on sale everywhere.

The Parc des Princes is showing its age these days. A stadium was first opened on this site in 1897 built for the 1900 Olympic Games, but the current ugly concrete stadium opened in 1972. The ground has hosted it's fair share of big matches including six European finals, two European Championship finals and of course numerous games in the World Cup codes for both football and rugby union as well as being the original finishing line for the Tour de France. The noise in the ground can be very intimidating but sit anywhere above row 5 in the upper tier and your view at eye level is of the sloping concrete roof. The PSG fans are famed throughout France for the intimidating atmosphere they produce. Normally at the north end of the stadium you have the Boulogne Boys, one of the most legendary sets of Ultras in Europe. For this game the fans had sensibly been split up, with the authorities worried of potential flashpoints with Porto's following.

PSG started the game with some Gallic flair, using the pace of the wide men to get in behind the Porto defence. The first real chance fell to Zlatan Ibrahimovic, no surprise there, but he seemed to have left his shooting boots back in Stockholm's new Friends Arena failing to convert Javier Pastore's cross. The centre-back pairing of Thiago Silva and Alex (once of Chelsea) were rarely troubled and every time they had the ball they had all the time in the world, only sporadically threatened by the Porto attackers who seemed to be here just for the shopping in the Champs Elysees. It was no surprise when the French side took the lead, with Silva heading home unmarked in the 30th minute from a deep corner. Surprisingly the PSG lead only lasted four minutes when Jackson Martinez headed home for Porto. Half-time and honours surprisingly even.

Was this going to be a dead rubber? The danger was that both teams would settle for the draw but the second half couldn't have been further from it. The final stats showed that there were 29 shots in the game, the vast majority in the second period. The referee somehow managed to brandish six yellow cards in the second half, trying to steal the show himself, but that honour fell to Helton the Porto keeper who seemed to push the ball into his own net after Ezequiel Lavezzi's weak shot appeared to have been easily covered at the near post. Two-one and that was enough to wrap up a very successful Champions League first stage for Ancelotti and his side, and one that would keep the daggers away from his back for a few months at least.

After negotiating the maze under the city I arrived just in time for last orders back in the Marco Polo. It had been a good night and whilst my taste buds were alive to the sound of my non-footballing colleagues stories of fine women, fine food and fine wine, my final Leffe of the night slipped down well with the sound of those Boulogne Boys ringing in my ears - "O Ville Lumière, Sens la chaleur, de notre coeur. Vois-tu notre ferveur, Quand nous marchons près de toi, dans cette quête. Chasser l'ennemi, enfin pour que nos couleurs...Brillent encore"

It had been a good night and one that had gone some way to restoring some love for the city. A hefty lunch on Wednesday afternoon topped it up even further, and finally a great training session in the office complete with a round of applause for my efforts had me brimming with amore once again. I love Paris – there, I've said it now. How could I possibly arrange an encore to the PSG game? Well how about another slice of Champions League just up the road in Lille? Sigh, if I have to. After seeing just one Champions League gravy train game in nearly two years, two had come along within 48 hours. Don't blame me - blame the 'Daggers Diary' team, they made me do it, it's their entire fault. It started with an innocent text message from Dagenham Dan a few weeks ago:

"Stu, we are driving over to Lille to watch them against Valencia in their new stadium in the first week of December. Only £65 a head including ticket, Le Shuttle and petrol"

"Sorry Dan, I'm in Paris for work that week"

"That's a shame. Hang on, what if you get a train after work to Lille and we can give you a lift home?"

Did I really have to answer that? Of course not. He had me at "new stadium". So after work I headed to Lille, just fifty minutes away on the train that goes very fast known as the TGV, a catchy name for Train Goes Voom. Lille Olympique Sporting Club, to give them their full fighting name, were domestic double winners in 2011 although the club haven't always had a history smelling of roses. They've had a traumatic and sometimes nomadic existence since formation in 1944. The fact that they now have their own stadium is a reward for the years where they probably felt the powers that be in the city didn't want a football team at all. But now they have a stadium fit for a club who have grand ambitions to be one of the powerhouses of French football. A 50,186 all-seater monster in the Villeneuve-d'Ascq area of the city no less, one which UEFA had given a shiny five star McDonalds badge. Build it and they will come said the Indian in Wayne's World 2 (and in some film about 'baseball' whatever that is), and so far the fans have taken quite a shine to the Grand Stade Lille Métropole, flocking here since it opened in August.

However, despite the plush new surroundings and memories of the trophies less than 18 months old, some of the fans weren't too happy with the team's performance in the UEFA gravy train this season. Four defeats in five games prior to the arrival of Valencia, including an embarrassing home defeat to the supposedly group whipping boys BATE Borisov and a 6-1 defeat in Munich, had seen the fans fume. Obviously the team lacked the midfield dynamo, the playmaker, the fox in the box, and the magician that is Joe Cole since he left in May.

Oh, and Eden Hazard, son of Mickey I'm guessing, he left for pastures new and Chelsea-shaped too.

Rumour had it that the fans would be staging a silent protest at the game to show the club officials exactly what they thought. So after a hard day's work in Paris (including the obligatory long lunch) I headed for the TGV. Fifty-minutes later I was enjoying my first beer in the world-famous 'Three Brasseurs' pub, the focal point for all new arrivals in the city. Alas one was all I could manage before I was diverted away from temptation by Dan and Brian, who both wanted to visit the LOSC 'superstore' in the city centre. I was still on the hunt for a Christmas present for the Current Mrs. Fuller and lo and behold the perfect present was staring me right in the face on the shelves of the club shop.

Sod your Efbe-Schott polka dot £500 toaster, the one I was looking at not only burnt Lille LOSC on your breakfast but also played 'Allez Lille LOSC' again and again until you took the toast out. Is that not the best Christmas present ever? Ipod Mini, Kindle Fire HD, vouchers, no, what every good wife really wants this Christmas is a musical Lille toaster. Hell, in fact Mariah Carey this is ALL you really want for Christmas and if you fancy popping over wearing that Santa Claus outfit, then I'll happily do you a few rounds of toast and Marmite.

After snapping up every LOSC-branded kitchen appliance in the shop we headed down to the stadium. Dan had parked close to the Cantons Metro and after a quick change that Clark Kent would have been proud of in the boot of his Ford Fiesta, we were headed to the stadium. Big tick for having accessible transportation, with metro stations on either side of the ground plus regular buses running from the centre. The plan was to meet a former work colleague, now living the high-life in Lille. Over a beer in the bar outside the ground we heard from Francois about the unhappiness of the LOSC fans that seemed to have it in for their manager, the chairman and nearly all of their players.

With the weather forecast predicting rain, wind, sleet and snow, the club had taken the decision to close the roof. Amazingly this would be the fourth time I was seeing Lille in the fourth different stadium. Eleven years ago I had seen a Champions League qualifier against Parma in the old Stade Grimonprez-Jooris, paying a whopping €80 at the time. Then I had seen them play Champions League games in the Stade de France and the Stade Félix Bollaert in Lens as their Stade Municipal stadium wasn't up to scratch to host Champions League games.

You would have thought it would be a tad warmer inside than out, but not in the indoor stadium. It was bloody freezing. Perhaps it was a plan to make the Spanish feel as uncomfortable as possible, although the fact they had taken the field to warm up in more layers than a mountaineer seemed to suggest they were used to the cold environment. People tend to forget how cold Madrid, Bilbao and Zaragoza are at this time of the year. We tried to head down to the edge of the pitch to take a couple of pictures. As we walked down the aisle an hour before kick off our way was blocked by a female steward.

"Billet."

"Can I just take a photo?"

"Billet."

"Ici."

"Votre siege n'est pas ici. Allez."

"Un picture?"

"Non. Allez. Il est illegal"

"Taking a picture is illegal?"

"Oui. Je vais vous arreter!"

It seemed that Lille had managed to pass a law just for their new stadium that made it an arrestable offence to take a picture. Congratulations LOSC for having the rudest stewards in the world. In a season where domestic and European success were far from likely, that's a badge of honour you can wear with pride. Such high praise takes some doing in my book having been to Stoke's Britannia Stadium a few times.

We headed upstairs to our real seats and watched as slowly the spaces began to fill up. With few fans in the arena the one word that summed up the atmosphere was sterile. The stadium blurb had boasted "…massive screens at either end of the stadium to show all the action". Unfortunately we couldn't see said screens as the TV gantry that hung from the roof was in the way, blocking the view at each end - very impressive. As you can tell by now I wasn't falling in love with the place. It was impressive and I loved it from the outside with the exterior made out of light tubes which lit up the Lille sky, but inside it was quite bland. Even the seats would have been classed as 'neutral grey' on the Dulux colour charts. Perhaps it was the complete lack of atmosphere (due to the fan boycott), the rude stewards or the fact it was bloody cold that was slowly getting to me. Still, ninety minutes of Champions League football would cheer me up I'm sure.

As the game petered out, with neither team particularly interested in going forward, the Lille fan next to me turned and said "ils ne sont pas digne de porter la chemise!" which I believe means that they (the players and not Brian and Dan sitting next to me) weren't fit to wear the famous red shirt of LOSC. It had been a toothless performance played out in almost silence. The 40,000 fans had indeed sat silently for virtually the whole game, bar for the occasional chant which was met with jeers from the other fans. Unfortunately it had no effect on the team who stumbled through the game without ever really testing the always comfortable Spaniards.

Lille coach Rudi Garcia named young forwards Ronny Rodelin and Gianni Bruno in an experimental line up and the duo combined in the second minute to create the first chance of the game, although Bruno was unable to turn in a cross from the left. Thirty minutes later and the home side had their next chance with little of interest going on in between. Our main excitement was coming from Twitter updates from games elsewhere which was a real disappointment not just for us, but everyone else in the stadium.

The only goal of the game came in the 36th minute when Jonas (the fourth Jonas brother, being the black sheep by not following

Nick, Joe and Kevin into the music business) converted a penalty after a soft foul had been conceded in the penalty area. At the other end of the pitch, ex-Chelsea player Salomon Kalou went down in the area. In fact Kalou spent most of the game on his bum, obviously having had some private lessons on how to fall over dramatically from Drogba before the two departed from Chelsea in the summer.

We were frozen to our seats by the time the first half ended. Our half-time entertainment came as we tried to move down a few rows so that we could watch the half-time highlights from the other games. Once again our path was blocked by a jobsworth steward. When we pointed out the rows of empty seats and our obstructed view he suggested we should have bought a more expensive ticket. Nice work mate.

The second half didn't ever get going although Lille did come more into the game. Valencia needed Bayern to stumble against BATE for them to finish top of the table, but that was never going to happen. The German machine was in full effect as they were cruising to an easy win against the Belarusians. The seventy-three travelling fans (Dan took a picture of them, enlarged it and then counted them) seemed to be enjoying themselves, knowing that this year a runners-up spot could give them an easier time in the next round. Full-time brought a few boos, although many fans had started departing with around 20 minutes to go.

We headed back to the car, tucked into Dan's girlfriend's home-made sausage rolls (not a euphemism) and I fell asleep. I know how annoying it is to have to drive people home at night and all they do is fall asleep, so apologies Dan. I briefly awoke at Calais when the guy at passport control shone a torch in my face to check I wasn't an illegal immigrant but then I went back to sleep, waking up finally as we passed Maidstone.

It had been a great few days in terms of work but up and down in terms of the football. I had looked forward to seeing some Gallic passion from the fans, especially in the new stadium in Lille but instead I was left feeling very cold. Oh well, I'm sure I would be back, perhaps when that big fiery ball in the sky made an appearance at some point in 2013.

The announcement of the "signing" of David Beckham by PSG in January certainly raised the stakes in French football. Many saw this as a masterstroke, the key to PSG going on to win the title, whilst others simply saw it as a way to drive the PSG brand across international borders. No sooner had the ink dried on his three month contract than queues per building outside the megastore on the Champs L'Eysee to buy their "32 Beckham" shirts at a snip at just €105. With existing "work" commitments and a serious lack of match fitness it was hard to see exactly how many minutes Beckham would actually get on the pitch for PSG. But that wasn't important. By signing possibly the world's most famous player, in a stroke they had become one of the most talked about football brands in the world. Poor, poor Ancelotti.

Nous sommes venus, nous avons vu, nous avons mouillé.

As the French would say.

Chapter Twenty

Dundee Derby Day Delight
Arbroathie smokies and self-proclaimed hotties

8th December 2012
Arbroath 2 Stenhousemuir 2
Gayfield Park

9th December 2012
Dundee 0 Dundee United 3
Dens Park

"...we tried to find someone who would run between the two
grounds in slippers to settle a bet..."

"There are two seasons in Scotland: June and Winter."

That quote from Billy Connolly rang in my ears and through my chilled bones as Danny Last and I alighted from the train at Arbroath on a cold Saturday lunchtime. In a recent survey only 10% of people could actually accurately locate the North Sea fishing port on a map. Granted I only asked ten people, of whom one had lived in Aberdeen for thirty years, but you know what they say – 93.23% of statistics are made-up bollocks anyway. Few people outside Scotland ever make the journey this far north, even fewer would come here out of choice on a Saturday, let alone one in mid-December with the temperature fighting to break freezing point.

But they're not slave to our master – football.

We believe in pushing the envelope, going where no sane Southerners have ever been before. Well, that was what Danny told me in an effort to refocus my attention when I suggested that I'd rather be at Lewes v Whitehawk today.

The master plan was to take in the Dundee derby, which for the pleasure of the millions from around the world who wanted to watch the game, had been moved to Sunday lunchtime for TV purposes. Not that it caused us a problem, it just meant we had an extra window - an opportunity to sample something new, extend our cultural reach and basically get tuts of disapproval from our respective wives. We had plenty of options but as soon as Arbroath was mentioned I knew I had found my raison d'être. Pints of Tennents all round, we now had a plan.

But as we opened our Dundee Derby advent calendar, counting down the days until we could have our Dundee cake and eat it, that darn weather got in the way. In the summer we have rain when we should have sunshine and in the winter we have snow and freezing conditions, when we should quite frankly have snow and freezing conditions. Frozen pitches had already begun to decimate the Scottish Football League programme as we prepared to board our private jet from London City airport, but they are made of sterner stuff in Angus-by-the-sea and there was never a doubt that Arbroath's clash with Stenhousemuir wouldn't go ahead. Like good boys well taught by our parents, we rang ahead anyway.

The first rule about visiting Arbroath is that you're not supposed to mention *that* match. The second rule is you're not supposed to mention the fact that the ground is located next door to a certain body of water and the third rule is that never, ever ask what a Red Lichtie is. Any hint of not knowing those would mark you out as outsiders. The fact we were from the South of England, spoke with an English accent, dressed like Englishmen and were acting like Japanese tourists at Buckingham Palace snapping every amusing sight going, didn't matter at all. It was all about being in the know.

Our journey had taken us from plane, to bus and finally to train. Train travel in England is a rip off but it seems that in Scotland you need to add on another 10% to that rip off. Our request wasn't too complicated - return tickets from Edinburgh to Arbroath but coming back tomorrow from Dundee. The initial quote at the station was £42.90 each. That's for a 70-minute journey each way. I know I give SouthEastern some pelters on a daily basis, but at least they only charge £6.60 for a similar journey although technically it should only take 20 minutes. We then asked for a return to Dundee and then a return from Dundee to Arbroath - total cost £33.20. Thanks a lot for that ScotRail.

I had done this exact journey once before on a Jolly Boys outing to Aberdeen. Due to an accident on the M1 we had missed our flight from Luton to Aberdeen so took a flight to Edinburgh and then the train. It has to be one of the best rail journeys on our Magical Isles. After crossing the Forth Bridge and past a couple of picturesque fishing ports you swing a right and head northwards, hugging the rugged coastline as you go. With the sun shining on the water it takes you back to a different age, when life was so simple. Then Danny interrupts your dream by jumping up and down because he has seen some floodlights in the distance. The ground gets closer and closer until we pass straight by Raith Rovers, there were even footballs on the pitch. What would make this journey even better would be a beer and as if by magic, a man with a trolley full of Tennents appeared at our side. £2.90 wasn't exactly cheap but as he explained to us, it was like staying in a five-star hotel overlooking the Bay D'Anglais in Nice. Beds are basically the same, but you pay a premium for sleeping on it.

We arrived in Dundee with seventeen minutes to check into our hotel and then get back on the train to Arbroath. Fortunately our executive guest suite was opposite the station. However the booking was in the name of Mr. and Mrs. Fuller and the trainee receptionist was all a fluster as to wheth-er to ask if we needed one bed or two. She became "all fingers and thumbs" as my Mum would say, another one of her rubbish northern sayings that basically means nothing – after all I would be worried if someone didn't have a) fingers or b) thumbs. Perhaps it should say "fingers for thumbs" or even worse "thumbs for fingers". Finally, we reassured her by liberal mentions of our respective wives that the twin-room set up was indeed correct and we were on our way, managing to hop back on the train with minutes to spare. We had feared this may be the Stenhousemuir special full of their top boys, ripping it up on their trip up from Falkirk. As it was it was just full of old women looking forward to a day out in Montrose. The excitement was palpable, so much so that we had to have another Tennents. We passed through Carnoustie, scene of so much golfing drama, before the train eased into Arbroath. Lucky old Arbroath as the old Hamlet advert used to say.

It would be rude of me not to introduce you formally to the biggest town in Angus, so allow me to give you a few facts.

1. Arbroath was the home of Dr Neil Arnott, one of the most revered people in the pornography industry although he probably doesn't know it. On a family holiday to Magaluf back in the 70s, he filled his dad's Lillo up with water "for a laugh" and created the waterbed, the most used prop from the early years of main-stream smut. Today, adult film studios still refer to a scene using a waterbed as an Arnott. Probably.

2. James Chalmers is another famous ex-Arbroathian. It's be-cause of him that we've all licked the Queen for he invented the adhesive postage stamp, fed up of using all of his sellotape posting his Christmas cards. He made the first adhesive out of chewing gum that he had used, then rolled it flat and used a cookie cutter to shape. Apparently.

3. Arbroath is the home of the Smokie - salted, dried and then smoked haddock that is unique (and protected) to the town. The locals eat more than 3,000 smokies per head per annum, making it the world capital of smoked haddock consumption. The town are in the process of producing Smokie perfume and bath-wash, Smokie air fresheners and Smokie shampoo to cash in on their fame. Possibly.

Oh sod this. You don't really want to know about such irrel-evant trivia. I know you, dear reader, want to talk about Gayfield

Park, Arbroath FC and THAT game back in 1885.

So let's start at Gayfield Park, the home of The Red Lichties. There is some mystery about where the club got its nickname from, some thinking it relates to a mysterious sea creature that used to be seen emerging from the North Sea at night. Others think it is related to how the locals used to believe the Chinese sweet fruit, the Lychee, was pronounced. We had discovered on the train up that it is neither of these. Davie was a mysterious old man who hoped on the train at Leuchers and off again at Dundee, who had joined us for a Tennents on the train and when he heard we were heading for Arbroath told us the story, but made us promise we wouldn't tell. Well, just telling a few people here won't really matter will it?

The club is named after the red light that used to guide ships home to the harbour at Arbroath. Today, the light can still be seen just to the north of the ground. Nothing too special about that fact, but then Davie told us more. It appeared our new friend, in his sober days, used to be a roadie for the Police and before they made the big time they played a gig in a pub in Arbroath. They got up to the town centre early and Stewart Copeland was a sucker for football and their gig just so happened to coincide with the Angus Derby against Montrose. As the light faded, the light was switched on sending a haunting red hue over proceedings. Sting, then of course using the ridiculous name Gordon Sumner as he hadn't yet been given that yellow and black jumper for Christmas which led to his nickname, asked a few locals who turned on the light. "That'll be Hamish Roxanne, the keeper of light. But he wants to pack it all in. Lighthouse keeping is not as glamorous as it used to be, and the on/off button was getting very stiff". So perturbed was Gordon that Hamish would get Repetitive Strain Injury by keeping turning the light on and off, he made an emotional plea for the installation of an automatic timer in the lighthouse. And so was born the song, 'Roxanne'. Sting laid out his wishes clear and simple – if the authorities would install the automatic switch, Hamish Roxanne would no longer need to "put on the red light". Quite a story indeed.

Davie was, of course, off his tits when he joined us.

Gayfield Park is the closest football ground to the North Sea, one long throw away from floating on the tide all the way east to Aalborg in Denmark, which means it's freezing in July, let alone on a Saturday in mid-December. I mean who would be mad enough to watch a game here at that time of the year?

Step forward Danny and myself.

Yep, it had snowed up here for the past few days. Yep, half of the Scottish Football League clubs had called their weekend games off some 48 hours previously. And yep, it was a long way up to travel for a game of football but we believe we have a duty as seekers of truth to get to the bottom of every unusual story, myth and fable. Which brings us nicely onto the real reason for our desire to come to here - Arbroath 36 Bon Accord 0.

So what about *that* game then? Let me take you back to 12th September in the year of our Lord 1885. Queen Victoria is still sitting on the throne in London and has been distinctly unimpressed by the action on ITV's FA Cup highlights show. Andy Townsend is once again confusing his false nines with his man in the hole and football fans are all urging him to get on his penny farthing and disappear into the pea souper. She flicks over the channel on her remote and finds a preview show for the Scottish FA Cup. The "game of the day" is from Arbroath where the Red Lichties were taking on Bon Accord in the good old Scottish Cup.

The away side weren't actually supposed to be playing in the competition at all. In fact they weren't even a football team. The invite to take part in the cup should've been sent to Orion FC but the postman, distracted by a something on his iPod I'm guessing, popped it through the letterbox of Orion CC who were a cricket club. Just like an invite to the Playboy Mansion (have I told you I've been there?) it would have been rude to decline, so they cut up their cricket pads to use as shin pads and headed down the coast for the game.

History shows us that the final score was 36-0 which was a world record in a first class game. Add to this that the referee actually disallowed a number of home team goals because he couldn't see if the ball went over the line (goal line technology in the 1880s hadn't quite stretched to goal nets). At the other end the Arbroath keeper sheltered under an umbrella eating a Smokie and reading a copy of Viz. So distracted was he at the events at the other end that he didn't realise the game had been finished for over an hour after the final flag had been waved (whistles were a few years off).

What are the odds of another game on the same day just a few miles away potentially topping that feat? Slim I would suggest, although Ray Winstone's big head may tell me otherwise. Whilst Arbroath's result saw them on Record Breakers ("Dedication, whoa, dedication") Dundee Harp had kicked off a few minutes earlier than Arbroath and put 35 goals passed Aberdeen Rovers. Or did they? The referee in that game actually recorded 37 ('thirty-seven' in time-honoured vidiprinter style) goals but the Dundee Harp secretary who phoned through the result had apparently missed two goals whilst he went and got the coffees in to enjoy with his Smokie. Either way, the record couldn't stand due to the debate.

So now you see why we had to come here - to breathe the air of record breakers. We wandered through the town, Smokie in one hand, can of McEwans in the other to blend in. We eyeballed DeVito's Night Club for later, hoping to swing a fast shoe with Danny himself as we wandered the coastal path to the ground. Pleasureland was in full swing (the indoor amusement arcade and not a German-style palace of adult entertainment) and we were tempted for a quick game of Time Crisis but instead we headed across the road to Tuttles Neuk Inn, which I understand is Angusian for Turtles Neck.

The bar was rammed. Thanks to their astonishing draw away at Celtic Park in the Scottish Cup last week, tickets had been on sale across the road for the forthcoming replay. Add in a smattering of "Stone Island" here for the Dundee Derby no doubt and we had to fight our way to the bar. It's not often you get to visit a bar which is expertly combines a potted history to the football club intertwined with stuffed animal heads that wouldn't look out of place on a game reserve, but the Tuttles Neuk did it in some style.

We skipped across the road with fifteen-minutes until kick off, hardly able to contain our excitement at visiting Gayfield Park. Twelve pounds (just £12!) saw us pass through the portal and within minutes we had a Bridie in our hands standing slack-jawed as we took in the view. To paraphrase my daughter Lolly "Oh My God". We could not only see the North Sea just over the top of the stand, but we could taste the sea air as well as hear the sound of the waves lapping against the rocks. Apparently the sea air, combined with the sandy soil meant games are rarely called off here. The pitch had been covered all night but you could clearly see the piles of ice on the side of the pitch, taken from the covers. Applause all round for the volunteers who had worked that morning to get the game on.

On the way up to Scotland Danny told me about his dream. Not the one featuring Holly Willoughby, or the one with the bath full of Harvey's ale, but the one where Stenhousemuir scored a late equaliser to secure a 2-2 draw. The reason he mentioned it as we passed a bookies earlier in the day was to see if I thought there was any hope of that happening. Of course I said "not a chance" and he put his tenner back away.

Oh how we laughed at that at 4:45pm.

We'd hardly had time to take 50 pictures before the away team took the lead. Bryan Hodge skipped through the Arbroath midfield, fed Darren "Smithy" Smith and he slotted home. It looked like the home side were already mentally lining up for the big game against Celtic.

A bumper home crowd of nearly 650, twice the average, had braved the freezing conditions and soon had something to cheer about as Steven "Dot" Doris thumped the ball home from the edge of the box. It was hard to take your eyes off the action on the pitch, despite the fact that we between us had managed to take over 200 pictures of the amazing setting sun over the North Sea. How on earth any of the players managed to stay focused I just don't know. "Just one more..." became the standard saying as the sky changed hue again. Girls Aloud could have run onto the pitch naked at this point and we would have been too busy turning our lenses skyward to have known. Probably.

The home side nearly took the lead in the final moment of the half when a free-kick was bent around the wall but struck the inside of a post. I actually managed to put my camera down long enough to see this as my hands by this stage had become frozen to the shutter button.

The second half saw the Stenhousemuir keeper emerge with white tights on, prompting Danny to remember those famous scenes of Leatherhead's Keith Deller (he meant Weller of course and not the Darts player) from the 1970s Tanner's Cup run. Who can blame him though (the keeper not Danny) as it was properly freezing out there. Stuart "Malkie" Malcolm fired the home side into the lead when a free kick caused all sorts of panic in the away defence and it looked like there could only be one winner. But Danny's prophecy came true as in injury time Stewart "Keano" Kean poked home from close range after Arbroath failed to close down Smith on the flank. A fair result? Perhaps not but football and players with nicknames had been the winners. Actually, scrub that, the real winner had been the truly outstanding sunset that had rendered us speechless.

We did think about offering to stay behind and help put the

covers back on the pitch but Dundee was calling. A swift half in the Westport followed by the worst chips with gravy in the world had put us in a drinking mood. Our fifteen-minute train journey back to the metropolis was livened up by the group of self-proclaimed 'Arbroathie Hotties' who decided the best way to be inconspicuous on a train full of football fans was to wear as little as possible. After all, it was only minus three by the time we got back to Dundee, positively balmy for this time of year we were told.

Danny had come up with the cunning idea of following the Dundee Real Ale trail and so we set off into the city centre, avoiding the temptations of Dundee's Premier Karaoke Bar, and into our first destination - The Bank Bar. Things could only get better D:Ream once told Tony Blair and the same was true of our first offering from Dundee. A God-awful pint (well almost as the barrel ran out and was topped up with something else) of Pentland IPA hardly went down at all let alone smoothly. Soon we were off and running in style. A long glass of Blue Moon (hold the slice of orange Duchess) across the road in The Trades, a thick treacly pint of Leffe in The Phoenix, a Deuchers IPA in Langs Bar and a wonderful Innis & Gunn Rum Cask Finished Ale in the Drouthy Neebors had us purring, ordering two more and talking crap for Engla..sorry Scotland.

Our evening would end with a nightcap, a bite to eat and Match of the Day in bed. Not together I hasten to add. Whilst our booking at the Premier Inn was in the name of Mr and Mrs Fuller, there were two beds in the room remember. Of course we went for an Irn Bru and vodka for our final wee dram, and a deep-fried Mars Bar, chips and curry sauce. What more could you possibly want from a night out?

"Gentlemen, to bed, for we leave tomorrow at noon for the Dundee derby."

Sunday morning, Dundee Derby Day! The sun shone into our room bouncing off the Tay, reminding us that days don't get much better than this. This is arguably Scotland's third biggest derby match, an argument we had last night, my vote was Ross County vrs Inverness Caledonian Thistle. Over breakfast the debate raged on as Ayr v Kilmarnock, Peterhead v Elgin City and Motherwell v Hamilton Accies were thrown into the mix by our waitress as she served us our full English. Passions run deep in the City of Discovery.

Danny had another good idea, or so he told me. "Let's go up to the Law, it has views over the whole city". After our excesses of Saturday I figured that a short walk would blow away our cobwebs. What he didn't tell me was the Law was an extinct volcano, the highest point in the city; in fact the next nearest highest point going eastwards was somewhere in Russia. So we got a bus up the steepest hill in the city, then we walked upwards, turned a corner and carried on walking upwards. As we stopped for oxygen at the midway point it became obvious that we had fought the Law and the Law had won. Or had it? A passing pedestrian told us that there was a bar at the top. As if by magic we were inspired to carry on, finally reaching the summit, knowing exactly how Edmund Hilary must have felt back on Everest in 1953. The bar in question was one to stop us toppling over the edge of the cliff but the views were stunning and whilst a normal person would have been drawn to the serene beauty of Firth of Tay, all we could look at was the reason why we were really here - Tannadice Street.

There aren't two football grounds in the United Kingdom that are closer together than Dundee and Dundee United. In fact apart from Spakenburg (remember those chaps from chapter one?) I cannot think of any grounds closer in the world. For years we had tried to find someone who would be prepared to run between the two grounds, wearing slippers of course, to settle a bet. I had always said that you could do the run in less than 20 seconds, Danny over 25 seconds. Today we'd find out.

The streets were relatively quiet as we descended the east face of The Law, and after a wander down Sanderson Street into Tannadice Street past both grounds, we found ourselves in the Troll Inn. No seriously, there is a pub, the closest one to Dundee United's ground that is a) called the Troll Inn and b) had numerous troll dolls on various shelves around the pub. After a few McEwans in here they would take on a life of their own. The excitement was palpable. The last derby game back in August had ended 3-0 to Dundee United, although recent form suggested a repeat result would be unlikely, or so we told ourselves as we placed a small wager on the draw. The last derby game played at Dens Park had been back in April 2005 so you could understand the excitement on the streets as we walked back up to the ground.

Everyone seemed quite jolly. There was no animosity on show, with a strong police presence out enjoying the sunshine rather than having to worry about fans having a go at each other. The ground was a sell-out with Dundee United given the whole of the Bob (brother of Bill) Shankly behind the goal and half of the Main Stand. The players warmed up on a pitch that was bathed in sunshine, ready for the 155th meeting between the two neighbours. Recent history hadn't been kind on the home side, having spent far too many seasons outside the top flight and a couple of near misses with the tax man. However, historically the two clubs have very similar records. Both have won the League Championship once (United the most recent 30 years ago during their golden period), both boast four cups and both have even reached the European Cup semi-finals. History is very special to the fans in these parts as we saw with a parade of some of the old legends at half time.

Danny had been in touch with the club as soon as tickets were on sale and managed to secure us some of the best seats in the Main Stand, right in the middle of WAG central. Great views to our left and right, although the incredibly strong sun shining in our eyes did make watching the main event difficult. We weren't going to complain; few football fans outside the city had experienced the event and it was our duty to document history with both pen and camera.

Some time later as the third Dundee United goal hit the back of the net with ten minutes to go, the home fans flooded out onto the streets around the ground with a sinking feeling that this could be the last derby game played here for another seven years. United had outclassed the Dee over the ninety minutes, pure and simple, earning the bragging rights over family, friends, work colleagues and strangers in the street for another four months until they met again down the road.

I grew up remembering the legendary Dundee United side of the early 1980s. I remember learning all about them as a youngster when West Ham bought a virtual unknown teenage right back called Raymond Steward in 1979. Tonka, as he was known by the fans, would go on to be a legend for the Hammers. Whilst many of my playground team mates wanted to be Rush, Dalglish or Hansen, I wanted to be Narey, Malpas, Milne or the legendary Paul Sturrock. After winning the league in 1983 they almost brought UEFA Cup glory back to Scotland, losing in the two-legged final (those were the days) live on TV against Goteborg. Today, despite the opinion of a very sad and frustrated Dundee fan who sat behind us (and accused us of being "Arabs" because

we took a picture of their second goal) we were actually supporting the home side.

Despite some initial home pressure down the flanks it was the
away side that drew first blood when a Dundee United corner was
flicked on at the near post and Keith Watson's well taken header
rippled in the back of the net. It was harsh on the home side
but they were always going to suffer if they couldn't put their
chances away. Dundee really should have been level on the half
hour mark when Matt Lockwood's cross found the head of Jim
McAlister, who nodded to Steven Milne but he volleyed over the
bar from eight yards out when he should have scored.

The home fans soon realised it wouldn't be their afternoon
shortly after the second half when everyone in the ground bar
the referee and his assistants saw John Baird's cross hit a United
player on the arm in the area. The humidity was rising in the stadium and the Dundee fans on the opposite side of the pitch were
getting agitated. Their mood didn't improve when the referee
bizarrely gave a penalty to the away side for a foul on Armstrong
after he had played a ball into the area. Stuart Armstrong wasn't
complaining and stepped up, slammed the ball past Rab Douglas
and Dundee United were as good as winners.

The third was simply icing on the cake when it came ten minutes later. There was an air of resignation when it came with
Willo Flood's shot from the edge of the area bouncing off Kyle
Benedictus, then off veteran keeper Douglas and onto a post. It
came back and hit the goalkeeper again and this time rolled into
the net. Insult, injury and all that business. By that stage our
furious friend had left, heading home to kick his cat no doubt.
The final whistle saw some muted celebration in the away end,
although they knew the pain that a derby day defeat could bring
only too well.

We still had time for a drink or two, so we headed to one
of the local pubs. You know the ones. Blacked out windows,
police car permanently parked outside and women breastfeeding
their babies whilst smoking a cigarette and drinking a pint of
Tennent's at the same time in the doorway. Inside it was heaving
with people watching the end of the Manchester derby, Dundee
and Dundee United fans sharing a beer and debating the lack of
a performance in the past ninety minutes. It was surreal to see
such a good atmosphere here whilst on the screen the hatred and
poison that two sets of fans in Manchester could generate was
all too evident. Some people take football far far too seriously.

In spite of what Bill (brother of Bob) Shankly said, football never has nor ever will be a matter of life and death. It is a game, a distraction from real life, a pleasure principal if I can paraphrase my good friend Janet Jackson for a moment. With all the trouble unfolding in Manchester it was amazing to take a look around our surroundings in a bar, lined with memorabilia of both sides, with fans from each end of Tannadice Street happy to share a beer together - exactly how local rivals should. This was a derby that still belongs to the fans. No racial hatred, no bitterness and no religious divide. Just two sets of fans who shared modest ambitions and a genuine love for their city who simply wanted the bragging rights for a few months. Dundee had been a good host and for that we thank you all. Perhaps we would be tempted to come back in March for the game just 21.1 seconds (in slippers) down the road...

As we headed back to Edinburgh I reflected on life as a Football Tourist. Just like my first adventure some eighteen months ago in Holland, the joy of watching football in a foreign land hadn't come at a big stadium with Champions League football, but one that has seen better days. And that is why I love this beautiful game. Modern football isn't crap. It is what you make it.

If you want to be ripped off paying through the nose to watch footballers who are only in it for the money then I can readily give you a list of places to visit, but you won't find me there (unless you have a ticket free, in which case it will be the best stadium in the world). Instead take a wander into the suburbs, look for a set of floodlights, a rusty old stand, grass covered terraces, a liberal sprinkling of dogs (preferably wearing club colours) and that's where you will find me and several of my good friends. Beer in one hand, camera in the other.

Ladies and Gentlemen, you have been a brilliant audience but all good things come to an end. It's time for me to move on to who knows where and, hopefully, I might even see some of you there along the way.

Acknowledgements

"Football, eh? Bloody hell!"

Sir Alex Ferguson

This is the part of the book that everyone who knows you skips to first to see what nice things you may have said about them. In truth I could thank a thousand people for helping me get my experiences down on paper (or iPad, Nook, Kindle, PC, ZX Spectrum or on several other devices now commercially available) but the editor has been mean and only given me 400 words maximum. So apologies if you have not made my list of acknowledgements. You know I love you deep down.

Any epic needs a hero and a villain and I am lucky to have had these in equal parts within my travelling companions who have cropped up during the past twenty chapters. The main protagonists have been Andy Hudson with his cheery disposition, sparkle in his eye, completely incomprehensible accent after three or four pints and his never ending list of teams he professes his undying love for; Kenny 'Tinpot' Legg for being Weymouth's number 1 fan in Düsseldorf and not taking the piss too much when I had my accident in Belgrade; Big Deaksy for his cheerful outlook on life; Luge Pravda and Ben Anderson for being great friends as well as fantastic work colleagues who have made me feel so welcome in their respective corners of the globe; Ditto Adam Lloyd for the hospitality in Rome in one of the best weekends we've experienced.

Finally for this part of the list, of course Danny Last. A better travelling companion you will never meet who sleeps with his shoes on, has an amazing ability to find an open door wherever he goes and takes some of the best pictures I've seen on a simple compact camera.

Normally authors doff a compulsory cap at their publisher but I am genuinely privileged to be writing for David Hartrick and Ockley Books. We talked long into the night back in the Bigg Market back in July 2011 about numerous projects and I am proud to say this will be the first of many hopefully successful ones to see the light of day. A genuinely great chap who has been full of support all along the way.

My family deserve a one-minute applause for their contribution to this project. My parents have always been on hand to help when I have been on my adventures and it is good to see some of my passion for travel is rubbing off on them, albeit as long as it is on a P & O cruise route. But the real dedication for this book goes to my three girls. They are the ones that get me through the long days in corners of the world that most rational humans have never heard of. Whether it be a post-it note in my bag or a photo sent to my phone they know how to lift my spirits. I hope one day that my two daughters will experience some of the wonder I have experienced on my travels. They make me proud, smile, laugh and cry every day of the year. And then there is the Current Mrs. Fuller. She knows there will never be another CMF because she is everything a Football Tourist could ask for and more. My only sadness is that she isn't able to share my adventures (yet). After all, what girl wouldn't want to stand in the Partizan Stadium with a flare in each hand? She never tires of my Petrol Station Flowers gags - in the words of Tina Turner she's simply the Nutbush City Limits.

Finally a big thank you to you, dear reader. You will never realise the kick an author gets when they see someone reading their work so thank you for improving my mood today by doing just that. I hope that in some way I've inspired you to 'try this one at home'. Go on, it doesn't hurt (unless you slide down a slope in Belgrade at 100 miles per hour) and in the words of Judith Chalmers, "it's cheaper than you think'.

Forza Football Tourism!